THE ROYAL NAVY

To Jo, Ben and Lucy as inspiration travels both ways; but especially to Jo, as without her this would not have been possible. 'A bird never flew on one wing.'

THE ROYAL NAVY

Birth of a Superpower 1793–1800

Mark Jessop

PEN & SWORD
HISTORY

AN IMPRINT OF PEN & SWORD BOOKS LTD.
YORKSHIRE – PHILADELPHIA

First published in Great Britain in 2018 by
PEN AND SWORD HISTORY
an imprint of
Pen and Sword Books Ltd
Yorkshire – Philadelphia

Copyright © Mark Jessop, 2018

ISBN 978 1 52672 033 7

Printed and bound in the UK
by T J International, Padstow, Cornwall, PL28 8RW

Typeset in Times New Roman 11/13.5 by
Aura Technology and Software Services, India

Pen & Sword Books Ltd incorporates the imprints of Pen & Sword
Archaeology, Atlas, Aviation, Battleground, Discovery,
Family History, History, Maritime, Military, Naval, Politics, Railways,
Select, Social History, Transport, True Crime, Claymore Press,
Frontline Books, Leo Cooper, Praetorian Press, Remember When,
Seaforth Publishing and Wharncliffe.

For a complete list of Pen and Sword titles please contact
Pen and Sword Books Limited
47 Church Street, Barnsley, South Yorkshire, S70 2AS, England
E-mail: enquiries@pen-and-sword.co.uk
Website: www.pen-and-sword.co.uk

Or
PEN AND SWORD BOOKS
1950 Lawrence Rd, Havertown, PA 19083, USA
E-mail: Uspen-and-sword@casematepublishers.com
Website: www.penandswordbooks.com

Contents

Preface

In 1792 Great Britain was at peace and her Royal Navy lay in slumber. Everything changed in 1793 when France declared war. Along the English Channel, Britain lay in sight of a powerful enemy. The British people had to react so they put their naval fleets to sea to confront the threat of invasion and take enemy sea-trade as prizes. To begin with there were barely enough warships to cope. Over the next eight years, war placed a heavy burden on the general public. Income tax had to be introduced, liberties were taken away, men departed their families to fight and many never returned. War became the fulcrum of people's lives.

Portsmouth, a large naval emporium[1] ninety-four miles from France, lay close enough to the threat of invasion that her inhabitants witnessed at first-hand how the war altered both the Royal Navy and themselves. At times civilians felt fear, uncertainty and sadness. They could have said,

> *It is our merchantmen that carry our goods and manufactures. Wherever they roam is where we gain influence.[2] It is our navy that protects our merchantmen, our shores, and our foreign interests. The greater our sea commerce the more powerful is our navy; the more powerful our navy the greater is our sea commerce!*

Their concerns were centred upon 'loss of the carrying trade', 'if one more bank fails we'll rue the day', and 'the costs to the country'. Battles and

---

1 The 1819 cyclopaedia referred to Portsmouth as 'this grand naval emporium.' From Rees (1819), 119.

2 No reliable tonnage figures exist prior to 1760 but 285,156 tonnes of shipping was cited for 1707, the year the Kingdom of Great Britain had been enacted. From *The Parliamentary History of England* (1818), 140. In 1800 Britain commanded 1,905,438 tonnes, according to figures put before Parliament, in McArthur (1801), 242; although 1,628,143 is given in *Hansard* 1849, 1371. Data also found in Robinson (1894), 39.

mutinies turned their heads. Dozens of warships foundered, burned, or were made wrecks. Mothers longed for peace so their sailor sons could return home. By 1801 the thousands of merchant ships that arrived, rendezvoused and sailed off had helped keep Britain from penury. Customs revenues and loans meant the Royal Navy had not rotted away. Despite communal fears warships had managed to keep Britain's coasts free from enemy occupation. British industry and commerce thereby continued and imports and exports climbed from £39,000,000 in 1790 to £70,000,000 in 1800.[3]

As the nineteenth century commenced the French threat remained. However, by then the Royal Navy had become a true Neptune capable of withstanding anything Napoléon could have thrown at it. So mighty were the efforts to strengthen her, a naval 'superpower' had been born. The birth proved arduous and bloody and her mother, Great Britain, passed away. Ireland, a client state of Great Britain and part of the exposed flank of the British Isles, lay open to a French invasion. That posed a terrible threat to Britain. Parliament therefore enacted an end to the Kingdom of Great Britain in favour of the United Kingdom of Great Britain and Ireland. The war continued, but the British had their navy to help bring about ultimate victory. People might have wondered what had helped create this naval 'superpower'.

---

3 Figures vary widely; these are found in Newmarch (1855), 47.

Major Events Between 1793 And 1800

The events mentioned in this book are based on fact and those named naval officers, politicians and Frenchmen were actual people. However, to represent the men and women swept up in the tide of history, often unknown and unnamed, the characters who recount their memories and thoughts within are mostly fictitious, such as the reporter, the ex-Cornish miner (based on a real group of men), the parson, the press-gang, the schoolmaster and his boys, the letter-writer, the ship's surgeon, Vinney, Solomon, Jennings and the crew of their ship, the petty-officer's wife, the old sailor, the sailor at St. Jean d'Acre, the foreign agent, and the West Indies ship owner.

1793
1 February. France declared war against Great Britain and the Dutch Republic.
22 April. The United States of America declared herself neutral.
28 August to 19 December. The Siege of Toulon.
5 October. Royal Navy ships 'raided' Genoa.

1794
23 March. Sailors and troops seized Martinique.
16 May. Suspension of habeas corpus.
1 June. Battle of the Glorious First of June.
4 June. British sailors and troops seized Port-au-Prince on Saint-Domingue.
17 June. The Anglo-Corsican Kingdom proclaimed.
November. Treason trials of members of the London Corresponding Society.

1795
5 March. The Quota Act decreed.
28 April. The Vagrants Act decreed.
16 and 17 June. Cornwallis's Retreat, off Brittany.
23 June to 21 July. Failed landing at Quiberon Bay.

25 August. Trincomalee seized.
September. Bread riots throughout England.
16 September. British sailors and troops seized Cape Town.
November. The Treasonable Practices Act, and The Seditious Meeting Act decreed.
Drinking lemon juice made mandatory on all British warships.

1796
May. The Batavian Republic declared war on Great Britain.
11 October. Spain declared war on Great Britain.
December. Failed French invasion of Ireland.

1797
14 February. The Battle of Cape St Vincent.
18 February. Great Britain took control of Trinidad.
22 February. A French invasion force landed briefly at Fishguard.
April and May. Spithead and Nore mutinies.
17 April. Failed attempt to take San Juan.
11 October. The Battle of Camperdown.

1798
23 May. The Society of United Irishmen launched a rebellion.
1–3 August. The Battle of the Nile.

1799
9 January. Income tax introduced.
12 July. The Combination Act decreed.

1800
2 July to 1 August. The Acts of Union 1800 created the United Kingdom of Great Britain and Ireland to begin 1 January 1801.

Chapter 1

The Sons of the Waves

At dawn, Captain Robert Barlow stepped onto the weather deck of the 14-gun *Childers*[4]. Looming grey skies, an increased swell, and a quick glance at the barometer told him that before nightfall a storm would rise up along the Breton coast and the chops of the English Channel. After a glance at the traverse board[5] he paced his customary spot and observed the dark rugged coast ahead. A spyglass helped him make out the church spires of Brest. The French Revolution had ravaged that port, but her roadstead[6] nonetheless remained one of France's finest. Nestled along the mouth of the Penfeld river the anchorage there could easily accommodate hundreds of French warships. Barlow could make out wispy masts of the French fleet, and with pleasure concluded that there were no obvious signs of an intent to make sail. With orders to stand in each morning, to reconnoitre the port, he needed to sail closer to make sure.

Between the *Childers* and those masts lay a difficult and dangerous coast. To larboard were the rocks and shoals of Pointe Saint-Mathieu, and the Bertheaume roadstead. To starboard lay the iron-hard Roscanvel peninsula, and the Camaret roadstead. Between both extremities lay the *Childers*, in an open bay that narrowed to a one-and-a-half-mile long passage called the *goulet* that led to the Brest roadstead. This difficult strait, barely half a mile wide, accommodated submerged rocks mid-channel and shore batteries upon the cliffs. Despite the riot of the revolution, such fortifications were well maintained. Barlow saw three of them with the naked eye. On the larboard side were the menaces of Fort du Petit Minou and Fort du Mengant. To starboard the 'Cornish Fort', a battery upon the Pointe de Cornouaille.

---

4 HMS *Childers*; James cites it to be a 16-gun brig-sloop. James, *The naval history of Great Britain,* Vol I (1837), 53.

5 A wooden board that showed a compass rose with stringed pegs. Over the course of a watch it showed the direction a ship had sailed.

6 Or 'roads', an anchorage where a number of ships can ride.

Due to the oncoming weather, this particular morning might be the last opportunity to observe the French fleet for some time. Barlow therefore navigated the *Childers* through the Passage de l'Iroise, one of three such approaches with greater width to deal with Atlantic swells and chaotic sea traffic. Slowly, with utmost care, the brig-sloop approached the *goulet* and the bay appeared to constrict upon her. The fearsome shore batteries came into range.

The crew of the *Childers* knew the situation was tense. Newspapers and dispatches reported how the French had finally put their king on trial. Louis XVI fell last summer, after a Paris mob stormed the Tuileries Palace[7] and, stripped of all powers, he had languished in the Temple prison ever since. He faced an uncertain future. The English king, the third George, bristled at such treatment of a fellow monarch. Rumbles of war had increased in intensity.

Things had perceptibly changed since they arrived off Brest. In recent days the revolutionaries had become openly bellicose. Fishermen shook their fists at them. French merchantmen, eager to intimidate, sailed far too close. The *Childers* had to endure every slight with an accommodating wide berth. Incidents must be avoided. But what if a battery decided to make a show?

Barlow stepped to the starboard side as the brig-sloop entered the *goulet*. Ahead he saw waves wash over the half-submerged rock the French called Roche Mengant. He ordered the quartermaster to maintain course and keep a small fleet of mackerel boats to starboard. He became aware of the loom of Fort du Mengant, slightly ahead, off their larboard side. Part of its twin batteries hovered high above on the cliff top, while at sea level there sat a small semi-circular emplacement. A couple of landmen[8] pointed at the visible faces of the French garrison, and made thin jokes about 'bloody Jacobins' and 'dare they to jail their king.' They knew that their meagre 4-pounder guns were nothing compared to the 48-pounders the fort commanded. The *Childers* could only manage a broadside weight of 28lbs of hot metal, and only then at the lower emplacement. Above them, the forts flew tricolor flags. Barlow struggled with that innovation because it represented old France overthrown. For most of his service life the French had flown the *drapeau blanc*, the Bourbon white flag.

Suddenly the wind failed, but the flood tide pushed them further along the *goulet*. Shivers ran down the captain's spine, and not just from the cold

---

7 In Paris, and where the French king had lived.
8 A landman had been a seaman with less than one year's experience at sea.

January weather. A sense of danger began to gnaw at the back of his mind. A veteran of the American War, he knew that if anything untoward were to happen it would be now. When a loud report, a deep throated rumble, resounded over the water he felt a momentary grip of shock in his vitals. A splash of water exploded skywards behind them and a cold spray landed upon the quarterdeck. The French had fired! Confusion gripped the watch. The men looked to their captain, as children to a stern father.

'Damn them and their antics!' shouted a seaman.

Barlow ordered quiet, and the off-watch to remain below. One of the young gentlemen caught his attention and pointed to starboard, where the soft haze of smoke wafted down from the Cornish fort.

'Sir, what if the other forts open fire?'

'Worry not,' he replied. 'See to your duties.'

He ordered the ensign aloft, along with the ship's pendant, to make sure the French knew they were neutral. Were they confused? Did they mistake them for a Prussian, or Sardinian, ship? Were they not at peace?

Satisfied the flags could clearly be seen, he ordered the ship to come about and sail upon the larboard tack. He scanned the Fort de Cornouaille once more and blanched when he saw another shot belch out. He traced the large black ball as it made a perfect arc to splash heavily in their wake. If the tide had not taken them they would have been hit.

To their relief, the breeze strengthened – a lack of wind would be their undoing. The mainsail filled just enough to push them around. Slowly, all too slowly, they moved out to sea. He glanced up for a third time, as the French hoisted their own ensign with a red pendant above. The signal repeated above the other batteries.

Another shot boomed out and this time it struck. With a loud thud, a 48-pound ball hit one of their larboard guns. Men jumped away in alarm, but surprisingly there was no blood. A group of wary sailors milled around the upturned and destroyed gun, gesticulating wildly, before the boatswain and his mate scooped up the remains of the warm ball in their hands and carried the three pieces to their captain.

Fort du Mengant added to the combined discharge of French cannons. All subsequent balls either fell into the water or upon the rocky shore. As the *Childers* gained distance, to make her way into the offing, the forts slackened their fire and eventually stopped altogether. The brig-sloop had been stung, but not damaged. A serious incident nonetheless and one that Barlow knew had to be reported to the Admiralty with all speed. With skies darkening in the west, swells now topped with whitecaps, the brig-sloop made as much distance from shore as possible to weather Ushant and head home. With luck, and a fair wind, London would know of this outrage within a few days.

In the end it required Captain Barlow nine days to inform the Admiralty. A storm blew the *Childers* off course, so he did not reach Fowey until 4 January 1793. He arrived in London with the cloven ball seven days later, after which the news spread rapidly. If then asked, a political reporter would have explained that tensions were high, and had been so for nearly four years. Since the fall of the Bastille, France had worried many in the British government. As had two other monarchies.

In 1790 Spain had claimed waters along the Pacific northwest coast of North America, and the fur trade there. Ships were seized in Nootka Sound, close to Vancouver Island. War had been thought possible. Although hostilities did not materialize it created a high level of activity in British dockyards, where 'there were 93 Ships of the line in commission considered to be in good condition...and not in the state that Guardships often were formerly, in time of peace.'[9]

The following year Russia moved against the Ottomans, the Ochakov Crisis, and that too had caused Britain to prepare for war. The Royal Navy had readied a fleet for the Baltic, and a fleet for the Black Sea. Public opinion had not been favourable. Regardless, by the end of 1792 close to sixty ships[10] of the line had been improved to a good state.

War happened to have broken out the same year, between France and a coalition made up of Austria, Prussia, Sardinia and some states of the Holy Roman Empire, but Prime Minister William Pitt had maintained neutrality. Why? Because of Britain's extensive trade. She had had much to lose. Britain benefitted from the Eden Agreement, that had brought to an end a long and bitter 'trade war' with France, and conflict would have ruined that agreement. Besides, the loss of her American colonies still cut to the quick. Pitt had felt obliged to pursue peace, and many applauded him.

Most people had been supportive of neutrality, but throughout Britain there had also been a strong undercurrent in favour of the French Revolution. The portly figure of Charles James Fox spoke for many, in 1791, when he said the French constitution was a great achievement. In 1792 some British political clubs had even supplied French armies with shoes and muskets. Pamphlets circulated in favour of 'rights,' to the great annoyance of the

---

9 Derrick (1806), pp.191 & 198.
10 James, *ibid*, 48. He writes, 'upwards of 60 of the 87'.

British king. Strong arguments were given against a conflict with France because it 'was not worth one year's expense of the contest; and that, while it was easy to see what England had to lose, it was difficult to conceive what she could possibly gain.'[11] Britain thereby remained divided. At one soirée the reporter had attended, a woman had shaken the *Annual Register* at him and said, 'read this!' An article within laid out how 'the Tories' were the most popular faction, Republicans the most active, and Whigs caught in between, ever conscious of trade interests. *But*, the woman had stressed, *there are more than three political groups. There are discontents of all stripes!*

The risk of insurrection ran high. A young Walter Scott, who lived through these years, later wrote that 'Britain had a far too ample mass of poverty and ignorance, subject always to be acted upon by hope and licence… societies were formed in almost all the towns of Great Britain… and seemed to frame themselves on the French model…. That state of things began to take place in Britain, which had preceded the French Revolution.'[12]

The reporter had previously written about the fall of Louis XVI and the atrocities carried out in Paris prisons shortly thereafter. He believed that those two events turned British public opinion away from sympathy for the revolution. British hearts and minds had hardened. At a literary party he came across Edmund Burke, who strongly argued that France had dragged her army and navy to the ground, and caused a perilous situation to arise. That man of letters ceaselessly tried to rouse the alarm, and encouraged French émigrés to take up arms. Others agreed with him. They believed the very course of the revolution had made the case for peace almost impossible. So, when the status of a European river became the issue of the moment it further darkened the horizon.

The closure of the Scheldt river had helped maintain a balance of power in Europe. The revolutionary French government wanted it reopened. They formally asked Parliament in December 1792 whether Great Britain would remain neutral over the issue or become a hostile power. Nootka Sound, Russia, the fall of Louis XVI, and then the Scheldt. The French ambassador, Marquis de Chauvelin, was forced to give his customary hard stare to British ministers and state coolly that a recent 'Decree of Liberty' made by his government had not been intended to arouse insurrection in Britain. It offered, he said, 'aid' to those peoples who had already achieved some form of liberty. He stressed how his country had no desire to molest the Dutch Republic, a nation who wanted the Scheldt firmly closed for their

---

11 Alison (1841), Vol 1, 111. This quote refers to war over the Scheldt, a 'most trifling cause of complaint'.

12 Sir Walter Scott (1833), Vol 4, 107.

own benefit, assuming she remained neutral. He argued that the opening of the river could not possibly be a reason for Britain and France to commence hostilities. For the British government such arguments sounded hollow. Strained exchanges followed.

Then occurred the *Childers* incident. Even 'Old Whigs' began to support the Tories. King George III recalled Parliament on 7 January 1793 and wrote, 'In this present situation of affairs, his Majesty thinks it indispensably necessary to make a further Augmentation of his Forces by sea and land; and relies on...the House of Commons, to enable...maintaining the security and rights of his own dominions; for supporting his allies; and for opposing those views of aggrandizement and ambition on the part of France, which would be at all times dangerous to the general interests of Europe.'[13] Britain accused France of hostile ambitions, and the French, by way of de Chauvelin, wrote, 'if we are still obliged to hear the language of haughtiness, and if hostile preparations are continued in the ports of England, after having done everything in our power to maintain peace, we will prepare for war, conscious, at least, of the justice of our cause, and of the efforts we have made to avoid that extremity. We shall combat with regret the English, whom we esteem, but we shall combat them without fear.'[14] France stumbled towards war against both Britain and the Dutch Republic.

The reporter had some contacts in Paris. He received reports that the French government, the *Convention nationale*, grew alarmed for they dreaded a naval war with Britain. The French navy stood strong but her manpower had been affected by the revolution. Furthermore, French colonies suffered neglect and disrepair. Reliant upon the wealth of her West Indies sugar islands France could not afford to relinquish them, nor hope to hold off the Royal Navy from ravishing them. Although some Frenchmen argued that Britain's receipts were never enough to sustain a war, some had countered that Britain's immense trade and relatively stable politics would help her sustain a long struggle. Great Britain would fit out far stronger fleets. Furthermore, revenues that Parliament controlled would support and supply coalition armies throughout Europe. So France had made attempts to maintain peace with Britain, through unofficial channels, even promising to evacuate Belgium and Savoy that they then controlled. However, talks were to no avail. In late January 1793 news of Louis XVI's execution travelled far and wide. When British ministers heard, they summoned Monsieur

---

13 Cobbett, Wright, and Hansard (1817), Vol XXX, 240.
14 Baines (1852), Vol I, 78.

de Chauvelin to tell him he no longer acted as a representative of the French king for Louis XVI lay dead. Orders were given for him to quit Britain. Official correspondence with France ended on 24 January.

Soon afterwards Jacques Pierre Brissot (de Warville) stood up in the National Convention and argued why 'England' desired war, and not France. In sympathy with his arguments the French government issued a decree, dated 1 February 1793, that stated how 'George, king of England...had drawn into the same league the stadtholder of the United Provinces; that... the English ministry had granted protection and succour to the emigrants and others, who have openly appeared in arms against France...to commit an outrage against the French republic, by ordering the ambassador of France to quit Great Britain; that the English had stopped divers boats and vessels laden with corn for France...contrary to the treaty of 1786...they have, by an act of parliament, prohibited the circulation of *assignats*. The convention, therefore, declare...the French republic is at war with the king of England, and the stadtholder of the United Provinces.'[15] With such a long build-up the declaration of war did not come as a complete surprise. Great Britain joined a cause then hell-bent upon returning the French crown to its ancient seat, despite that hope seeming less and less likely.

Parliament considered it important to increase Britain's overseas interests, and ensure her continued prosperity. Through her 'industrial revolution', years of innovation and relative freedom from government restraint, she had brought into being powerful trade and industry concerns. As an island nation with far-flung colonies, factories in India, and envious European neighbours, she could never hope to protect herself with just an army. It had always required a large and powerful navy to provide the protection she required, to maintain the security and rights of her dominions, support her allies, oppose France's views of aggrandizement and ambition, protect her trade, gain colonies as useful to her as the ones she had lost in North America, and to defend herself from seaborne invasion. The Royal Navy would have to be Britain's aegis. Likened to Jove, her fleets had to propel thunderbolts across the globe.

Efforts needed to sustain a navy in peacetime were onerous. Stores, food, guns, ammunition and countless other needs had to be provided for. Funds were not always plentiful. Some ships had to be placed 'in ordinary', that is out of commission and in reserve. They were moored, without masts, denuded of guns and sat draped under tarpaulin almost empty of life.

---

15 Kelly, C. (1820), 100.

They appeared squat and dull in the water and had to wait patiently until called back into commission. After Parliament issued a manifesto[16] on 11 February 1793 that laid out reasons for war and how general reprisals were permitted against French ships, goods, and subjects, ships in ordinary had to be brought back into commission to conduct most of those reprisals. After a decade of peace this would normally have been difficult, but the crises of 1790 and 1791 had made the navy semi-prepare. The legacy of one man, Sir Charles Middleton, also had an effect. When Comptroller of the Navy he had introduced the expedient of putting aside articles of furniture and stores for every seagoing ship of the fleet, and had made it a requirement for every English naval dockyard to maintain well stocked magazines[17] of non-perishable goods. Such foresight proved very useful in the early days of the war. Ships had had to equip themselves for an unknown amount of sea-service. Their masts, rigging and ordnance had to be supplied and fitted and crews found to work them. Thanks to Middleton there was less delay in readying the fleet. Within a few weeks of France's declaration of war commissioned ships of the line were augmented from twenty-six to fifty-four in number. Commissioned 'cruisers' also increased steadily in numbers, from 136 to almost 200, although, some argued, far too slowly. Thunderbolts were soon cast far and wide, but in those first days only the quick dispatch of a few precious ships to various stations, and the filling of certain vacancies, could be done. Put into commission were the *Crescent* (of 38 guns), the *Nymphe* (36), and *Queen* (98). Lord Howe was appointed commander in chief of the Channel Fleet. A note placed in the Admiralty lobby in London asked for lieutenants to come forward and seek employment. Hundreds of desperate men were allowed to seek gainful employment. The increase in the fleets commenced.

The British public expected successes. The march *Heart of Oak* returned to the lips of sailors and civilians alike. The reporter often whistled the tune as he wrote. The song referred to the 'wonderful year' of 1759 when a British fleet had foiled a French invasion of Britain, and people who sang it in 1793 had expectations of a similar wonderful year. The Royal Navy had protected Britain's shores many times before. People assumed she would do so again.

Already a large organisation, the role of this 'wooden wall' had been understood by many. A few even knew the costs involved. It required large amounts of government expenditure to maintain warships fit for service.

---

16 Kelly, *ibid.*
17 James, *ibid.*

In peacetime, according to Charles Derrick, it required £300,000 per year just for basic maintenance and repairs.[18] For 1793 Parliament agreed to £171,448 for building, £198,780 for rebuilding and repairs, and £67,532 for improvements of the navy. A total of £437,760, with a total 'charge' for supplies of £6,031,706. 16s. The wooden walls were expensive. Derrick also wrote that 'such a state of preparation for war, so far as concerned the Navy, as had never before been seen at the beginning of a war.... And happy was it for the country that the Navy was in the state described; for... the French... possessed a very powerful Navy, though inferior to our own.'[19] – the Royal Navy could not claim to be the only powerful sea-force in Europe.

The French had, on paper, an equally impressive fleet. She had worked hard to make her *Marine nationale* comparable to the Royal Navy. In 1793 warships stood on their stocks, and she had commissioned many ships' cannons. Whereas the revolution inflamed her *matelots* it had also sowed distrust and discord, and had allowed the persecution of naval officers. A depressed state of morale ensued, and incompetence bedevilled her fleets. Fortunately for the French, by the time war was declared against Great Britain steps had been taken to end the excess of violence in her ports. She had 'put a little life into the navy, and prevented the absolute break-up which would have occurred had the French fleets met those of England in the early days of their complete disorganization.'[20] Opposed to her, Britain had a stable government, an extensive naval organisation, experienced naval leadership and a sense of endeavour. No one could foresee the future. Some observers thought it a close call as to which of the two naval powers would eventually prevail. For many throughout Great Britain, and her colonies, the first verse and chorus of *Heart of Oak* summed up their feelings:

> *Come, cheer up, my lads, 'tis to glory we steer,*
> *To add something more to this wonderful year;*
> *To honour we call you, as freemen not slaves,*
> *For who are so free as the sons of the waves?*

> *Heart of Oak are our ships,*
> *Jolly Tars are our men,*
> *We always are ready: Steady, boys, Steady!*
> *We'll fight and we'll conquer again and again.*

---

18 Derrick, *ibid.*, 198.
19 *Ibid.*
20 *The Atlantic Monthly*, Vol LXXI (1893), 557. The (unknown) author refers to Mahan.

Chapter 2

Heart of Oak Are Our Ships

The promise of a major French prize lay somewhere over the horizon. The 32-gun frigates *Cléopâtre* and *Sémillante* had been chased into French ports but they could venture out again any time in search of plunder. It would be the Cornishman's ship, the *Nymphe*, that had to fight them and she awed and appalled him in equal measure. Before the war he had been a tin miner near Bodmin and had never been to sea, but unemployment made him desperate enough to take the bounty and volunteer as landman in the Royal Navy. He had brute strength and could pull a rope, and the navy needed as many men as possible. He joined his ship with seventy-nine other Cornish miners, and soon found himself at sea. His first days had been a nightmare of complaints, curses and kicks, until their captain had pressed sailors out of two British merchantmen. Only then had things improved.

Through days of bad weather, sea-sickness and bone-aching fatigue he slowly fathomed what his job involved. The way the ship moved, with unexpected lurches and rolls, made him think more than once he would end up in Davy Jones's Locker. All the ex-miners had been teased mercilessly by the regular seamen – 'Look yonder, my lads, see that evil spirit up there in the rigging? A storm to send us down will surely come.' No such storm ever arrived. But he pulled more than a few ropes. Dozens of them, all rearing up amongst the sails and masts. Stays. Braces. He struggled to name and comprehend them all. Never a man of learning, he felt confounded. The regular seamen talked a language of obscure words that excluded him; but at least he could converse with fellow Cornishmen. Everything on board made him feel at odds. Considered a mere landlubber, incapable of redemption, the boatswain's mate had had to remind him what to do and where to go, often with the end of a rope.

Until the ship had anchored in the Carrick Roads he never knew where he was. He then lingered on deck. Each and every Cornishman had the same thought in his head: *There lies Falmouth!* If any one of them could swim he would have been over the side. Yet no one took the plunge. The prospect of employment and prize money kept them on board, and shortly afterwards they were back at sea.

Now he can see dark green Devon countryside fringed with a line of surf. Pilchard boats tarry nearby, and the waters of the English Channel are busy with coasting merchantmen. Most seem eager to gain as much distance from them as they would a French frigate. He knows why: none of them want to lose a man to the press. War has made every seaman a target.

A sudden thud of the dreaded rope's end forces him back to work.

As the ship approaches Start Point Captain Pellew appears on deck with his brother, another Royal Navy officer who acts as a volunteer. His chest swells when he sees them, for they are both men of Penzance. His captain's quiet orders are law, likened to an old time prophet, and his words command instant activity. When Pellew orders the ship to wear, and head south towards France, men instantly run up to the tops, sails are trimmed, and ropes attended to. The two brothers remain upon the quarterdeck for hours, but no enemy sails are sighted. By late evening they turn back towards Devon. Start Point is reached by the early hours of the next morning.

The Cornishman stands on deck when dawn approaches. The whole of the western horizon resembles a huge painting, a seascape of golden light upon a dark horizon. His thoughts race with the promise of breakfast, when a shout from above grabs his attention. Off to the south-east lays a ship, hull down, with sails yellow from the rising sun. All eyes move to the quarterdeck where, as expected, the captain soon appears. Pellew calmly notes the log, compass, wind and wheel; his ruddy face looks stark and foreboding below a mop of greying hair. Start Point lies off their larboard bow and apart from the sighted sail no other vessels can be seen. The usual rhythm of the ship continues but within one run of the glass they all know that the other ship is the *Cléopâtre*. When the enemy hauls all sail, orders are given to make chase.[21]

The crew feverishly work the ship, take to the guns, and know their breakfast will be delayed because the French allow them to approach. They do not seem to recognize them. By four bells (six o'clock of the morning) they converge within hailing distance. The French ship is two points off their larboard bow when a French accent comes across the water, with what seems to be a question. Pellew leaves the quarterdeck and walks to the prow. The crew begins to discuss the situation, until the boatswain[22] tells them to be quiet.

---

21 James, Vol I (1837), 106.

22 This was John Burke, as stated in the logbook of HMS *Nymphe,* that also states how she saw 'strange sail' and 'made the private signal which was not answered' (ADM/L/N 212).

When the captain reaches the bitts he shouts out an indistinct 'Hoa! Hoa!' and quietly issues an order for the entire crew to give three cheers. This sudden opportunity to raise a mighty noise allows everyone to roar with glee. It creates a thrill of excitement. In comic disbelief the men chuckle when the French *capitaine* holds his hat high and returns with 'Vive la nation!'[23] One thickset seaman, a real hearty cove, leans back and manages to both stifle a laugh and whisper loud enough for everyone to hear, 'Bloody Frenchies! Ha! Ha!' Dozens of eyes look to their captain. What will happen now?

Quietly, Pellew speaks to his first lieutenant, who in turn faces the men. Orders race down the length of the ship for the larboard guns to fire, the signal being when the captain places his hat upon his head. Until then the tension mounts. Soon enough, the hat is raised and firmly clamped back upon the captain's head. A second later the foremost larboard guns open fire, with a report that makes the ex-miner jump. A cloud of gun smoke and a strong smell of powder waft by. Action has commenced! Before long his teeth begin to rattle. Never shy of noise, being well used to mine explosions, he nonetheless makes a prayer for deliverance. It only requires one stray metal ball to knock him on the head for an eternity of sleep to follow.

The two ships separate as the *Nymphe* continues upon her course, while the *Cléopâtre* veers off to larboard. For one whole turn of the glass this continues. Both ship's fires remain constant, the deep boom of their own guns mingled with the occasional thrum of enemy shot overhead, until the French frigate can no longer fire her starboard cannons. Veteran seamen wonder what course is it that the enemy takes, only her stern chasers can fire, *yet we can rake them!* The larboard guns send a withering fire down the whole length of the French frigate and the sight of blood and mangled bodies made him look away. Around seven o'clock the *Cléopâtre* receives a double blow. Her wheel is shot away and her mizzenmast falls over her starboard side with a stomach-wrenching crash. Amid a break in the smoke he sees a splintered stump some twelve feet high where a mast used to be. There are gleeful shouts from the *Nymphe* and he joins in. The French are brave souls however, for they haul up and turn their bow towards them. With horror he realizes both ships will collide.

A boy staggers by under the weight of small-arms. A sword appears in his hand, thrust there by a wild-eyed gunner's mate. Other sailors prepare to board the French ship, with cold determination on their faces.

---

23 There exists another version of this scene whereby the British replied with 'Long live King George!' and the French captain held up a red phrygian cap.

He understands that he must fight, but he has never held a sword before. Not sure what to do with the weapon, events take a turn so that he does not have to think at all. With a sound as from hell the prow of the *Cléopâtre,* with wood, rope, rigging and sails, falls upon them. Her jib shoots by above his head, midway between the fore and main mast. The shock of the collision knocks him down. The guns and small arms momentarily stop firing. As he clumsily regains his feet, he thinks of all the hours spent on cleaning the brightwork, holystoning the deck and countless other menial jobs here and there. Everything has been ruined! Men fall about him, either shot dead or thrown over by exploding grenadoes. Shards of wood and hot metal cut flesh and graze heads, but all he can think about is the waste of his labour. A dark rivulet of blood flows upon the deck, and he struggles to remain upright. Ahead of him a midshipman suddenly spins around like a corkscrew, to look in his direction in wide-eyed astonishment. A dark red stain spreads on his chest, and the Cornishman can only watch as the young man adopts a thousand-yard stare and falls down dead. Anger, frustration, fear and bravado all entwine within him – Frenchmen, as many as possible, must die! A red mist envelops him, darkened with every boom of a gun, every musket fired by a marine, every scream of agony thrown heavenwards by a dying sailor. Death to the enemy!

There follows a terrible scraping as the two ships settle side by side, each prow pointing in the opposite direction. To the relief of those able to keep a calm head about them, the jib of the *Cléopâtre* falls away and fails to damage their own mainmast, but both ships remain clapped together like two sisters refusing to let go in a time of distress. The *Nymphe*'s mainmast takes another juddering blow and some seamen, lost to his view, race up the rigging to cut the two ships apart. Such nautical considerations remain far beyond the compass of a 'landlubber' like himself, and buffeted by the boarding party he only has eyes for the enemy. Given a jolt in the ribs he ascends the side and jumps over the gap of grinding wood, roiling sea and strangely quietened guns below, to disappear amid a wall of smoke and land heavily upon a Frenchman on the other side. Their heads collide and both are knocked senseless. Luckily for him he lands on top with his sword deep in the Frenchman's chest. As he comes to, he vaguely feels the last breath upon his cheek. He would have fallen to one side, but fellow *Nymphes* appear through the smoke to pin him there.

By the time he regains his composure the enemy ship has been taken. The *Nymphes* had successfully forced their way to the quarterdeck and caused many French sailors to seek safety below – to their doom, as it turned out, for they came upon British sailors who had gained entrance by way of the gunports. With a sense of groggy relief he witnesses the tricolour hauled down in surrender. The enemy ship has no fight left. Some enraged British seamen continue to butcher men regardless, and finally there are only faint cries of mercy. A seaman, in obvious pain with a broken arm, still manages to lead a chorus of victory. The *Cléopâtre* has been taken a prize!

Enemy sailors, now prisoners, are escorted across to the *Nymphe* and confined below decks. He escorts them. By the time he returns on deck the two ships have separated, and he cannot help but notice their beaten and sorrowful appearance. He feels a sadness like he has never felt before. Looking at his trembling hands he has to clench them shut to stop their shaking. 'Don't worry, lad,' a marine tells him, 'Blood rush 'tis all. Think of the prize!' He returns a thin smile and wonders how many have died.

This action is quick but costly. The butcher's bill runs high with twenty-three *Nymphes* dead and a further twenty-seven wounded. Of the dead there are the boatswain; Richard Pearse, master's mate; the three midshipmen, Samuel Edfall, John Davie, and George Boyd; and fourteen seamen. The French lose sixty-three men dead and wounded.[24] He has killed a man. The enemy, yes, but a man nonetheless. Perhaps he too has a family.

That night the crew discuss whether they have the honour of taking the first French frigate of the war. Wooden cups and wine glasses are lifted in salute to the King, and the warm hope of many more prizes to come. Sitting amid the dim surroundings of the gun deck he senses the Cornishmen have finally been accepted. They have helped defend the honour of their ship and acquitted themselves well.

Looking deep into his cup he thinks about the men. Their movements, focus and sheer determination recall to his mind a complex dance he once saw in Helston. They were lissome, coordinated and purposeful. He finally understands that the *Nymphe,* with her guns, sails, rigging and decks is a community put to sea to cruise and capture the enemy. He has struggled to fully appreciate her finer points but at least he has had a glimpse of what she can do, and he likes what he has witnessed. A sense of pride forms within. These rugged men eat ravenously, complain far too much, sleep untroubled when allowed, often bemoan their lot, yet they always return to their duties, move dangerously high above the rolling deck, laugh in torrential downpours, shrug at life's misfortunes and look forward to the

---

24 James, *ibid*, 106-8. The French *capitaine*, Mullon, died in agony. His left hip was blown away by a shot. He tried to eat what he thought were the signals before he passed away. These were later found and eagerly taken by the British.

warmth and companionship of friends. The ship would be nothing without them, and they would be nothing without the ship.

Unbeknown to the Cornishman, other naval ships and vessels sail over the horizon. Large ships on their way to blockade duty, and frigates off to foreign stations. All sail closer to their fates. Some will gain fame. Others will founder. Harsh are the ways of the sea.

The *Nymphe* soon found out she had indeed been the first to take a French frigate a prize in this new war. She proudly escorted the *Cléopâtre* into Portsmouth on 21 June 1793. With relish the Admiralty received the news, and the captured signals from the hand of Captain Pellew himself. Delighted, indeed bewitched, for such an early return Britain gave the *Nymphe*'s captain a knighthood one week later. Such a victory deserved a public celebration! Put into commission the prize was renamed *Oiseau* and she faithfully sailed under the British flag until sold off in 1816. The Royal Navy seldom failed to put to use a foreign-built ship.

The exploits of the *Nymphe* and the *Cléopâtre* demonstrated to the general public the nature of frigates, and the role they fulfilled. These 'fifth-rate' ships had a sense of adventure and derring-do. However, the truly remarkable thing about the *Nymphe* proved to be her crew. William Schaw Lindsay considered, 'When war was declared by the French in February, 1793... Pellew, finding it impossible to get seamen for his frigate, at once put eighty Cornish miners on board his ship, and a few months later fought and won the celebrated action with the *Cleopatra* - most of his crew never having seen a shot fired before.'[25] That so many raw recruits managed to achieve such an excellent result gave an impression of British fortitude in the face of the enemy. Leadership, discipline, the advantage of surprise, superior gunnery and motivation all had a part to play. The build quality of the ship also proved vital.

For the Royal Navy to emerge victorious from a war against revolutionary France (and by 1795 her client states) she had to rely, in large measure, upon her ships and vessels. There were countless men and women who asked, how fit was the Royal Navy in comparison to the French navy? In 1800 a retired parson remembered the first weeks of the war when most people had only wanted to point out the good aspects of the fleet. For instance, how copper sheathes had been introduced to keep ships and vessels weed-free and allow them to remain at sea for longer periods; that back in 1788 Patrick Millar,

---

25 A footnote to page 182 of *History of merchant shipping and ancient commerce*, Vol. III (1876). This source gives a peacetime establishment of 16,000 sailors and marines, and does not agree with other sources that give 20,000.

James Taylor, and William Symington had placed a steam-powered engine on a boat and had reached seven knots; that in 1791 the Society for the Improvement of Naval Architecture had been formed. All very positive, but he had argued that they were only innovations, and they had nothing to do with the build of ships. He also remembered the time when the *Nymphe* had made the news. What some had then failed to mention was how that ship had been built in a French yard. In fact, the Royal Navy then had a small collection of French and foreign-built ships, all captures from previous wars. He often saw them from his window: the *Gibraltar* (80) (ex *Fenix*), *Courageux* (74), *Bienfaisant* (64), *Hebe* (38), *Concorde* (36), *Magicienne* (32), and *Orestes* (18), to name but a few. There had also been other captures that had served as receiving ships, or accommodation for new recruits; and sheer hulks, or 'cranes', that helped step masts on ships and vessels. Those captured men-of-war were a happy breed because they tended to have their lower tier gunports higher above the waterline than British ships, they had incurred no costs to build, and they were often better built ships with superior sailing qualities. Whereas British shipwrights and surveyors had undoubted skill, he had often complained about the policy to save money through repair and rebuild of ships rather than replacement. He believed neglect had been caused because to repair an old ship meant the mistakes of previous eras persisted into the present, and the knowledge of shipbuilders had not always been done justice.[26] He believed such a situation still persisted. An article published in 1800, by Ralph Willett, talked about the consequences of such neglect before the Seven Years' War (the 1750s). He had written that 'A long peace made us inattentive to the farther improvements of the Navy. We idly imagined that the neighbouring Powers had been as remiss as ourselves; and that our own Navy, still equal to what it had been, was still as able to combat theirs as ever…we supposed, by having a greater number of Ships that we had also an acknowledged superiority of force; but we saw with surprize how active our enemies had been, and what advantage they had taken of our indolence.'[27] When captures were made they had their designs and armaments minutely pored over. It had always been so. Some people liked to stress that when the French captured a British warship they rarely put her into their own service, and if they did it tended to be at a lower rate than a British classification.

---

26 Murray and Creuze (1863), 18. It reads: 'the forms and dimensions of a previous century passed down, in many instances, into the succeeding one, and justice was not done to the shipbuilding knowledge of the surveyors.'
27 Willett in *The Naval Chronicle* Vol III (1800), 462.

Even the timber used to build ships had received criticism. The parson's study had hundreds of books and papers on the subject. One, from 1777, complained about Stettin-sourced lumber. Temple Luttrell had reported to Parliament that such timber had caused ruinous builds and endangered 'the health of...seamen, who are frequently set afloat in their hammocks, from the water soaking in, over-head, through the planks.'[28] HMS *Mars* (74 guns) had been rebuilt with such wood and found to be unusable for service. To Luttrell's mind foreign-built ships had stood better. 'Neither are the ships of war belonging to other maritime nations so bad, in these times, as those of the British navy. The Spanish two-deckers, of 80 and 74 guns, are the strongest and most durable in the world; not only those built in the island of Cuba, of cedar-wood and mahogany, but even such as have been constructed in the European ports of Spain, by English builders, and upon the same models with our own. We have few men of war on our list that have proved so lasting as the Centaur, Bienfaisant, and the ships of war in general that were taken from the French 20 years ago; they have stood us but in little for repairs, compared with others of the same class built in England.'[29]

Critics continued to make their cases throughout the war. In 1794 HMS *Anson,* that had spent the first thirteen years of her life as a 64-gun ship, was cut down (or *razéed*) to transform her into a 44-gun frigate. 'Although in all other maritime states the science of naval construction was well understood, yet so culpably ignorant were the English constructors, that this operation, so well calculated, when properly conducted, to produce a good ship, was a complete failure. Seven feet of the upper part of the top sides, together with a deck and guns, making about 160 tons, were removed, by which her stability was greatly increased; but, by a complete absurdity, the sails were reduced one-sixth in area.'[30] When put to sea she sprung several top-masts and had to return to the yard, and the same problem affected several other warships that underwent the same process. In 1801 a 'disinterested observer' had a letter printed in the *Naval Chronicle*[31] in which he argued that the custom 'to discontinue in time of peace' the building of ships in the river Thames had led to 'no encouragement for the builders, their officers, or workmen, to take apprentices'. Thereby ensued the diminution of professional shipwrights, so that when war returned the yards could not manage the sudden demand. A lack of professional workers increased wages and the

---

28 *The Parliamentary History of England etc to the Year 1803* Vol XIX (1814), 883.
29 *The Parliamentary Register* Vol IX (1778), 26. Stettin is spelled 'Stetin'.
30 Morgan and Creuze, *Papers on Naval Architecture* Vol III (1831), 80.
31 *Naval Chronicle* Vol VI (1801), 480-2.

prices of materials. The need to build and commission warships in quick order only created an inferior build quality that decreased the useful life of warships. A prejudice existed against ships built by contract, despite how the 'disinterested observer' believed such ships were stronger built. Some yards, he wrote, knowingly constructed ships with inferior materials. In 1805 a debate in Parliament[32] stated how it had been found that one half of all sided timber then at Deptford designated to build ships had been rotten. Loans to a few timber merchants had enabled them to 'drive all competitors out of the market'.

The Royal Navy designated her wooden warships by rates, signified by the number of guns they carried. The parson distinctly remembered when, in 1793, he had visited The Point in Portsmouth to join a large crowd that had looked out upon the fleet as it prepared to put to sea. They saw a dull white blaze of new canvas limp under the spring sun. Over towards Priddy's Hard there had been a bomb vessel and a fire ship, a hospital ship further on and brigs aplenty. The harbour exuded a sense of the strength of the nation. Civilians marvelled at the obvious cost needed to build, furnish, and crew them all. The guns of a massive first rate had glinted in the sun and made them all squint. Eight hundred men called that ship their home, more than the parson had known in his childhood village. Such colossi required years, and thousands of loads of timber, to construct. To lose even one had to be considered a national disaster, and one had famously been lost off Portsmouth. The *Royal George* (100 guns) sank at her anchors on 29 August 1782. She had been considered one of the finest vessels in Europe, and 'carried the tallest masts and squarest canvass of any English-built ship in the navy, and originally the heaviest metal.'[33] The water pipe, for cleaning her decks, needed repair so she had been heeled over on her larboard side to reveal the pipe under the keel. To do so her lower ports were opened. A squall later passed over and threw so much water into those opened ports it filled the ship and sank her in less than three minutes. Close to 700 men died. Dozens of bodies later washed up on shore. The shock of that event lasted for years. In 1793 her wreck could still be seen.

When the crowd at The Point had expressed their curiosity about one particular ship they could not recognize, the parson had told them she was a second rate, a type that foreign navies shied away from building for *they thought their lower rated warships could compete*. He patiently explained

---

32 *Parliamentary Debates* (1812), 149.
33 Slight (1843), 7 & 8.

that, *a ship's broadside needed to be superior to an enemy broadside, therefore a three decker second rate had to be superior*. He said it stood to reason, and even a Frenchman agreed. 'It is really the cannon which alone gives the law at sea,'[34] he said. He finished off by stating that this war would decide the issue.

When a third rate 74 warped past, the crowd had cheered. Sailors liked them[35] and they could stand up to the largest enemy warship. They needed to because, sadly, the fourth rates below them were too old and too weak to serve for much longer. Certainly those of fifty guns. He told the crowd that two of them were then with the West Indies fleet as flagships (some were later purchased from the East India Company, and converted to transports and convoy escorts).

So there they had stood, amazed with the industry required to make such mighty craft, and he had told everyone that the four top-rated ships acted as 'ships of the line'. They formed up in 'line of battle' and provided the bulk of the 'wooden wall'. But the lower rated ships[36] and vessels did as much damage, and not just to warships. Frigates, brigs, and sloops supported their much larger sisters, destroyed enemy merchantmen and menaced foreign shores. He had looked for one example of the two-decker 44-gun class, but they were then nowhere to be seen. His nephew had wanted to join one and go on a detached and independent cruise, as one of the 'eyes of the fleet'. Either that, or on a 36. The harbour had been mostly crowded with unrated vessels, with their perplexing array of sail-plans. Small craft, compared to the mighty first rates, they were ideal for annoying the enemy as gadflies. He knew that at the time the Royal Navy commanded 411 warships and vessels spread far and wide over the globe, but many were in ordinary. In 1800, when he read that the fleet had increased to 757 ships and vessels with 124 ships of the line, he had been staggered. The efforts needed to reach that number.

Great Britain eventually put into commission more warships than anyone else, but what about the amount of broadside weight those ships propelled in anger? A warship had to be built 'making proper accommodations for guns, ammunition, provisions, and apartments for all the officers, and likewise

---

34 Maw and Dredge in *Engineering* Vol LIV (1892), 52. The Frenchman was Pierre-Alexandre-Laurent Forfait.

35 *Ibid*. The book states, 'they drew less water, and usually had superior sailing qualities, while they could hold their own against the largest vessels of our enemies.'

36 James, W., Vol I (1837), 75. He wrote that ships 'may cruise about, and interrupt trade, or levy contributions on some comparatively insignificant colonial territory.'

for the cargo.'[37] Each gun had to stand with enough space to recoil. With a need for a larboard and starboard battery, plus space for masts and other deck furniture in between, the width of a ship became self-determined. But no ship could be too long in proportion to her width. A longer line of guns to face the enemy could never be the answer. Instead, a ship had to be built upwards by means of decks. The more decks built, the more guns a ship could carry, but the number of decks could not exceed three full gun decks due to the weight above the waterline. A major consideration always had to be stability.[38]

If there were shortfalls in ship quality the Royal Navy held her own with ordnance. What mattered were fleets superior in numbers with a greater weight of broadside metal to throw at the enemy.

The parson could have made a comparison of a British 74-gun ship and a French 74-gun ship as found at the end of 1792, something James later wrote about: 'the smallest British 74 carried 32-pounders on the lower deck, while the smallest French 74, although upwards of 100 tons larger, carried only 24s.'[39]

Ship's guns were not the only source of firepower. In 1759 Lieutenant General Melville had invented a 'smasher', produced at the Carron Foundry near Falkirk. This ordnance gained the name 'carronade'. By 1781 warships mounted 32-, 24-, 18-, and 12-pounder versions. This new type of ordnance turned heads when the *Rainbow* (44) fired off a whole broadside of them and forced the French ship *Hébé* to immediately strike her colours. At close range carronades were lethal. Not all captains[40] liked them, due to their overheating, constriction of range, and the way they were mounted. Unlike a gun, a carronade rested upon a wooden slide. Carronades might have been smaller and lighter, and required less gunpowder and men to fire, but the Royal Navy much preferred a gun for its greater range. However, ships were equipped with carronades and swivel guns.

The British needed as much ordnance as possible, for France stood 'ready to second her efforts to humble, if not overthrow, her great maritime rival.'[41] She had 250 ships and vessels and a further 71 had been ordered. The parson argued, like later writers, that after taking away ships ordered,

---

37 Murray, M., (1754), 1.
38 The Spanish ship *Nuestra Señora de la Santísima Trinidad* had four decks with guns (not four full gun decks) but this was highly unusual.
39 James, W., *ibid.*, 63. Part of a longer exposition on the size difference of French and British naval ships.
40 *Ibid.*
41 *Ibid.*, 74.

or on the slips, there actually stood 113 British ships of the line to 76 for the French. It was their aggregate weight of broadside metal that mattered. In 1793 Britain commanded 8,718 guns[42] to France's 6,002. As French cannons were of a larger calibre than British guns the cumulative broadside weight narrowed to 88,957lbs for the British, to 73,957lbs for the French. Superiority of numbers therefore made sense. The Royal Navy had to put more ships to sea to increase her broadside weight of metal.

The parson understood the prohibitive costs of the British fleet. In 1792 expenses amounted to £1,485,000.[43] In 1793 it had climbed to £3,900,000. By 1800 it had reached £13,619,000. Five weeks prior to Britain entering the war Parliament voted for 20,000 seamen and 5,000 marines, at a potential cost of £1,300,000. After the declaration of war a further 20,000 men were voted at a further £1,040,000 of expenditure. That made an establishment of 45,000 men.

This pushed up consumer prices. Poor harvests of 1792 and 1793 resulted in profits for some but distress and bankruptcies for others. The cost of grain doubled, and the parson had prayed for an end to suffering.

The British government had to take out loans to conduct the war. In March 1793 the first one raised £4,500,000. There were three loans in 1795 that raised £40,600,000. A 'loyalty' loan in 1797 added to a then combined total of £101,600,000 raised over four years. There were eighteen loans made between 1793 and 1801. Archibald Alison later wrote, 'Power at sea, unlike victory at land, cannot spring from mere suffering, or from the energy of destitute warriors with arms in their hands. Fleets require nautical habits, commercial wealth, and extensive credit; without an expenditure of capital, and the gradual formation of a nursery of seamen, it is in vain to contend with an established power on that element.'[44]

British warships might have fallen short of the best quality build, but there would eventually be more of them, and the amount of destruction they unleashed was mighty. To emerge victorious from the war against revolutionary France, Great Britain had to rely in large part upon her expensive warships. The need to have superiority in numbers charted a course towards the Royal Navy becoming a true naval 'superpower'.

---

42 Ibid., 74. A separate abstract for 1793 shows a total of 411 ships in the navy, of which 135 were in commission; 113 were ships of the line (26 in commission). James states there were 115 ships of the line. The abstract for 1800 shows 757 ships in the navy, of which 124 were of the line (100 in commission).

43 Alison (1854) Vol V, p, 176. Data also comes from the *Journal of the Statistical Society* Vol XVIII (1855), 108 onwards.

44 Alison, *ibid.*, 363.

Chapter 3

Jolly Tars Are Our Men

'Landlords should make a list of men they want rid of. That would help matters.'[45] Old Hanway, the more thoughtful of the gang, often gave his opinion. His rheumy eyes glazed over with some memory or other, and despite being what their Regulator called a 'sea-lawyer',[46] most people tolerated his Messianic utterances. Not so Kemble, who uttered, with a mouth full of chewing tobacco, 'As if those tallow-breeched fools will help us out, old man!'

Old Hanway gave a sideways look. 'Are you woolly crowned?[47] They have in the past.'

Ruspin happened to be the smallest of them, who looked the least threatening with his childlike face, but none dared mess with him. He took quick offence, had a dark aura, and a back ruined by the strap. 'Shut your gobs, both of you, the lieutenant might hear.' Gang members close by became attentive and peered out from the doorway onto the busy street.

Their lieutenant, a derelict of a man, stood across the street near to the *George Inn* with the other half of the gang. Recruitment posters festooned the walls but only two men had volunteered, both out-of-work barristers eager to take the thirty shillings bounty for a landman. They had looked downright miserable when told they would have received £5 each if they had been able seamen. The navy wanted skilled men, but anyone young, strong and sane enough to serve would be accepted.

From amongst the crowds, coaches, and wagons a man and woman appeared. As they passed the Town Hall the gangers, who stood with Ruspin, instantly readied themselves. The couple had obviously been at the

---

45 *Chambers's Journal of Popular Literature* (1895), 347. A common method where landlords handed lists to press gangs.
46 A 'lower deck lawyer', a rating who gives opinions or makes complaints.
47 Then a colloquialism for 'dumb'.

fair to celebrate Howe's victory.[48] The woman, dressed like a Bartholomew Doll,[49] sported a large feather on her head and waved a small British flag. A ditty performed but two days before, in Drury Lane, remained on her lips and although her voice could not reach the true notes she gave a good rendition nonetheless.

When in war on the ocean,
we meet the proud foe,
With ardour for conquest our bosoms do glow,
Shou'd they see our vessels Old England's flag wave,
'Tis worthy of Britons, who conquer to save![50]

The man with her touched his hat at passers-by. Tall and thin he walked with a strange rolling, sailor-like, gait. Ruspin smiled, for the woman's beau seemed to fit the bill. With a low whistle he gained the lieutenant's attention, who noticed the man and minutely nodded his approval. So, with cudgel in hand, Ruspin walked out of the shadows and said to the beau, 'Yo, ho! You should come with me.'[51] The man must have assumed that Ruspin was a part of festivities as he nodded and walked on. Ruspin, unperturbed, gave a loud whistle and the wide expanse of Beckett staggered out from a doorway further along the road. A giant of a man with huge hands he took one look at the young man and grabbed his collar. The suitor recoiled quickly and, before anyone could react, sat down hard upon the road with a bloodied nose and tears in his eyes.

The festive crowd, mainly apprentices and young women, turned and either scattered or faded away to nearby courtyards. The traffic halted and no one moved. The lieutenant's face turned red with anger. Why hit the man? Silence fell, apart from the snort of a horse. A hand to his nose, the escort looked up to the man who had assaulted him, a large figure with a dank face and a stench of tobacco and spirits. The large man looked sad and embarrassed at the same time. The betrothed remained transfixed as a shadow fell across him, and what appeared to be a small youth stooped

---

48 The first major fleet engagement of the war took place on 1 June 1794. The British reckoned it a victory and called the battle 'The Glorious First of June'. The French called it *Bataille du 13 Prairial an 2*, referring to their revolutionary calendar.
49 Gaudily dressed like a St. Bartholomew's Fair wooden doll.
50 *Songs, Duets, Choruses* (1794), 8.
51 Smollett, *Roderick Random* (1824), 182-3.

down to whisper in his ear. 'You should be proud. Today you get to protect and defend our good King.'

'Protect?' the bleeding man asked.

'Aye. You walk like a sailor. I bet you've got tattoos, eh? Jump ship did ye? Or are you a damned patriot like them Corresponding types?[52] Sign our book, and it's a bounty for you.'

'Leave him alone!' The pressgang looked to the woman, who had one arm outstretched. 'Look at his hands!'

Old Hanway looked. Already troubled with the wayward hit he visibly sagged as though a great burden had been placed upon his shoulders. 'Ah! They're ruined.' The beau's fingers were crooked, deformed and some were missing. Ruspin spat in disgust. 'Is it rickets?'

The lieutenant arrived and took command. 'Didn't any of you notice? He can't pull a rope.'

Willoughby shrugged his shoulders and turned his dark chops towards the officer. 'We thought you gave the signal, sir.'

'This won't do,' the officer stated. 'Pick him up.'

The pressmen helped the betrothed to his feet. Under the gaze of the officer they touched their hats and stood aside, while the naval lieutenant made an apology. 'Mistaken identity. Thought you might be someone else. Easily done.' The suitor nodded while blood streamed from his nose. 'Quite understand.' With wild wide eyes he watched the ten men and their officer stride off down the road and disappear from view.

The pressgang had bungled that one so they had to set their sights elsewhere. Since the main sweep of the river the night before, all men good enough to be pressed had long since gone[53]. London knew of them and few were left to volunteer. As they neared London Bridge a local crimp[54] caught up with them. He whispered a few words to the lieutenant then ran off towards the rendezvous.

The lieutenant turned to his men and gave the news. 'A woman has eloped from Sheerness with her two children and a black servant. It appears she arrived at the *Nag's Head* only to meet her estranged husband waiting

---

52 There had been arrests made earlier in 1794, of men considered seditious and possible traitors. Some of those men were members of the London Corresponding Society, and were thrown in jail until trials took place in late 1794.

53 A normal press could not take apprentices, hard-to-find craftsmen, or men of a certain age, but no one was safe in a 'hot press', where any man found fit enough could be taken.

54 A crimp took men for the merchant service.

there. Supposedly the servant fired a pistol and has holed himself up in the stables.[55] We should take a look.'

They all nodded. Some were perplexed, but others hopeful for a brawl. Either way there might by a few collars to touch and thus gain a greater reward. They were paid per head. So they walked back the way they came, heedless of those people who recognized them, and soon arrived at the inn. It proved to be a sprawling affair with rights of way to King Street, its cobbled yard dominated by a large crane and a roof sporting a prodigious chimney. A woman stood silently beside a crowd of stable boys, and a strong smell of stale ale made them slaver for a tipple, but they had work to do.

One stable boy ambled over to greet them. 'Turns out the husband took away the children. He told her she could go where she pleased, damn her eyes. The lady replied she only wants to live with Solomon.'

The lieutenant gave his thanks and a small coin. 'Who's Solomon?'

'Why, the servant, who else?'

The officer looked towards the men, all eager, and told them to get to it.

'Come on lads,' Ruspin said, with a gleam in his eye.

Solomon turned out to have no more bullets for his duelling pistol but he had the muscle to fend them off. Ruspin and Beckett piled in. Willoughby and Kemble came from the sides. Two others tried to get on the roof. Bridles and bits were thrown, and almost knocked Old Hanway senseless. When the man had been subdued they tied him up with a rope and waited until the lieutenant came inside the stable. Duly satisfied, he proclaimed Solomon pressed for His Majesty's Navy and God Save the King! Did he want to take the bounty? Made to stand up, blood on his cheeks, the servant refused to answer so they led him along the street towards the river. The only noise they heard, until they turned a corner, was the wailing of the woman he left behind.

As afternoon waned they approached the rendezvous[56] at an old tender opposite the Tower, freshly painted, with a large flag flapping in the breeze. Solomon had his name entered into the books and disappeared into the hold to join some volunteers and the pressed. When the gang reported to the Regulating Officer, they collected their reward, knuckled their hats and stood idle long enough not to be noticed. Curses of pressed men failed to turn any of their thoughts away from the prospect

---

55 Inspired by a true story, from Rendle and Norman, *The Inns of Old Southwark* (1888), pages 225-6. The description of the inn comes from the source.

56 Hall, *Retrospect of a Long Life* (1883) Vol I, 86. The rendezvous was where press gangs took their captives.

of hard liquor and a warm pie at *The Talbot*; and they knew the women of the town would be in plentiful supply. They wanted to get as drunk as Davy's sow.

The lieutenant stated the press had ended. As though released from bondage, the gang, all grizzled locals and none of them sailors, made their obeisance and walked off the tender. As night fell they found themselves back along the Borough Road, full of people and traffic once more, but with no sight of the woman and her lover. None of the gang uttered a word until they arrived at the inn and had downed a pot of strong beer. They relaxed, began to laugh, and soon got riotously drunk. Old Hanway remained quiet. As he drew deep on his pipe his thoughts wandered to the time he had been pressed many years ago. He had then lived in Liverpool and ended up on a warship for the term of her commission. Five years, and the trauma still lingered. How would his life have turned out if he had remained on his farm? Whatever happened to his wife and son? Painful memories, but at least tomorrow would be another day, and the reward in his pockets was handsome.

Parliament voted to raise the naval establishment so by 1800 it stood at 120,000 men,[57] but disease, death and desertion required manpower to be constantly replenished. Disease took away the largest number, followed by desertion. Nelson believed that between 1793 and 1802, 42,000 men deserted. As it required £20 to train each one,[58] that amounted to a loss of £840,000. A paper by a Mr Hodge was read to the London Statistical Society in 1856, titled 'On the Mortality arising from Naval Operations'. It stated that between 1793 and 1815 a total of 6,663 men died in action, 13,621 died by wreck,[59] and 72,102 died from disease or by accident,[60] for a total of 93,386.

The majority of British sailors had volunteered, but bounties and pensions could not provide a sufficient enticement to replenish such losses. There had also been competition: men knew, for example, that they would generally be offered better pay and better conditions in the Newfoundland fishery trade.

For recruitment of ordinary hands there had been the bounty or, as a last resort, the Impress Service. Britain had resorted to the 'press

---

57 This figure was soon reduced by 10,000 (Fincham, 1851, 137).
58 Southey (1890), 353.
59 Naval losses are difficult to ascertain; this figure comes from the *Illustrated Naval and Military magazine* Vol IX (1888).
60 This figure came from the *Edinburgh Medical Journal* Vol I (1856), 272.

gang' for centuries. Arguments in support of the brutal practice stated it necessary for national defence. Many volunteered for the navy, but without the press, never enough. The 1597 Vagabonds Act[61] had 'rogues, vagabonds, and sturdy beggars arrested, whipped, put to work, sent overseas, or placed in a galley'. The 1703 Recruitment Act[62] limited those who could be taken, but still permitted the 'press' to operate. Threat of invasion had been the issue. In the first weeks of war impressment generated large numbers of men and warships could be to put to sea to build the 'wooden wall'. Some people considered compulsion to serve no different to the ballots then used to raise militia, and they thought no viable alternative existed. 'We have learnt to endure, the ills we cannot cure.'[63] A German wrote, 'Every friend of humanity must revolt at the idea of a press gang in a free country; a practice that entirely overturns every principle of English liberty... but the doctrine of necessity has hitherto stifled every other consideration.'[64]

Some later writers thought that such a 'doctrine of necessity' created sailors who showed 'reckless courage and contempt for death', who remained loyal to good captains and officers, and yet brought into the service some of the worst elements of British society. Press gangs were said to have lurked around jails with the aim of taking newly released prisoners. The navy took 'Scapegraces in respectable families, disqualified attorneys, cashiered excisemen, dismissed clerks, labourers who through idleness or drunkenness had lost their employments, men from every walk of life, who, through want of capacity or want of character had found other careers closed to them.'

After Britain entered the war, the United States clarified her neutral position (22 April 1793)[65] and thereafter accused the Royal Navy of impressing American sailors. This continued to be an open sore until 1812. Charles Grey,[66] member of Parliament for Northumberland, raised the spectre of evils that resulted from impressment. He brought attention to events of 26 April 1793 when a press gang entered the town of Shields:

---

61 *Country Gentleman's Magazine* (1876), 805.
62 Its full title was 'An Act for raising recruits for the land forces and marines, and for dispensing with part of the act for the encouragement and increase of shipping and navigation, during the present war'.
63 *Impressment of seamen and a few remarks on corporal punishment etc* (1834), 10.
64 Archenholz (1791), 263. The author goes on to argue that bounties held out to seamen had little effect, and that many men joined merchantmen to avoid a warship.
65 Winsor (1888) Vol VII, 461-6.
66 The future Earl Grey who had the tea named after him.

'They entered not only public but also private houses, and conducted themselves with such violence as to become the general terror of the whole town. In one house they entered the chamber of a person by force, and at another took seven women naked out of bed, thrust their bayonets into closets, under beds, and many other places, under pretence of authority for searching for seamen for the service of His Majesty's navy.'[67]

Criticisms continued after the fall of Napoléon in 1815. Thomas Urquhart[68] asked why a whole generation of British subjects, having been raised during a time of conflict, had bred so few seamen. He placed the cause upon an 'improper mode of impress', where insults, bad conduct of officers, and a reliance upon 'the refuse of mankind' to make up the impressment service, resulted in an aversion to the navy. With men taken from merchant ships, those ships often struggled to get into port, and had to procure hands to do so, incurring further expense upon their owners. Thomas Trotter[69] had thought this might have been why merchant traders sometimes opposed the 'efforts of government' by hiding their men, or sending them far inland to avoid impressment. Some men even resorted to self-mutilation of fingers and hands, or offered bribes, just to be left alone. If a man was taken by the press, but found to fall outside the required age range or to be an apprentice, he would be set free so long as he could prove his age and work status. If he could not prove those things, then he remained 'pressed'.

The main need for the Royal Navy had been expert seamen. Without them the war would have been lost. Skilled sailors, known as able seamen or 'topmen', worked a complex set of spars, ropes, sails, equipment and manned the great guns. It required years to become competent in their role, and they had to start young. This explains why many sources refer to a 'nursery' of seamen. Nurseries were provided by the coastal, coal, Baltic, Newfoundland fishery, West Indies and American trades, that had thousands of seamen in employment. In peacetime they were left alone, but in times of war the needs of the state took precedence. A man who could work high above the deck, while a ship pitched and rolled on rough seas, and deal with sails when winds howled all around was a precious resource. It was dangerous work, so only for the young and hearty. Volunteers did come forth, but for the shortfall there had been impressment.

---

67 J. Almon in *The Parliamentary Register* (1793) Vol XXXV, 525. Grey was a member of the 'Friends of the People'.

68 Urquhart (1816), 9.

69 Trotter, *A Practical Plan* (1819), 17.

The merchant trade was a rich source of men to be pressed, so most impressment took place at sea. Naval ships and vessels would confidently stop and board a merchantman returning home or arriving upon a distant station, and take the men they needed. An officer could often tell at a glance whom to press. A man so pressed, sometimes in sight of home, might never see his family again.

An Act of 5 March 1795[70] made it obligatory for 'counties and districts to provide able-bodied men to serve in the Royal Navy'. This 'Quota Act' required parish officers to assemble and determine how best to raise their allotted number of men and the bounty they would offer. The Act was imposed nationwide, not just on coastal parishes and counties. For example, the 1795 quota for Birmingham had been forty-four men allotted by a 'general Session of the Peace at Warwick'.[71] This quota was completed by May 1795, and those who came forward were paraded through the streets with fanfare. The County of Cambridge received a quota of 126 men. The town and University of Cambridge[72] had to find thirty-two men. A parish suffered a fine if it failed to hit its quota, so when men no longer came forward quotas were sometimes fulfilled by forcing prisoners to join the navy rather than languish in jail at the expense of the parish.

Further legislation in 1795 brought into being 'An Act for enabling the Magistrates in the several Counties, Cities, and Boroughs of Great Britain, to raise and levy, under certain regulations, such able-bodied and idle persons as shall be found within the said Counties, to serve in his Majesty's Navy'. The term 'idle' then implied a man who had no lawful calling. In June 1795, 'An Act for augmenting the Royal Corps of Artillery, and providing Seafaring Men, for the Service of the Navy, out of the Private Men now serving in the Militia', allowed volunteers to serve with a bounty of ten guineas for each man. Britain thereby became heated with recruitment, and some nefarious fellows appeared to have taken advantage. A printed caution of 13 April 1795[73] in Birmingham warned of 'Crimp Sergeants' who had illegally 'engaged' men for the navy without any authority, and stated that such men so engaged would be discharged at full liberty and the names of the sergeants sent to the War Office for punishment.

This was an era of theories and ideas sponsored by civilian groups, such as the London Corresponding Society, who caused alarm in government

---

70 *Report of the Committee appointed to enquire into the subject of boy enlistment* (1876), 519.
71 Dent (1880), 300.
72 Cooper (1852) Vol IV, 453.
73 Langford (1868) Vol II, 50.

circles. Founded in 1792 by Thomas Hardy, a shoemaker in Piccadilly, Corresponding members met once a week at the Bell public house in Exeter Street, London. They advocated greater democracy and reform of how Parliament represented the people, while against them stood those who confounded such ideas with revolution. Some members of this society had been seconded as members of the 'Friends of the People', a far wider Whig group who sought a stronger Parliament, free trade and an end to slavery. Newspapers spread their notoriety, and their ideas seeped throughout all levels of society. A labourer soon came to know of them as well as any barrister. However, the French Revolution, and what occurred at the guillotine, had made the idea of 'rights' a dirty one for many. Parliament resisted moves towards reform. A war had to be won that made people in authority shy away from liberal thoughts and liberal ideas.

In 1794 arrests were made against 'perceived' seditious individuals. Thomas Hardy, John Thelwall, John Horne Tooke and others were thrown in jail. Although later acquitted, their treatment had been seen by many as the slow erosion of British liberties. In the same year Parliament suspended the ancient right of *habeas corpus,* the protection against unlawful arrest. Reinstated in June 1795, further suspensions followed in 1798, 1799 and 1800. When King George III drove through London to open Parliament on 29 October 1795, there had been bread riots. His carriage was surrounded by a large crowd and a bullet broke a window. Potential groups of 'beau nasties' (similar to members of the gang that had pressed Solomon) looked on. Parliament, fearful of an outbreak of the violence that France had suffered, reacted with a Treason Act and a separate Seditious Practices Act. The Treason Act permitted the arrest of anyone who wrote, spoke or caused hatred to be directed towards the king, the king's authority or his heirs during the remaining lifetime of the king. The Seditious Practices Act disallowed large political meetings, unless advertised beforehand, and two justices could disperse any meeting they considered dangerous. Sailors mutinied in 1797, and in 1799 Parliament introduced a Combination Act that forbade the formation of any trade society.

In 1799 Lord Grenville[74] argued that the press had proven to be injurious to Britain so that 'the country might be armed, and its income expended, but every effort was useless if this intestine ulcer was suffered to prey upon its vitals.'[75] Lord Holland replied that a warlike enemy, and the disaffection

---

74 *Parliamentary History of England* (1819) Vol XXXIV, 171.
75 *Ibid.*

of the people, should not be enough to take away habeas corpus; that Parliament had got into an argument of 'sacrificing a part to preserve the rest'. He considered suspension of habeas corpus to be inappropriate 'thanks to the bravery and skill of British seamen; and above all, thanks to the victory obtained by lord Nelson; and thanks, no less, to the vigour and activity of the Admiralty, the danger of invasion was not only removed, but wholly destroyed.'[76] Regardless, habeas corpus had been suspended.

A man's faith could also make him 'seditious'. Since the Test Act of 1673 Catholics had suffered discrimination due to their obligations to the Pope and some doubted their loyalty to the crown. They had been ousted from public offices. If a Royal Navy ship worked in Irish waters a Catholic officer could serve on board, but he could not if the ship transferred to other waters. In effect, he became barred from many naval positions. Until 1801 Ireland remained financially independent of Great Britain and in 1782 had voted funds[77] to raise 20,000 men for the Royal Navy. A large proportion of Royal Navy sailors happened to be Irish, and many followed the Catholic faith. They could not openly follow their religion while onboard a British naval ship outside Irish waters and the first Article of War required them to conform to the rites of the established church. Officially no warrant or commission could be given until the recipient had taken an oath, and made declarations to prove he would uphold the requirements of the office.

If political ideas changed, then so too did the very social structure of Britain. A widespread redistribution of population had already occurred before 1750. With no official census returns until 1801, and then only limited, the number of people who lived in Britain before that date is hard to state. Finlaison, an actuary, estimated in 1831 that Britain's population stood around 6,000,000 people in 1750, but had risen to over 9,000,000 by 1801[78]. In the middle of the eighteenth century the population of certain counties altered significantly, especially in Lancashire, the West Riding, Warwickshire and Durham. They were the main centres of cotton and wool manufacture, potteries and hardwares, and coal mines respectively. This shift altered the balance of population between rural and urban areas. In 1688 it had potentially been 3:1 in favour of a rural population, but sometime around 1770 it reached parity. Thereafter it continued to grow in favour of

---

76 *Ibid.*
77 *Royal Commission of the financial relations between Great Britain and Ireland* (1895), 321.
78 Toynbee (1887), 34.

the cities.[79] By the time of the war against revolutionary France, an industrial class had begun to arise. The old relationship of master and servant had started to break down in favour of a relationship between manufacturer and worker, of employer and employee. Britain slowly converted from a rural population tied to farms, to one that predominantly lived in towns and cities, tied to manufacturing. Many of these cities stood on or near to the coast. By 1800 Newcastle had 28,000 people, Portsmouth 32,000, Bristol 68,000, Liverpool 77,000, and London had ballooned to more than 1,000,000 people. Sea trade dominated these towns, and Britain's merchant marine drew upon a large pool of young hearty fellows eager for work. This could only help the Royal Navy.

The redistribution of population incurred social changes, that in turn brought distress for many. Manufacturers made enormous fortunes but rural rents rose sharply[80]. The continuing enclosure of land, consolidation of farms, and high prices of corn during the war caused hardship. Landowners became conspicuous by their consumption, yet workers struggled to live with high prices and low wages. The debt the American War had incurred still lingered, and foodstuffs had become expensive. A typical man of the times, Vinney, had been a labourer whose wages had not kept pace. Bad harvests caused scarcity, prices rose even further, and he could not afford to feed himself and his family. In 1790 his wage purchased 169 pints of corn. If he had not ended up in prison, and eventually upon a warship, his wage would have dropped so that by the mid-1790s he could only purchase 83 pints of corn.[81] A colossal amount of national wealth had been created in his lifetime but not for Vinney. Many found themselves in his position. Monies spent on poor relief stood around £2,000,000 in 1785 and had increased to £4,000,000 by 1801[82], but Vinney would have done anything to earn a wage. When the Royal Navy offered bounties, in 1793 and 1794, he had been unable take one as he lived too far inland. The Quota Act changed that. What made men like Vinney seek employment with the Royal Navy was need. Defoe said, 'It is poverty makes men soldiers.'[83] It also made them sailors.

Those volunteers who took the navy bounty, soon realized that wages were not as high as they had expected. Vinney, who ended up on the same

---

79 Mackay (1889), 132.
80 Toynbee, 92.
81 Toynbee, *ibid.*, 124.
82 Pashley (1852), 247.
83 Marshall, H., *Military miscellany* (1846), 26. Defoe talked about conditions at the time of Queen Anne for the army.

warship as Solomon, soon found that the cost of articles for a sailor's simple subsistence had increased, but a sailor's pay and allowances had not. Annual payment for all Royal Navy sailors had been fixed in 1653. A bill of 24 January 1758, for the 'Encouragement of Seamen employed in the royal navy, and for establishing a regular method for the punctual, frequent, and certain payment of their wages,'[84] had brought certain improvements, but wages remained static. Vinney cared nothing for history. When he received payment it seldom came to the full amount, as there were deductions, and he resented it. Seamen might go long periods without any payment at all. Only when a ship had been 'paid off', or put out of commission, did a sailor normally receive his full due, if he remained on board. This non-payment was often a deliberate method to stop desertion. As landmen, Solomon and Vinney earned £10 a year. Those able seamen they came to know earned £14 a year, petty officers £27 a year. Commissioned officers fared better: a lieutenant received £100 a year, and a captain of a first rate ship more than £330 a year.

Ordinary sailors could reason and communicate their grievances as never before. For an equally fundamental change had taken place: education. In 1698 the Society for Promoting Christian Knowledge first began to distribute Bibles and scripture books amongst the poor. Between 1733 and 1840[85] they distributed close on 51,000,000 books. After 1782 Sunday schools became widely established with an aim to educate poor children. Vinney would have been one such child, and in 1795 he was an adult with his own children. A 'society for the establishment and support of Sunday-schools' had, at the end of ten years, 'distributed 91,915 spelling-books, 24,232 Testaments, and 5,360 Bibles, which had been applied for use in 1,012 schools containing about 65,000 scholars.'[86] If only at a rudimentary level, more seamen could read. They could also write, and wrote letters[87] to people they thought might read them. There were numerous desertions – Vinney and others eventually fled their ships – but the majority of sailors waited for an opportunity to be heard. That finally arrived in 1797 when grievances about their lot became loud and raucous. Until then they had remained quiet because the Royal Navy was a strict mistress.

---

84 *Parliamentary History of England* (1813) Vol XV, 839.
85 Buddicom (1840), 8.
86 Gregory (1877), 104&5.
87 Sailors did so before the Great Mutiny of 1797.

Critics at the time thought impressment was responsible for excessively strict discipline. 'It is impossible to consider the subject of impressment, as connected with naval discipline, without at once discovering and admitting, that to this unjust and oppressive practice, is to be mainly attributed, the severity that had become common in the discretionary exercise of the power to punish for all breaches, as well of the articles of war, as the private rules and regulations established by each captain in the service, for the governance of his particular ship.'[88] The Royal Navy was a military service, and the Articles of War imposed severe punishments for various misdemeanours. They aimed to put resolve in the men, and they applied as much to an admiral as they did to a landman. The 25 December 1749 Articles of War,[89] an 'act for amending, explaining, and reducing into one Act of Parliament, the Laws relating to the Government of His Majesty's Ships, Vessels, and Forces at Sea', made no reference to punishments where a man might be flogged, but instead referred to punishments 'according to sea customs'. Vinney suffered more than one punishment 'according to sea customs'.

The Articles did not exist solely for misdemeanours. They set out the standards by which a sailor should conduct himself. All seamen were warned regularly to follow the public worship of Almighty God according to the Liturgy of the Church of England. Never to get drunk, curse, be unclean, pilfer or be scandalous. Never to entertain a rebel or his letters, for fear of death. Never to be shy of an engagement with the enemy, for fear of death. Never to desert, for fear of death. Never to make any mutinous assembly nor stir up trouble. Never to attempt to hit a superior, for fear of death. Never to sleep on watch. And so on and so on. Officers heard the same Articles. In 1792 a statute made the Articles of War be read 'to the end and intent that every Seaman employed in the royal navy of Great Britain, may at one and the same time hear and know the forfeitures and punishments he is liable to for any neglect or disobedience, and likewise the encouragements and benefits to which he is entitled, by a due and faithful performance of his duty; and that upon suffering any oppression or injury in such service, he may be better enabled to lay his complaint before the lord high admiral of Great Britain etc.'[90]

John Lockwood, a US naval surgeon with no ties to the Royal Navy, wrote in 1849 that the articles 'did not prevent seamen in British

88 Haly (1822), 1.
89 22 Geo. II, c. 33.
90 *The Statutes at Large of England* (1811) Vol XVII, 816.

men-of-war from being greatly oppressed. Scarcely at any period in history has civilized man been exposed to more gross injustice, and more barbarous usage, than were British sailors at and before the close of the 18th century. The British government professes to have necessity to plead in extenuation of such atrocities. Immense fleets were to be manned and sailors could be procured in no other way than by the instrumentality of the press-gang. Thus...it was not rare for excesses to be committed or violence threatened, requiring summary and severe measures to punish and restrain.'[91] Lockwood went on to say that by the end of the era the situation had altered after the Royal Navy introduced punishment books for ships, and enforced regular reports about punishments to the Admiralty. However, before then it appears few men complained about the Articles of War or arbitrary rules of warships.[92] When sailors mutinied in 1797 they made no mention of grievances about punishment. Sailors assumed a man punished had committed a wrong. Besides, most ships' captains preferred to be as lenient with their men as possible. Good motivation in battle led to success, and most knew it.

As soon as pressed men like Solomon, quota-men like Vinney, and volunteers like a man called Jennings, found themselves on a warship, their lives changed drastically. After an inspection by the ship's surgeon they received their hammocks and were shown where to hang them. They were then placed either with the larboard or starboard watch, or as an idler.[93] They would have found their ship a strange and dangerous place, a wooden world where men talked in strange phrases, acted in a manner unlike anything they had known before and lived amid spaces difficult at first to comprehend. A world of hard wood, rough rope and stinging salt spray. From dangerously high spars that towered above, down ratlines and rigging to a cluttered deck below, thence down hatchways to a dim and foetid interior of muffled sounds, stooped gaits and the smell of damp wood. An unforgiving world that lurched and moved. Unsure of themselves they had to adapt to survive. Jennings, an ex-printer thin of chest but broad of mind, could easily blend in. So too Solomon. Vinney proved to be awkward, sharp-angled, with ribs that stood too proud of

---

91 Lockwood (1849), 5.

92 One anonymous writer pointed out how ships were constructed on the same lines of classes (and rates) and navigated by the same rules and principles, but were not 'governed by the same regulation'. *Observations and instructions for the use of the Commissioned, the Junior, and other officers of the Royal Navy* (1804), 1.

93 where men who did not 'work' the ropes were placed.

his pale skin. Resentment ever burned in his belly. They soon came across men who had long served at sea, and who considered lubbers like them a nuisance. The likes of the cook, with his mangled left hand, the gunner with a voice as sharp as flint, the boatswain both loud and bluff, the carpenter busy with repairs, the purser who most did not care for. Everyone had their place upon the ship, from the captain down to the boys, and most stood a watch. Solomon, Vinney, and Jennings quickly found out that the rear parts of the ship were places they would seldom venture, for there the officers resided. Their sea-lives would generally be conducted in but two thirds of the ship, unless they acted as a servant. It became their home and place of work with hundreds of other men who lived cheek by jowl, jumbled upon a long, thin and skittish wooden horse.

At sea, Solomon and Jennings followed a two-watch system, opposite each other, that reset every two days; four hours on, four hours off, apart from dog watches in the evening. They seldom had much time together. Day in, day out, for weeks on end. Bad weather often required they remain on deck even when off watch. A tiring system, even worse when the ship was short-handed. The ship always needed repair and attention. Rigging needed tightening, ropes had to be coiled, brightwork required cleaning, the upper deck had to be holystoned, the lower decks swept, the big guns attended to, and small-arms drill performed. They were either on watch, at work, eating, drinking, going to the heads, sleeping or savouring a few hours of rest and relaxation. Their life became set by the ship's bell (though sudden yaws could cause it to 'strike without leave') and the thud of the boatswain's rattan cane. A rigid, relentless system where everyone was kept busy. A sail upon the horizon, the odd drama, an outbreak of disease, spates of boredom, the state of the sea, the weather, meals and an occasional sight of land marked the passage of days. Jennings and Solomon thrived. Vinney fell prey to the 'black dog'.[94]

It required time and effort to come to know and appreciate the ways of a warship, to 'learn the ropes'. But Jennings and Solomon had aptitude and a first lieutenant who encouraged them. As neither of them cared for the sight of blood the position of surgeon's mate had been out of the question. Jennings made the best of it and worked hard. He learned how to hand, reef, steer, work the rigging and stand a watch so was rated ordinary seaman within a year.[95] He became an able seaman in quick order and

---

94 depression.

95 Handle sails and ropes, reef (furl and unfurl) sails in poor weather, and steer a ship; he should also be able to handle the lead, row a boat, splice a rope, strop a block, and make all kinds of knots. As found in Brown (1853), 69.

within five years he could have been made petty officer, a position with responsibility. He proved to be good at seamanship, so either boatswain's or quartermaster's mate beckoned for him. Solomon struggled at first, but he did the best he could. His natural strength proved an asset. He excelled at the big guns, his muscles perfect for the rear of a gun, so either gunsmith or gunner's mate was for him. Vinney proved to be hopeless. Pulling a rope literally did him in. He therefore became a 'shifter', a cook's aid, as he could manage the 'steep-tub'. He could read and had hoped to catch the eye of the captain. That dreadful, remote, figure of utmost authority needed to maintain many books and logs, but he already had a clerk. If Vinney had secured that position he might have ended up as purser. Ultimately, either due to death, disease or desertion, none of them attained the central triumvirate of gunner, boatswain, or carpenter. That set of most experienced sailors had received their warrants from the Navy Board. The gunner held responsibility for all the ship's ordnance,[96] the guns, small arms and powder. The boatswain managed those men who 'worked' the ship. The carpenter cared for the ship's boats, masts, yards, leaks and damage. Above these three, 'The higher warrant officers, as the master, purser, and surgeon [were called], were in a different position from the other officers, by reason of the power intrusted to them and their connection with guilds or departments on shore. The masters were all Trinity House men, the surgeons were nominated by the governing body representing their profession, and the pursers were, in a sense, the representatives afloat of the Navy Commissioners, to whom they gave bond for the proper performance of their duties.'[97] The purser doled out required provisions at least twice a day, and provided wood, candles, lanterns and controlled the storage of provisions. The likes of Vinney, a man never satisfied with anything, had contempt for this man because of his perks. A purser could deduct one-eighth of every seaman's food allowance.

The ladder of promotion ensured every warship had a mixture of hands, from men learning the ropes to expert seamen, warrant officers and commissioned officers. Warrant and commissioned officers provided advice and leadership for their captain, and diligence through upkeep of ledgers aimed to lessen embezzlement and fraud. The upper levels of a ship were never closed to a man of talent. James Clephan had been pressed from a merchant ship in July 1794 and soon made able seaman on board the *Sibyl*

---

96 Sadler (1891), 41.
97 Robinson (1894), 342; and Steel (1801), 31.

(28 guns). In 1795 he became master's mate on board the *Doris* (36), and in 1801 a lieutenant. The year 1805 found him aboard the *Spartiate* (74) at Trafalgar. He died in 1854 a full captain. Whereas a warrant officer received the title 'officer' he could not be called a 'gentleman'. Only a commissioned officer could claim to be a gentleman. Warrant officers were permanent to a ship, commissioned officers came and went.

Every ship had its own small band of commissioned officers, commissions granted by the Admiralty. None suffered impressment to become one, although a pressed man could eventually be promoted to one. They came from all strata of society, but were considered to be 'gentlemen'. James Cook began his sea career as a ship-boy.[98] There had long been a form of corruption with regards to how some had begun their careers. It had been known for a captain to place the name of a friend's, or patron's, son on his ship's muster book. Often the child would be as young as 10 but did not actually go to sea until much older, possibly 15 or 16. By then he was said to have 'gained' five or six years sea experience. On his arrival, totally green, he would have been rated midshipman and made eligible for lieutenant. In 1794 an Order in Council forbade any 'youngster' to be entered on a warship's muster book as 'servant'. The rank of 'boy' had to be used instead. To mollify ships' captains, who made complaints at the time, four servants could be taken for every one hundred men of a ship's complement, and an officer could have one servant each. Therefore, no 'boy' could be placed on the books of a warship under the age of 11.

'Officers in training' commenced with midshipmen, the 'young gentlemen', who one day hoped to be made commissioned officers. If new to the navy they were mustered as first class volunteers or, if already experienced, as midshipman or master's mate. After six years experience, with a minimum two years served as either, they could take the examination for lieutenant. The 'cockpit'[99] of midshipmen and master's mates therefore formed a bridge between the gun deck, where the likes of Jennings, Solomon and Vinney messed, and the wardroom. This meant Jennings and Solomon could hope to become officers one day, so long as they had the requisite period of time at sea, with responsibility, and had become master's mate.

Superior to a midshipman stood a lieutenant. Every warship had a number of them, dependent upon its rate. A first rate could have six, a

---

98 In the merchant service.
99 Name given to where they messed.

frigate three, and an unrated ship one. In 1793 the Royal Navy had over 1,400 lieutenants. By 1803 she had more than 2,400.[100] Not all were on full pay. If at sea they too stood a watch and were linked with a gun division. The senior lieutenant was the first lieutenant. He had executive control of the ship and ran it day to day. He controlled the lives of ordinary hands. His understanding of what the captain required was fundamental to the effectiveness of the ship, and seamen prayed for a good one. As he remained in the wardroom with other officers he needed to be both forceful and sociable in equal measure. Above everything else he had to know every man who served on his ship, and encourage the boys, landmen and seamen to succeed. Along with the senior petty officers, the first lieutenant examined every sailor seeking promotion. He reported to the one man who ranked above him – on first and second rated warships a flag officer might have been present, but normally the highest ranked officer was the captain or commander.

A captain had to decide the manner in which his ship was rigged, fitted out, and stowed. His authority was absolute to the point 'of a petty German prince'.[101] He had to keep a journal, make weekly accounts to both the Admiralty and navy offices, oversee all stores, and receive regular, if not daily, reports from his warrant officers. Along with his clerk he kept an eye out for possible fraud and embezzlement, had responsibility to maintain effective manning of his ship, and kept the ship's muster book up to date. Under no circumstances could he have more men onboard than the rate of his ship allowed. Not every hand on board would have been his personal choice, and with men like Vinney he had to perpetually guard against desertion. He would have fretted over his sails,[102] made sure all fires and candles were extinguished at night if not contained in a lantern, and made certain that the correct number of men be trained in small arms. He preferred to have commissioned officers who had chosen to serve with him, especially his first lieutenant. As soon as he received promotion to commander (nominally the captain of a vessel of war) he was placed on a seniority list. The passage of time, and the natural 'wastage' of death and retirement, allowed him to progress up that list.

Vinney failed utterly to appreciate the ranks he never came across. He understood 'captain' well enough, even 'post captain', but flag officers he never did work out. Rear, vice and full admirals were people who never

---

100 *Encyclopaedia Britannica* (1884) Vol XVII, 303.
101 *An Enquiry into the present state of the British Navy etc by an Englishman* (1815), 44.
102 Steel (1801), 27.

ventured upon his ship while he served onboard. Jennings eventually served on a second rate, so he did meet an admiral. A marine friend on that ship had explained how a rear admiral was equivalent to a major general, a vice admiral to a lieutenant general, and an admiral to a general; that the titles admiral 'of the blue', 'of the white' and 'of the red' were then no longer equated to actual squadrons as they had once been, only seniority; that men like themselves had a certain worth and if ever exchanged as a prisoner the enemy would expect one seaman in return, but sixty men for a full admiral.[103]

Jennings's marine friend formed part of a complement[104] found onboard every warship. With war their establishment had been increased to 9,000 men. By 1800 it stood at 24,000. They were comprised of three divisions based upon the three main naval ports. Their numbers were also dependent on the rate of a ship. A colossal first rate carried more than one hundred marines.[105] A frigate carried close to thirty. A sloop of less than 18 guns could have claimed eighteen marines. Privates were sentinels at sea. They mustered for inspection every evening, at quarters, and were often at small arms drill. During punishment they formed up between the commissioned officers and the men. Vinney would have testified to that. In an engagement a marine might have climbed up the rigging, encumbered as he was, to fire down upon the enemy. Apart from their different uniforms, both marines and seamen shared similar stories and backgrounds. However, their desertion rate proved to be far lower.

On board Vinney's ship there had lived a woman. The purser's wife shared her husband's life at sea. Like any wife on board a warship she had to share her husband's rations, expect little or no privacy, and often needed to absent herself from sight. The purser's wife assisted the ship's surgeon.

In port, bumboats brought women on board for a few hours. Some managed to stow themselves away. In 1799 the *Proserpine* (28) became wrecked off the Elbe river on an uninhabited island. All her crew disembarked and walked to safety through thick snow. Two women went with them. One had had her husband taken by the press and brazenly followed him on board, despite being heavily pregnant. When 'discovered' the ship had already

103 *The Annual Register, or a view of the History, Politics, and Literature for the year 1798* (1800), 172.
104 *Encyclopaedia Britannica Dictionary* (1890) Vol XV, 545.
105 They did not become the 'Royal' Marines until 1802.

put to sea; she had her child before the ship was wrecked.[106] In 1816 it was ascertained that 'Amongst the crew of the Queen Charlotte...recently paid off, it is now discovered, was a female African, who had served as a seaman in the Royal Navy for upwards of eleven years, several of which she has been rated able on the books of the above ship by the name of William Brown; and has served for some time as the captain of the foretop, highly to the satisfaction of the officers. She is...about five feet four inches in height, possessed of considerable strength and activity...about twenty-six years of age. Her share of prize money is said to be considerable... she exhibits all the traits of a British tar, and takes her grog with her late messmates with the greatest gaiety. She says she is a married woman, and went to sea in consequence of a quarrel with her husband, who it is said, has entered a caveat against her receiving her prize money.'[107] Vinney once spent time on a hospital ship, and he got to know the female nurses and the women who did the laundry.

To emerge victorious from the war against France, her client states, and eventually Spain and Denmark, the Royal Navy had to rely upon her men *and* women. With never enough sailors the fleet resorted to the press and offered bounties. Government policy was to put more warships to sea than the combined total of her enemies. Through training, discipline and promotion they maintained just enough skilled hands to help the Royal Navy become a naval 'superpower'.

---

106 Gilly (1857), 17.
107 Taylor (1816), 139.

Chapter 4

To Receive Them on Shore

Dear Sirs,
No doubt you are sensible to the work of John Evelyn,[108] *who once wrote*
upon the plight of our national trees. Through his foresight and efforts he
lived to see a prodigious replenishment of the national stock. The quantities
of oak timber consumed by the Royal Navy, since the commencement of this
war, have come primarily from the Royal Forests or private plantations made
after the Restoration. The Comptroller of the Navy, Sir Andrew Hamond,
should consider the current situation as demand far exceeds supply.[109]
I humbly present to you that without a constant, and sustainable, source
of timber the instrument for our salvation will perish. If adequate supplies
of oak reserves, or suitable hardwoods, are not protected future merchant
and naval ships will struggle to be built, refurbished and repaired. Without
supplies of Baltic timber we could not replace spars and masts, and the
war might widen to put at risk timber from Baltic contractors.[110] *Remember*
what happened in 1791 with the Russian crisis! No longer should we look
to the present. We should look to the future. Without redress we will have
incontrovertible proof within the next few years that availability of our oak
trees has reached a perilous position.

---

108 Evelyn wrote *Silva, or a Discourse of Forest-trees and the Propagation of Timber in His*
     Majesty's Dominions in 1662 – a highly influential book.
109 Sir Andrew reported on this in 1802. Between 1793 and 1800 the fleet had expanded so
     much the future supply of oak timber was a concern. It was later reported 'a melancholy
     fact, as shewn in an account laid before the House of Commons, dated November 26,
     1803, that in the New Forest, of 66,942 acres, "the number of oak trees in an improving
     state, which may be considered fit for naval purposes, were only 8,012, containing but
     8,322 loads" of timber; which, from Parliamentary records, appear not to be equal to
     three months' consumption in the King's Dock-yard only.' From *The Naval Chronicle*
     (1804), 281. In 1804 the Navy Board asked for 'competent' persons to look into the
     purchase of timber.
110 After a general discourse on the subject by Viscount Melville, June 1810, as found in
     Nichols (1813) Vol LXXXIII, p. 22.

Prior to Christmastide I had recourse to visit the yard of Mr George Parsons, situated on the Hamble River at Bursledon. Excitement rests upon supplies of timber for their current build, the 40-gun Cambrian. This ship is important for it will be the first Royal Navy frigate to carry 24-pounders. Construction continues apace. Shipwrights are already out of the Mould Loft,[111] and they have laid-off the ship. I saw the keel scarfed, bolted and clinched.[112] The ribs, stern-post and the stem take shape. The yard has enough timber to construct the ship's bottom and sides but more loads are required to complete her. You will no doubt recall that Mr Parsons launched the 32-gun Galatea last year, and took upon himself construction of the 16-gun Rattler at another yard,[113] so he is acutely aware of timber supply. He has many years of experience. Despite the narrowness of the Hamble he successfully constructed the 74-gun Elephant, back in 1786. That ship must have been a prodigious rare sight upon the blocks. She needed more than three thousand loads of timber to construct.

We currently have on the stocks, in various private and naval yards, numerous warships and vessels. It is thanks to Mr Parsons, and other master shipwrights, that warships protect our shores. These estimable men must be reassured about future timber supplies. For it would be a tragedy if their yards ceased construction due to a lack of timber. The silence of their mauls and caulking mallets would be a tocsin of doom.

Our naval timber requirements are not in isolation. They are in direct competition with[114] the necessity to build and refurbish mills, docks, dock gates, slips, sluices, piers, boats, barges, bridges, harbours, mines, coal works, buildings and barracks. That kind of construction requires tens of thousands of loads of timber, mostly oak. I regret to say that by my own calculations private plantations have little more than twenty years of adequate supply of oak remaining[115].

As to the Royal Forests, close to 115,000 acres support the navy. I understand that from a survey conducted in 1783 it had been found that only 50,000 trees sufficed for naval needs, whereas 35,000 trees stood in a decayed state. In the five decades before 1783 there averaged an annual

---

111 A large space where templates are drawn out from detailed plans and wood formed to follow the shapes drawn.

112 Lengths of wood joined together.

113 *The Hampshire Antiquary and naturalist* (1892) Vol II, 79. Data taken from a letter to the magazine submitted by Robert C. Leslie in 1899. Many ships cited here fall within the American War period, and the source mentions that a typical 64-gun ship required 3,070 loads of oak and other timber for construction.

114 A reference to an article on naval architecture as found in Smedley (1845) Vol VI, 399.

115 A figure 'admitted' in 1802; Nichols (1813) Vol LXXXIII, 22.

output of 1300 loads from these estates, barely enough to support the construction of one 32-gun frigate per year. It is a situation found elsewhere. I regularly visit the Forest of Dean, so I can attest to this. Our navy quickly approaches a need to consume more than 100,000 loads of timber per year, an amount that does not account for masts. The New Forest, one source of supply, provides 9000 loads of timber per annum. This suffices to cover our naval needs for just three months. There is an obvious necessity[116] to replant trees upon a national scale. Land planted ought to be cared for as diligently as those stands that reside upon private estates. Only by such an expensive, and extensive, measure could we hope to secure our future supply needs.

There should be an enquiry made into the procurement of naval timber. Contractors make large profits. It remains in their interest to make supplies difficult; certainly if the navy continues to pay a fixed rate for timber. There is much wastage involved. We become ever more reliant upon foreign supply, and whereas Canadian timber remains constant we should begin to look for oak supplies from the Great Lakes. Merchants involved in the Norfolk Island trade tell of tall pines that grow indigenously upon that remote island. And there are far more substantial trees found in New Zealand, that Maori call kauri. These thoughtful and considerate merchants believe that these types of trees would make excellent ship timber for our fleets.

We should not be despondent, but we should be cautious. We soon enter upon the third year of a war with no end in sight. Our sacred duty to the crown demands a proper investigation and further reflection. The Royal Navy must safeguard supplies of compass timber[117] for now, next year, and the years to come.

I am Sirs, your humble servant,
G. B.
28 December 1795.

The sea force of Great Britain were the ships and vessels put into commission, the men (and women) who worked those ships, the men who *directly* staffed her yards and offices, and the thousands of men and women who *indirectly* supplied timber, food, drink, cloth, rope, naval stores and all other necessities required to keep warships at sea. By the year 1800 estimates of naval manpower exceeded the population of any British city apart from

---

116 The future Lord Melville reported such in 1810.
117 Timber able to be steam-bent to shape.

London. The naval sea service had become so large and pervasive it resided at the very heart of national affairs. Industry and commerce across the length and breadth of Britain had to be substantial to support the fleets. To emerge victorious from a war against revolutionary France, and Spain after 1796, the Royal Navy relied upon the organisation of such a vast enterprise. It began with the top level of government.

National governance was made through Parliament, then a body of men with deep commitments to Britain's trade, industry, merchant and naval fleets. They understood that much of Britain's wealth came from customs and excise revenues. Most customs revenue came from sea commerce, and sea commerce required capital. The Bank of England had made loans that had in turn allowed enterprise and ideas to flourish. Inventions and new industry gave rise to the production of more sea commerce. More sea commerce increased state revenues. After William Pitt became Prime Minister in 1783, his policies favoured both British commerce and a strong navy. He strengthened the nation's finances[118] and various duties of Customs and Excise were consolidated. He improved administration of various departments that benefited the navy. Funds for the naval treasury had to be placed in the Bank of England before withdrawal, and annual accounts provided by the naval treasurer. A 'body to inquire into "the fees, gratuities, perquisites, and emoluments" received in public offices, and into all abuses connected with them' was created.[119]

The Royal Navy continued to be 'the great instrument of our influence and dominion'.[120] In war, Britain expanded and wielded a large and powerful navy because her government could access the funds to do so. Her expanded fleets then provided British colonies with a presence strong enough to deter other powers from encroachment and a potential loss of trade.[121] Regiments were transported abroad with some measure of impunity.

Immense pressures were placed upon her economy, so that in 1797 the Bank of England believed that loans to Germany would have ruined her, and an Order in Council had to be made to prohibit the Bank of England 'from paying their notes in specie - a measure shortly afterwards ratified

---

118 He brought in additional taxes on a whole range of items.
119 Lecky (1891) Vol VII, 301.
120 Robinson (1894), 19. He was writing of Tudor times, but it applies to the eighteenth century.
121 Robinson, *ibid.*, 4. He wrote, 'that only by the possession of maritime strength has the development of England, and the growth of Greater Britain, with its world-wide commerce, been made possible.'

by the Bank Restriction Act'.[122] Britain continued to bankroll her allies and create a navy unlike any known before. It became obvious, to some foreign observers, that Britain had surged ahead in her industrial capacity enough to warrant the term 'industrial revolution'. Parliament, industry and finance together created a colossus of the seas.

The means to beat France had been to confine her ships to French ports rather than allow them to prowl the seas. That required blockade, in all weathers, which caused a terrible strain upon British warships and vessels. Storm damage and wear and tear required frequent access to nearby friendly yards for repair and refit. Enough ships and vessels were needed to cover for this. France and Spain had naval arsenals and ports far from British waters, so the Royal Navy had to control, or possess, her own ports, safe harbours and anchorages in foreign waters. In the Mediterranean, Britain had Gibraltar, but Port Mahon, San Fiorenzo (Saint Florent) and Malta became targets to strengthen the capabilities of her fleets. If and when taken, those places required funds to garrison them and build and maintain adequate facilities. Likewise the West Indies, the Cape,[123] India, the Indian Ocean and the Pacific. In 1797 Parliament reported, for example, on such 'extraordinary' expenses as £2,280 for 'Forage for the Cattle employed on the Works at Gibraltar.'[124] The Royal Navy was a global organisation that required a complex and extensive set of departments to run it.

One fine summer's day in 1800 a schoolmaster, with a few students in tow, strolled through London to study some of the places from where the Royal Navy was administered. The teacher called it a tour of the 'guiding lights'. It happened to be the boys' last lesson before they left school. They started outside the Palace of Westminster to consider the men who most influenced the destiny of the nation. *Boys,* he said, *all our warships are 'His Majesty's Ships'. Only the king can declare war and make peace, but Parliament over there controls how many men are raised and paid for. Remember, we fight to preserve ourselves and stop the French from imposing their ideas upon us. The revolutionaries would do away with our king and Parliament. We fight to stop Jacobin oppressors bringing anarchy, and the guillotine, to our shores. They would end our civil institutions and do away with the church if they could. We continue this war to preserve our very way of life! Yes, it is a burden, but one we shoulder gladly. Our cause is just, and it was not we but the French who started the war.* He explained about the Prime Minister

---

122 Waterston (1847), 187. This act was strongly criticized at the time.
123 Southern Africa.
124 *Journal of the House of Commons* (1796) Vol LII, 133-5.

and his cabinet, and Henry Dundas, who acted as both Secretary of State for the War Department and Treasurer of the Navy. He painted a verbal image of that firm and resolute Scot, a man who feared nought and truckled to no one. He told them that if that 'great man' happened to walk by they should raise their hats in respect. [125] *The cabinet decides national policy, but it is the Board of Admiralty*[126] *and her subordinate Boards that continually, day to day, manage the navy.* He had reminded them because he felt they were a bunch of blockheads who could not remember anything.

The Board of Admiralty (*Boys, remember it is officially the 'Commissioners for Exercising the Office of Lord High Admiral', although there is no Lord High Admiral, for the navy is far too large for one man to manage*) comprised a 'political' body of seven men, either naval lords or civil lords, who often served as Members of Parliament. These men resided elsewhere, so the schoolmaster marched the boys up Whitehall to stand in front of the Ripley building.[127]

The road outside the Admiralty was busy with carriages, and men and women going to and fro. Blue-coated naval officers mixed with black-coated civilians. The schoolmaster gathered up his boys and pointed to several windows that were, he believed, accommodation for the First Lord and the boardroom on the top floor. *That is where the Lords Commissioners meet!* He made them imagine how the men who they saw enter and leave under the arch[128] might well be from the Hydrographic Department, solicitors, officers, paymasters, representatives of the king or translators of foreign papers. *They're probably messengers, sir!* They saw a red-coated marine, a captain and two lieutenants. They looked nervous, no doubt keen to discuss promotion and employment, and were likely to be stopped by a huge porter. That man was a Cerberus without so many heads,[129] who generally said that unless they had either preferment, a title or widespread acclaim, in no circumstances could their lordships be disturbed! The boys giggled,

---

125 Dundas was put on trial in 1806 for 'misappropriation of public monies'. He was acquitted.
126 *The Gentleman's Magazine* (1872) Vol VIII, 233. 'The affairs of the Royal navy were managed without interruption by the Board of Admiralty and the subordinate Navy and Victualling Boards.'
127 the Admiralty.
128 An 1817 account considered the building a 'magnificent edifice of brick and stone'. From Hughson (1817), 222. Many thought it ugly, and only improved by 'a screen designed by Adam.'
129 *An Enquiry into the present state of the British Navy* (1815), 26: 'A gigantic porter, who generally possesses all the attributes of a Cerberus except the additional heads.'

more at the schoolmaster than the image he painted. He then launched into a long-winded explanation the boys had difficulty following, about how the seven board members reported to Parliament upon weighty matters. Naval finance and expenditure, construction of warships and vessels of war (*they approved ship designs, boys, but did not actually make them; and did you know that Mr Fox considered the main responsibility of the board ought to be the improvement of our warships?*), manpower,[130] prize court decisions,[131] and offences against the articles of war (*if committed outside the limits of common law jurisdiction, that is*). They had to make sure all superior commands never fell into 'improper' hands[132] (*No, that would not do*). He told them how the Admiralty gave instructions to numerous subservient boards. *Boys!,* he said with feeling, *the Admiralty manifests a strong and willing navy. The navy lords have to have long experience at sea. Never listen to those wits who call them 'signing lords!*[133]

The schoolmaster had wanted to instil a love of country in his students. He did not mention how, at the beginning of the war, the First Lord had been the indifferent Earl of Chatham, who had been bundled off by means of another appointment. The next was Earl Spencer, and in the schoolmaster's opinion he was more than suitable to hold such a high office of state. He also brought to their attention another man, Evan Nepean, the First Secretary to the Admiralty. *Boys, he is one of the very best lights; never mind he had once been a purser! That man receives hundreds of letters from ship captains all over the world. Imagine that, boys. Letters from Martinico, India and Ultima Thule!*

The Admiralty gave instructions, but everyday administration at that time lay with the Navy Board.[134] Britain's oldest naval administrative office, it had originally been sited at Tower Hill, but by the time the school group strolled the streets it had moved to Somerset House. The group stepped round to the Strand, by way of Charing Cross. Compared to the Admiralty building, Somerset House had a more pleasing aspect with larger offices and direct access to the Thames. *Remember boys, Henry Dundas resides within.* The composition of the Navy Board[135] changed by Order of Council on 8 June 1796 and various new commissioners were created. *Boys, it means*

---

130 The Admiralty received returns from regulating officers, as reported in *The Times* of 9 April 1795 (Ashton, 1885, 90).
131 Smyth (1867), pp.203&4.
132 Stockdale (1802) Vol XI, 153.
133 *An Enquiry into the present state of the British Navy* (1815), 26.
134 It was abolished in 1832.
135 I give here the composition of the Navy Board after 1796.

a leaner board with better administration...Sir, did you not say the Board dislibes change? The schoolmaster gave a stern look and the ruddy-faced boy went quiet. He told them, slowly, of the Board's eleven members. Only seven resided in town; the other four resided at the dockyards. *The seven in London meet twice weekly, so we might see them. Men of influence, boys! Their Comptroller is a naval man of senior status and long service. Remember who? Yes, Sir! Sir Andrew Hamond, Sir.* Not sure if they were feigning interest he kept to himself how the Board had 'to transact, to the best advantage, all affairs tending to the well-being and regulation of the Civil Establishment of His Majesty's Navy',[136] such as 'bills and accounts, domestic and foreign, payment of seamen's wages; to controul the payment of half pay at the navy pay office, the payment of artificers and labourers at Deptford and Woolwich yards, and of the ships paid off at those places.'[137] Instead, he told them how Sir Andrew took a chaise every week to inspect the Deptford and Woolwich yards, and that Dundas held responsibility for funds received from the exchequer. *A lot of money!*

The boys sat on a bench to eat a small pie. While they did the schoolmaster could not help but continue, pacing up and down. *There is an Inspector General of Naval Works...and a Surveyor.* They did not listen. Regardless, the schoolmaster talked on, of how the master shipwright *sees the world differently and understands how things fit together before they do. Think of all the ships' plans he has...all those surveys of hulls, masts, and spars...so much wood.* The schoolmaster thought to himself of how the ruddy-faced lad had been correct: the Board did not like change. *The Inspector General of Naval Works, Sir Samuel Bentham, happens to be the brother of Jeremy Bentham* and had been tasked to seek 'improvements in relation to the Building, Arming, Navigating, and Victualling Ships of War, and other Vessels employed in [His] Majesty's Service, as well as in relation to the Docks, Slips, Basons, and Buildings, and other Articles appearing to... Naval Establishments.'[138] *Improvements mean innovation,* or change, and he would not be surprised if Bentham championed the use of steam engines and steam-dredging machines for the yards to pump water and clear silt.

The schoolmaster spied some clerks over towards Somerset House. Acutely aware of his own status in society he appreciated what they did. The Board needed such clerks to deal with the necessary tedium of fees and

---

136 *Fourth Report of the Commissioners for Revising and Digesting the Civil Affairs of His Majesty's Navy* (1806)
137 Adolphus (1818) Vol II, 251.
138 *Fourth Report of the Commissioners, ibid.*

accounts of slops, stationary, binding, salvage, pilotage, freight, demurrage (a penalty incurred if a chartered ship had not been properly stowed, or discharged to a set schedule) and the need to 'take cognizance of the Receipt, Issue, Remains, and Returns of Stores of every description.'[139] Even a small vessel of war required a long list of stores to remain at sea. Scaled up to hundreds of naval vessels, spread far across the globe, it was obvious that much paperwork was needed to account for everything. Messengers had walked by, weary men who brought for inspection numerous pay and muster books, slop and prize lists, journals and papers sent in by officers. Such things held little interest for the boys. What they wanted to hear about were the battles, actions and lives of heroes.

The Navy Board took responsibility for all the navy yards, but individual commissioners regulated everything connected with their particular yard. If the schoolmaster could have done so he would have taken the boys to Chatham, Sheerness or Deptford to study their work, or sites even further afield. Perhaps to the naval storehouse and refit yard at Harwich, or Portsmouth, Plymouth, even Kinsale in Ireland. The boys would then have learned first-hand how all naval yards had to be secured, patrolled, stocked, replenished, paid for and worked. Perhaps one day his boys would, as men, venture to Port Royal on Jamaica, Kingston Dockyard on Lake Ontario, Gibraltar, Antigua, or Halifax in Nova Scotia (the only true British dockyard outside the mother country) and see for themselves how the Royal Navy had a reach far beyond London and Great Britain. Perhaps, he thought, some of them would join the navy one day.

He wanted so much to discuss the yards. His sister had married a yard storekeeper. However, the boys fidgeted, so he kept himself from telling how the Commissioners for the yards administered oaths for commissioned and warrant officers, accounted for widows' pensions, and made regular reports for the Navy Board and Admiralty. Neither did he say how, below the commissioners, each yard had 'a master, or master's attendant, a master shipwright, a clerk of the cheque, a storekeeper, and a clerk of the survey; each of whom...have a certain number of clerks employed under them. There are likewise at each yard, a surgeon, a boatswain, and a master porter, and at all the yards, except Sheerness, a purveyor; likewise at all except Sheerness, and Deptford, a clerk of the rope yard, and a master rope-maker.'[140] What he did tell them was how the yards gathered stores, docketed and accounted for them, delivered them to ships, kept the sail-lofts and rigging houses

---

139 *Ibid.*
140 Adolphus, *ibid.*, 205.

at full capacity and helped take ships in ordinary to commissioned status. *Back in 1792 naval dockyards contained over £1,800,000*[141] *worth of stores. Imagine what sums there would be today!*

They had returned to school. Sitting at their desks the schoolmaster made his students read from an old book. *Boys, the Navy Board could never manage everything. Our navy is too large. Read here about the Victualling Board. See how it mentions their offices at Somerset Place, and the Red House at Deptford? Look at the picture of Deptford and all the storehouses, the slaughterhouse, cooperage, brewhouse, bakehouse, flour mills and oat mills. Every sailor and marine, and soldier in transit, receives a food allowance and Deptford helps provide that. What was their food allowance, Sir?*[142] *Thank you, Adams. The food allowance was set in 1731. The weekly ration for each man was seven pounds of biscuit, four pounds of beef, two pounds of pork, three pints of oatmeal, two pints of pease, six ounces of butter, twelve pounds of cheese and seven gallons of beer. Yes, Jones, when abroad the beer ration might be wine, brandy, rum or arrack. Yes, Stimpson, olive oil instead of butter. True British sailors prefer hard butter. It's only natural!*

The schoolmaster omitted to tell the boys that after many weeks at sea, sailors became 'palled and sickened, even to disgust, with salt junk, as hard as mahogany - Irish pork, twenty years old...strong and rancid...musty meal, and still mustier flour - cheese absolutely alive - and the still more detested villainous sweepings of a hard-up bread-room, where a piece of biscuit the size of a square inch, accidently showing face in the mess's daily allowance of twelve or fourteen pounds, was a prize that was frequently fought for.'[143] He did not tell them that after the mutiny, sailors had eventually received 'savings', a refund given if a mess of men failed to receive their full allowance. He did give his opinion that for some seamen a regular meal and intake of alcohol was a diet better than they could get elsewhere. To provide the navy with victuals, the Victualling Board in 1797 expended £4,578,788.[144] A Commissioner Superintending the Department of the Accountant for Cash accounted for this. He acted as chairman of the Victualling Board, and a Commissioner Superintending the Department of the Accountant for Stores.

The schoolmaster wondered whether naval seamen ever considered where their food came from. The average warship carried hens, cattle and

---

141 Derrick (1806), 198.
142 *The State of the Nation* (1800) Vol IV, 269.
143 *Blackwood's Edinburgh Magazine* (1825) No. CII, 41. This quote comes from a piece called 'The Man-of-War's Man', a satire.
144 *Reports from Committees of the House of Commons* (1803) Vol XIII, 508.

goats when they could, but were usually dependent upon casks of meat and dried foodstuffs to feed their crews. Meat and fish fell under the purview of the Comptroller of the Cutting-house, who ran the naval slaughter yards at Deptford and Weevil (just outside Gosport, across the harbour from Portsmouth). Drovers delivered herds of pigs, sheep and cattle, much of this 'flesh' purchased in Ireland.[145] Testimony given during the libel case of Captain Thomas Baillie[146] in 1778 stated that up to 5,000 oxen were killed in a winter. Herds and passels were allowed to 'cool' upon arrival, before a master butcher inspected them. If this man, and the resident officer of the cutting-house, approved them then they were killed. If not they were sent away. After slaughter, the animals were butchered and salted by teams, and then turned over to coopers for packing into barrels.

The naval brewhouses at Deptford and Weevil, and the production and procurement of alcoholic beverages, was then managed by the Comptroller of the Brewhouse. Beer for the fleet had to be produced in large quantities to supplement water, but beer soured quickly. Contractors provided rum and wine, as these kept longer. Sailors' work was hard and thirsty and they received a daily allowance of half a pint of rum, watered down. Grog was all important to sailors, 'For grog is our larboard, our starboard, Our mainmast, our mizen, our log; At sea, or on shore, or where harbour'd, The mariner's compass is grog.'[147] The dispensing of grog had an almost religious symbolism on board a naval vessel. For sailors it softened their hard lives and helped rid their minds of the horrors of war. It also kept a tenuous connection with life on land, where grog shops were found in most ports and towns. It was a misconception that 'Jack dances and sings and is always content; knew nothing of the value of money; and could put up with every hardship if he had plenty of grog,'[148] but certainly the amount of beer, wine and spirits provided aboard was considerable.

The Comptroller of the Bakehouse dealt with the baking of bread, or 'soft-tack', and ship's biscuit, or 'hard-tack'. Each bakehouse had a master baker, and hardtack offered an essential form of reserve food. At Deptford, the dough for sea biscuit comprised flour and water and had to be worked by a large machine. A second workman sliced it, then passed it to five bakers: a

---

145 Irish 'flesh' was destined for foreign service, but first had to be sent to England. This was considered more economical than running an Irish victualling yard, and easier to maintain checks on quality and abuses.

146 Howell, T.B. (1816) Vol XXI, 142.

147 Old ditty.

148 Knight, C. (1814) Vol VII, 339.

moulder, a marker, a splitter, a chucker and a depositor. 'The business [was] to deposit in the oven seventy biscuits in a minute.'[149] Twelve ovens baked in one day enough biscuit for 2,000 men.

After bread and biscuit had been baked, beer brewed and 'flesh' apportioned, they became the realm of the Commissioner for Cooperage who collated them with separate deliveries of flour, hops, malt, molasses, oatmeal, groats,[150] cheese, rice, sugar, pease (flour and pease often came from Ireland) and flesh, to be sealed, tallied and placed in storage. Meat, bread and some alcohol had to be stored in barrels. William Thompson, an inspecting Cooper of the Pickle-yard of His Majesty's Victualling Office London, gave insight into this work.[151] He professed that salters should take care not to mix the 'dirt of their shoes' with the flesh placed in the barrels, and that barrels 'should' be made from timber that did not suffer from 'putrid filthy stenches'. Barrels were, he believed, less subject to leaks if not put together when snow lay on the ground, or when the wood was sodden, and that 'what is still worse, many hundred Casks being exposed to the Weather, during the whole slaughtering Season, and one, two, or three Months usually expiring before they are cooper'd and made tight, not only hurts the Casks, but the Flesh also'. Thompson complained that sometimes labourers failed to drain old barrels before reuse, and that casks were often left out in the open and therefore leaked and ruined shell and salt flesh within to cause 'scorbutick disorders[152] in the men belonging to the Royal Navy'. Offal had to be removed soon after slaughter, before it began to 'stink',[153] and 'Blood and Excrements' had to be cleared away in 'due Time'. Oftentimes barrels when opened at sea were found to be spoiled. Every spoiled barrel had to be accounted for and returned.

After coopering, the barrels were moved to storage and the realm of the Commissioner for Dry Stores. Dutifully tallied and accounted for, they waited until delivered to ships. For those warships in British waters this was by way of cart, or small vessels that shuttled them around the coast. Victualling ships fell under the responsibility of the Hoy-taker, who hired and commissioned hoys, or armed sloops and cutters, for victualling the crews.[154]

---

149 Mortimer (1810), 'B'.

150 That is, grains.

151 Thompson, W. (1757)

152 The reason for scurvy was little understood at this time, but this quotation does point to a cause of the ruin of so many casks before they even reached the fleet.

153 Thompson goes on to mention the 'stinking of 1,500 Hogs in 1743' because of this.

154 *The State of the Nation* (1800) Vol IV, 246.

He inspected hired river craft and had to make reports, always reports, on hired or owned vessels' sailing qualities and seaworthiness. The total value of vessels and their contents were noted down and approved, in case they were lost to storm, wreck or the enemy. Between June 1795 and December 1796 the list of ordnance store-ships taken, or lost, came to fourteen, with eleven in the West Indies, two while sailing for Gibraltar and one off the Saint-Marcouf islands near Cherbourg.[155]

Possible fraud, either with false claims or inflated losses, concerned the Board. A prodigious amount of stores and provisions were transported to yards, storekeepers, pursers, masters of transports, and designated agents throughout Britain and overseas upon a regular, if not daily, basis. The victualling yards could not fulfil everything needed. Ships upon far distant stations had to allow pursers to purchase local stores, keep receipts and later provide evidence of those purchases to the Board. Men had to be fed and watered with an adequate and varied provision to maintain morale and fighting efficiency.

Throughout the eighteenth century much had been written about scurvy. It had been found during the American War that French warships suffered far fewer cases of that debilitating disease than British warships.[156] Some pointed to the mode of French victualling and their use of light vegetables and wine. Resistance to change meant the British navy long ignored possible remedies. John Woodall, a naval officer, published his *Surgeon's Mate* in 1636 and argued for fruits to be introduced into the sailor's diet. It required an outbreak of scurvy in the Channel fleet in 1795,[157] a calamity that put at risk the ability to defend Britain's shores, for Sir Gilbert Blane to successfully introduce lemon juice to sailors' diets, despite how the majority of medical opinion remained set against it. 'The Records of the Royal Naval Hospital at Haslar...shewed that one thousand four hundred and fifty-seven cases of scurvy were admitted in 1780, whereas in 1806 there was only one single case,'[158] so he was ultimately vindicated.[159]

---

155 *Reports from Committees of the House of Commons* (1803) Vol XIII, 506.

156 In 1792 the *Monthly Review* stated how in 1778 a French squadron arrived off America without one case of 'scorbutic' onboard, whereas a British squadron had a large number of cases of scurvy due, it was argued, to a 'want of vegetables, a wholesome nourishing diet, and of fermented drink'. *Monthly Review* Vol VII (1792), 280.

157 Macdonald (1881), 203.

158 *Chambers's Journal of Popular Literature* (1877), 190.

159 Lemon juice was not particularly pleasant to take: 'In order to preserve the juice from mildew, to which it its peculiarly liable, sperm oil was floated on the top, which it was necessary to remove by means of wool before use.' Robinson (1894), 141-2.

The schoolmaster could have talked to his boys for hours about the victualling boards and other boards and departments that dealt with important aspects of running the navy, but he knew their interests mainly ran to the press-gang. He also did not mention how before the war the Transport Board had been abolished and only reinstated in July 1794 to deal with the extensive business of transporting army regiments, ordnance and victuals. In 1799 this board took on added responsibility for the management of prisoners at home and abroad.[160] It had the usual array of commissioners (five), a secretary, various clerks, an inspector, a surveyor, storekeepers, messengers and porters. Between its re-inception in 1794 and June 1797 it hired more than 278,000 tons of shipping at a cost of £4,088,524.[161]

The schoolmaster briefly told the boys about the Sick and Hurt Board that dealt with ships' surgeons, naval hospitals and the welfare of sailors and marines. This Board provided ships' surgeons with supplies of medicines and utensils, but encouraged them to provide their own. As the war continued, the board faced increased pressure to disband. In 1795 it had been considered 'advisable to relieve the Sick and Hurt Board from the care of the prisoners of war, and two additional commissioners had been placed at the Board of transports for that particular service.'[162] Between 1793 and 1800 it remained active and spent as much care upon prisoners as British sailors and marines. It maintained Royal Naval Hospitals at Haslar near Portsmouth, Stonehouse near Plymouth, Great Yarmouth, Port Mahon in Minorca after 1798, Port Royal in Jamaica, Gibraltar, English Harbour in Antigua, Halifax in Canada and to some extent the Royal Hospital in Greenwich. A hospital at Deal, Kent, opened in 1800. Management of these hospitals had been conducted by individual councils, comprised of a physician (a professional doctor), chief surgeon, steward and an agent.[163] After 1795 a naval captain became Governor of each one.

Then the schoolmaster spoke about the Impress Service. How it held responsibility for the forced recruitment of naval men, that it had been devolved down to ports throughout Britain where either a captain or lieutenant, known as the Regulating Officer, took control of 'gangs'. Due to their very public presence, and more than a century of stories and mythology,

---

160 *The Parliamentary Register* (1798) Vol V, 202.
161 *The State of the Nation* Vol IV, 257.
162 *An impartial report of the debates that occur in the Two Houses of Parliament* Vol IV (1796), 319.
163 *The Fifth Report of the Commissioners for Revising and Digesting the Civil Affairs of His Majesty's Navy* (1809), 4. This report was for 1806.

this part of the navy had gained a public image far greater than any other part of naval administration. Not so the Sea Fencibles, who provided coastal defence for Britain after 1798. Districts had recruited and trained men in artillery, with assurances they would not be pressed.[164] Most of the Sea Fencibles would have been seafarers and they received permission to accost privateers in coastal waters, with a mouth-watering promise of profit. One of the schoolboys had a cousin who served as a fencible.

Although not part of the sea-service, the Board of Ordnance was very important for the navy.[165] The relationship between them had always been intimate, as naval transports shipped guns and powder abroad for the use of the army. Hundreds of ships and small vessels had sailed with their holds crammed full of powder, stacked both on deck and below, to help keep far flung land and sea forces active. With offices in the Tower, and a manufactory at Woolwich, this board remained independent with a civil and a military branch. It maintained stores throughout Britain and Ireland, on Gibraltar, some West Indies' islands, Halifax in Nova Scotia, Bermuda and at Newfoundland. The military branch supplied the navy with all ordnance and necessities and dealt with powder-makers, gunsmiths, ironmongers, matchmakers and saltpetre producers. Once approved by the board all naval guns and powder were either delivered to storekeepers in a naval port, or to a ship's gunner and his team. Dockyards had storehouses set aside for guns, small arms and gunpowder. The Citadel kept powder for Plymouth; small arms lay within the town of Portsmouth, with gunpowder at Priddy's Hard in the harbour; Upnor Castle acted as the store for Chatham. As the navy commanded thousands of guns the upkeep and replacement of ordnance and powder was always vital.

Boys! We must conclude our lesson. Know that those things we witnessed and read about today inform us that the seamen of the Royal Navy are not the only heroes, but so too are the commissioners, men of the boards and the yards, even your own mothers and fathers if they supply the fleets. Every one of them is as important to our national success as a first rate or a Nelson. Without them the navy could not succeed. He wished them well for their future and shook all their hands. He never met them again. Two later died in Portugal during the Peninsular War, three were lost at sea, and two went to live abroad. Some did later think about those nameless men and women who worked the yards and helped supply the 'superpower' that was the British Navy.

---

164 Seventy-eight commanders, according to *The Naval Chronicle January to July 1799*. It was disbanded in 1810.

165 There was a lieutenant general, surveyor general, ordnance clerk, storekeeper, delivery clerk, secretary, under-secretary and a whole raft of clerks.

Chapter 5

As Free Men, Not Slaves

Sitting at his desk in the sick berth, as close to the hot stove as he could manage, the surgeon reflected upon the ludicrous need to wait upon the roll of the ship until it reached the midpoint. Only then could he put quill to paper and write a few words, until the roll continued on and made it too difficult to write. His right hand held the quill. His left arm lay across the desktop at such an angle as to pin the paper under his elbow and hold the inkpot in his left hand. So far there had not been a single blot. His letter, a request for the captain to make a survey of his stores of medicines and bedding, was an important part of his position as ship's surgeon. He hoped to conduct the survey as soon as possible. Without a completed survey he could not order a replacement of stores. An opportunity to dispatch a completed survey report, and a copy of his daily journal for the Commissioners for Sick and Wounded Seamen, beckoned. After weeks at sea, and numerous winter tempests, the ship was to anchor off St Helens.

Between the times he could commit quill to paper he cast an eye over two books kept open by two bone nippers.[166] One, the 1731 *Regulations and Instructions*, lay open at chapter five. A turnscrew pointed to where it said 'cleanliness, dryness, and good air are essentially necessary to health, the Captain is to exert his utmost endeavours to obtain them for the Ship's company in as great a degree as possible.'[167] The second book, Trotter's *Observations of The Scurvy*, had been opened to where the author mentioned his time off the Gold Coast.

Quill touched paper. He managed three words. He turned his eyes to the *Regulations*. His thoughts crowded in like bumboats around a moored ship. Terrible weather made holystoning of the weather deck impossible, gunports had not been opened for three weeks, and the free circulation of air had been impossible. At least sailors could scrub the lower decks with sand.

166 One of the medical instruments all ship's surgeons were expected to purchase.
167 Privy Council, *Regulations and Instructions relating to His Majesty's Service at Sea* (1808), 138.

His quill moved. Five words. Another dip in the ink pot. Hand held ready.

The men had had to sleep in wet clothes. Everywhere there was a sticky dampness. What about the drunkenness of sailors? Half a pint of spirits every day to every sailor regardless of their age. A sudden sea lurch caused the inkpot to tremble. A 17-year-old consumed a pint of rum every two days. Knocks and injuries were common. Deplorable! Two words written. Vinney's complaints of 'bullock's liver',[168] and a request not to tell his mess-mates. The quill dipped into the pot.

Vinney had a reputation for ill health. He exhibited one of the worst cases of persistent melancholy the surgeon had ever seen. On recent examination he had ulcers in his mouth; he complained his gums were sore, but they did not bleed. Eyes naturally dull, there had been a sallow bloated look about him.

Three more words, then his thoughts returned to the medical inspection of Vinney.

'Are you costive?' A blank look from eyes as lifeless as a shark's. 'Have you voided your bowels recently?' 'No, sir. I haven't been to the heads[169] since before we put to sea.'

His quill added six more words. Perhaps not scurvy, then? A need for a laxative?

'Don't tell others, sir, for they will make my time awful cruel-like. Especially Jennings.'

He had pressed a finger into Vinney's left thigh. The impression remained longer than expected but less than he feared. Time to write, but no ink on the tip! He had failed to dip the quill. A missed opportunity so a dip and a further wait. His mind continued to wander.

The effects of too much salted meat and smoke-dried fish. Vinney had been a Quota Man, hadn't he? Upon arrival he had stood on deck emaciated and frail and had said he had not eaten well in months. Some form of dyspepsia long suffered. Will these storms end in scurvy? A whole sentence this time.

Eyes back to Trotter. 'Of all the women only eight were affected.... Few boys were tainted, from being out of irons, and allowed to run about the ship.'[170] Exercise! Vinney required a course of strenuous labour! He forms part of the afterguard, so a regimen of daily exercise would suffice. For him and others. The older sops would especially benefit.

---

168 ulcers, and a symptom of scurvy.
169 the toilets for seamen on a warship.
170 Trotter, *Observations on the Scurvy* (1786), 38.

I remain your dutiful servant, etc.

His mind wandered in line with the rhythm and lurch of the ship. Stores of lemon juice had run dry days ago. He had once thought scurvy could be alleviated with liberal doses of brandy. Or physic.[171] Or both. He had continued in that vein until he had read Trotter. Yes, there is only one type of scurvy! All this time confined at sea. Where will the French land their blow? Gibraltar, Portugal or Ireland? If Ireland, then he and his ship would have to confront them. Surely Gibraltar, for that immovable rock had long confounded the French and Spanish.

He folded his letter and put it aside. The heavy sea continued to rise, but he had duties to perform. Loblollies[172] were eager for his attention and the purser's wife needed assistance. Her husband's opinion, given over their last dinner: *We've been sent west as nought but a show. You'll see, the French won't venture out this time of year.* Days of torment, and now possible scurvy. The sick berth would have to be washed down with vinegar. As surgeon he would make sure iron pots and cinders were walked throughout the ship to alleviate the damp and effluvia. Damn Vinney and his like. Damn the whole drunken lot of them! There will be no scurvy on his ship.

In 1796 Parliament voted a naval establishment of 110,000 men.[173] By then France had rid herself of her *Convention nationale* and was able to focus more upon her external enemies. To help Great Britain emerge victorious from this war the Royal Navy had to care for and motivate her sailors. Medical care had importance because sailor's effectiveness lessened through hardship, and sailors suffered 'unparalleled hardships...from the nature of their employment.'[174] This encompassed constant toil, danger, disease and privation. Doctor Samuel Johnson had done much to colour civilian perceptions of the harshness of sea-life. He had written, 'A ship is worse than a gaol. There is, in a gaol, better air, better company, better conveniences of every kind; and a ship has the additional disadvantage of being in danger. When men come to like a sea-life, they are not fit to live on land.'[175] A warship certainly had to confront danger, often with a lack of conveniences, but as to 'air' and 'company' that was debatable. A gaol did not then care much for health and rewards, as men like Vinney would have testified, whereas the Royal Navy did to a certain extent. As to the provision

---

171 purging.
172 Assistants to a surgeon's mate.
173 James, W. (1837) Vol I, 437.
174 Trotter, T., *A Practical Plan* (1819), pp.15&16.
175 Macaulay (1884), 132.

of health and medicine for sailors this ran parallel with medical developments in general. There were slow improvements throughout the era. Thomas Trotter wrote, 'When we reflect on the vast sums of money that have been spent on the recruiting and support of our navy, we must at the same time lament how sparingly it has been applied where the health of a sailor is at stake.'[176] He pointed out how, in previous conflicts, British warships on foreign stations had to bury a 'whole complement' of men carried from England.[177] Up until this war, and throughout, yellow fever[178] wracked British ships on tropical stations, especially the West Indies. 'Ship fever', or typhus, could be found everywhere.

Concentration of people on warships placed them at risk of disease. Whereas the Royal Navy kept in commission hospital ships, hundreds of men nevertheless succumbed. James Lind[179] wrote upon naval hygiene, and he thought impressment of ex-convicts a direct cause of disease. Improvements, and possible cures, were always welcomed. Fumigation 'with the vapour of mineral acids'[180] was one method used to keep jail-fever at bay. In 1795 the Sheerness hulk *Retribution*[181] held prisoners of war, and suffered an outbreak of typhus fever; 150 captives contracted the disease and 'Ten females and twenty-four men of the crew were attacked; three medical officers...died.'[182] With hopes of a cure the Admiralty brought in Dr. Carmichael Smyth, who had promoted use of nitrous oxide[183] for many years beforehand, to conduct experiments onboard the *Union* hospital ship[184] at Sheerness. After fumigation of the ship, in 1796, only one man further contracted the disease and those already with the fever appeared to have their symptoms lessen. The experiment was successfully repeated in 1797, and the widespread adoption of soap and keeping bilges clean added much to the improved health of the fleet.

Indifferent victuals, and the length of time ships remained at sea, maintained the blight of scurvy up until 1795 when a virulent form broke out amongst the Channel Fleet. Within five years Trotter could observe how 'the preserved lemon-juice being now a part of the surgeon's stores,

---

176 Trotter, *ibid*, xiv.
177 England was often synonymous with 'Great Britain'.
178 The French called this disease *Maladie de Siam,* or *Fièvre Matelotte.*
179 He died in 1794.
180 Creighton (1894) Vol II, 118.
181 Hulks were old warships converted into prisons. All their masts, rigging, and ordnance were taken off.
182 Hamilton (1887) Vol IV, 343.
183 Another source, *The British Critic* (1796) Vol VIII 22, states it to be nitrous acid.
184 Hamilton, *ibid.*, 343.

and regularly supplied when demanded, the certain relief is at hand. When I contrast the present state of the Channel fleet [in 1800] with what it was many years ago...there is much reason for exultation. It was no uncommon thing in those times, for a ship, during an eight week cruize, to bury ten or twelve men in scurvy, and land fifty at an hospital. There was an instance last war, where so many were landed at Haslar, on the fleet coming from sea, that the hospital could not contain them; they were lodged in the chapel, and in tents erected for the purpose...many died in the boats between Spithead and the hospital; and in the hospital also many perished.'[185]

The Royal Naval Hospital Haslar opened in 1762. Designed to complement wooden type hospital ships it had been built close to Gosport, across from Portsmouth, with fine views of Spithead. Two rows of three stories stood around three sides of a square, with open spaces and lawns in between. Situated close to the waterside, sick sailors could land easily with the tide and be accepted into the hospital, but there always stood a guard to deter desertion.[186] Wards were built uniform in size. They could hold ninety patients, with side apartments for nurses. Other brick-built hospitals followed because the Royal Navy needed her men to be as healthy as possible.

During the last decades of the eighteenth century, medicine remained rudimentary but two men made notable advances that had direct effects upon the health of the fleets. Appointed naval surgeon in 1782,[187] Thomas Trotter worked in the Africa trade, went into civil practice, returned to sea on Admiral Roddam's flagship and in 1790 wrote *A Review of the Medical Department of the British Navy*. Physician at Haslar, he was made physician to the Channel fleet in 1794. In 1803 he wrote *Medicina Nautica, or an Essay on the Diseases of Seamen*. He helped promote good health throughout the navy. The actions and words of Sir Gilbert Blane resonated many years later when William Guy, who lectured at King's College, looked back at the mortality rates of the Royal Navy in both the American War and the French Revolutionary War. He repeated Blane's assertions that if the same rate of death that occurred in the first war had continued in the second, 'our stock of seamen would have been used up, and "men would not have been procurable by any bounties, however exorbitant."' So that it was not the seamanship and fighting qualities of our sailors alone that carried

---

185 Trotter, *Medicina Nautica* (1803) Vol III, pp.387-8.
186 Allen, *History of Portsmouth* (1817), 179.
187 Chambers and Thomson (1856) Vol V, 582.

us triumphantly through that terrible contest, but a reduced mortality due to the sanitary discoveries and reforms which first recruited our population by saving lives in infancy and childhood, and then cut off from our forces by sea and land, the destructive supplies of jail-fever, scurvy, dysentery, and smallpox.'[188]

Dysentery, or 'bloody flux', had long been a curse of naval life. It continued to rage well beyond 1815. Surgeons had resorted to Peruvian bark, a febrifuge, to lessen fevers. Opinions varied as to whether the best cure for dysentery was retention, or evacuation, of bodily fluids. An 1810 medical book[189] considered ripe fruits suitable to help void the stomach and rid a patient of the flux.

Another blight of the navy, and society in general, was smallpox. Edward Jenner worked on a cure with matter taken from cowpox lesions. In 1799 he shared his findings in *An inquiry into the Causes and Effects of the Variolae Vaccinae, a disease discovered in some of the Western counties of England, particularly Gloucestershire, and known by the name of The Cow Pox*. He laid out how cowpox progressed from horse to cow to 'dairy-maid', and 'the person who has been thus affected is for ever after secure from the infection of the Small Pox; neither exposure to the variolous effluvia, nor the insertion of the matter into the skin, producing this distemper.' His observations found favour throughout Europe and North America. After 1800 France and Spain conducted their own experiments with vaccinations. In 1801 President Jefferson[190] vaccinated his own family and close neighbours; and British men of medicine arrived in Gibraltar, Minorca, Sicily and Malta to introduce vaccinations to the fleet. A British expedition to Egypt had all its sailors, marines, and soldiers inoculated whether they wanted to or not. Trotter wrote how 'the introduction of the Jennerian inoculation will be deservedly recorded as one of the greatest blessings to the navy of Great Britain that was ever extended to it.'[191]

As part of their crews, naval ships and vessels could muster a ship's surgeon, plus a surgeon's mate or two[192] to care for the men. Whereas a physician was a graduate of a school of medicine, any man could become a ship's surgeon

---

188 Guy (1870), 5.
189 Robertson, *Synopsis Morborum* (1810) Vol I, 304.
190 Collinson, *Smallpox* (1860), 34.
191 Collinson, *ibid.*, 35.
192 The means to procure a warrant for a surgeon's mate is given by Smollett in his satire *Roderick Random*. Although first published in 1748 much was still relevant in the 1790s.

so long as he had first served as surgeon's mate. According to John Bell, himself a surgeon, physicians were expected to have 'respectable' general knowledge, while surgeons had to be 'perfectly dextrous, well informed in anatomy, and accustomed to operations'.[193] At sea a surgeon needed to be well organized, and prepared, to give instant attention to sailors as soon as the drum beat to quarters. His skill in surgery had to be examined by the Court of Examiners of the Company of Surgeons of London (after 1800 it received a royal charter to become the Royal College of Surgeons in London); his skill in physic had to be examined by the physicians of Greenwich Hospital. Apart from these two examinations a surgeon needed to present his instruments and medicines to show he had 'the Sorts, Goodness, and Quantity required, and to give him a Certificate thereof'.[194] His knives, forceps, catlins, saws, tenaculums, turnscrews, bone-nippers, bone-rasps, trocars and ball-scoops were all examined.[195] Thereafter, his medicine chest was sealed until arrival onboard his ship. His captain had to verify the chest, and could only accept it if it had been sealed. The exigencies of the service no doubt made such visits, and examinations, difficult if not impossible at times.

Many sailors must have been alarmed on first sight of a surgeon's instruments. Designed for amputations, bleedings,[196] trephination and examination of wounds, they looked menacing. Disinfectants were rare, so sailors were at constant risk of infection if their wounds were not quickly attended to. Often amputation was required just to keep a man alive. Bleeding was a standard practice of relieving fevers, along with forced vomiting, purges, sweating, salivation and blisters. Trephination, or trepanning, was a common means to remove a compression from the brain, often caused by head injury, 'whether it be bone, serum, blood, or pus.'[197] A surgeon had to make sure he had enough bandages, tourniquets, sponges, lint, linen and compresses in expectation of normal day-to-day injuries and the trauma of battle. He often worked in low light, on a moving and unstable platform, with injured men arriving at his operation table at a brisk rate. His patients might be horribly burned, lacerated by splinters, concussed or near death.

---

193 Bell (1800), 5. Bell thought such examinations to be too slight, that a man might gain experience at sea but not necessarily knowledge of medicine. He argued for a School of Naval and Military Surgery.

194 Privy Council, *ibid.*, 138.

195 A catlin was a double sided knife; a tenaculum a slender, hooked, scissor-like, forceps; trocars drained fluid.

196 Rush (1796) Vol IV, 184.

197 Lara (1796), found under 'Trepanation'.

In Bell's *A System of Operative Surgery*, 1816, a surgeon reflected upon the type of wounds he had personally witnessed in the era then passed. He considered how the American War had had sea engagements conducted at a distance, so splinters caused by cannon balls hitting a ship's side had been common. In the period 1793 to 1815 ships tended to approach within range of muskets, so injuries accrued through musket shot, grapeshot and canister shot were common.[198]

The boarding of enemy ships often resulted in wounds from 'pike and cutlass' and sword. For cutting out expeditions, oftentimes a surgeon's mate accompanied the men but all he could do was stop the bleeding of wounds. However and wherever injuries took place, if a man survived the initial ordeal, his wounds were dressed and then he was secured safely in a cot. Presence of mind and a calm demeanour were two characteristics a physician and surgeon needed to succeed in a life at sea.

A ship's captain and first lieutenant also had to be mindful of the health of their crew. One means was to circulate as much air throughout the ship as possible. Weather permitting, hammocks were taken to the upper deck as early as possible, and placed along the stanchions of the ship to get an airing. Once a week the lower decks were washed and scrubbed. Time was given over for 'the ship's cooks...to boil water for washing the ship's company's clothes...clothes lines, cut out of white-line [were] kept for that purpose...between the main and mizen shrouds, at sea.'[199] If possible the crew were inspected every evening at quarters and mustered by divisions on Sunday mornings to check their 'cleanliness' and presentability. Most Sunday afternoons the men off watch could 'make and mend', and attend to their clothes.

The harshness of eighteenth century ship life was lessened by small civilities and formal modes of address. They added a genteel layer of civilian mores upon what was a cold hard platform of war. Officers received a servant or two, and their meals were conducted with a convivial formality to help make them memorable and something to look forward to. John Galt wrote of a sailor fresh from the West Indies who said, 'Ah...for all that, a sailor's life is a heartsome life - If we risk limb and life, we are spared from the sneaking anxieties that make other men so shamefaced. Besides, Sir, there is a pleasure in our dangers, and common suffering opens the generosity of the heart, so that, when we have little

---

198 Page 440.
199 *Observations and instructions for the use of the Commissioned, the Junior, and other officers of the Royal Navy* (1804), 39.

wherewith to help one another, we make up for it in kindness.'[200] A hard life, but sailors lived it as best they could. Tiredness could be lessened with the adoption of a three-watch system, rather than the more gruelling two-watch system. This permitted a sailor who stood watches to get a full night's sleep every third day and have longer periods off watch. In daylight hours he would then be more productive with ship maintenance. It depended on whether a ship or vessel of war had enough crew, and space, to allow a three-watch system. Every common sailor received fourteen inches to sling his or her hammock. In small vessels it was essential to have only a two-watch system, to place almost half the men on deck at one time and give enough room for the off-watch and idlers to set their hammocks. Commissioned officers always received their own cabin.

It required a mutiny to encourage Parliament to raise seamen's wages. After 1797 an able seaman's pay went from £1 4s. per month to £1 9s. 6d.; an ordinary seaman had his 19s. per month raised to £1 3s. 6d.[201] There was also the prospect of prize money. With its origins in the Cruisers and Convoys Act of 1708, prize money was part of the scheme of wages, pay and allowances for seamen. The Spanish ship *La Hermione* was taken a prize off Cape St Vincent in 1762 and ordinary seamen of one of three ships involved received a share of £485 5s.; the captain received a colossal £65,000 13s.[202]

The Prize Act 1793 applied to a list of nations at war against Great Britain. Prize money encouraged British sailors and their officers to sweep enemy trade and warships from the sea. Most sailors knew it as a means to ready money, and not just for the navy. The Admiralty issued letters of marque and reprisal to anyone with a vessel so long as they made lawful application, posted a bond and made an oath. Any prizes taken by them belonged to their owners and crews, but prizes taken by warships belonged to the 'flag-officers, commanders, and other officers, seamen, mariners, and soldiers on board every vessel of war' involved.[203] Prizes could be taken at sea, in enemy ports, harbours, creeks or roads. Even enemy fortresses could be taken. To do so no commander or captain of any naval vessel could willingly abandon a convoy, nor seek a prize if carrying dispatches, for fear of a court-martial and loss of shares. After being taken a prize, a ship could never be ransomed. It had to be sent to a friendly port, with any goods

---

200 Galt, *The steam-boat* (1823), 37.
201 Derrick (1806), 207; £1 9s. 6d. means 1 pound, 9 shillings, and 6 pence.
202 Whitlock, *Prize money* (1862), 8.
203 Mortimer (1810), under the lengthy article titled 'Prize'.

carried liable to customs duties. The Victualling Board could purchase any captured naval stores.

There existed rules of engagement, and not all prizes were 'condemned'. The likes of Jennings, Solomon and Vinney cared nothing for the process. When their ship captured a prize, others dealt with the paperwork. They were happy so long as they received their shares. The finer points of law and the deliberations of the high court of the admiralty left them cold, though they probably knew that a prize could be any ship that sailed under a standard other than the state from whom it received its commission; or had no proper paperwork such as a charter, invoice or bill of lading; or carried contraband goods, equipment or material that could be used by the enemy; or carried goods that had once belonged to the king. Oftentimes those things could only be known after the fact. Seamen no doubt knew of the 'prize agent'[204] who acted on behalf of their ship; and they would certainly have cared deeply about the total sum awarded for their prizes, and how it was divided into eighths. For example, a prize later found to be worth £20,000 would have equated to £2,500 per eighth. Three eighths would have gone to all captains involved in the capture, for a total of £7,500 of prize money, unless an admiral happened to be involved who received one eighth himself; captains then received two eighths between them. One eighth went to the commissioned officers, and in a lower rated ship with two lieutenants that would have equated to £1,250 each, or twelve years pay. One eighth was apportioned to all warrant officers to share between them. One eighth went to the petty officers. Two eighths went to all of the 'common' men onboard, for £25 each. For Jennings, Solomon and Vinney that would have meant two years pay. They received their shares before being paid off. If the captured ship happened to have contained British prisoners then each one would have received £5 for being held captive and assumed to have been involved in the capture of the prize.

With prize money finally in their pockets, wide smiles and warm hearts would have been the result. If a man had been injured while taking the prize, and later dismissed from service, he received a pension from the Chest at Chatham.[205] This chest was literally an iron-bound chest with a number of locks. Every sailor's pay had sixpence deducted per month to help fund it. Pensions were given after a man (or woman) was invalided out of the service, not because they were old, and it did not keep a recipient from penury.

---

204 Mortimer, *ibid.*
205 This ceased in 1803.

In 1808 it was reported that 'An old woman, generally known by the name of Tom Bowling, was lately brought before the Magistrate, for sleeping all night in the street; and was committed as a rogue and vagabond, and passed to her parish. She served as Boatswain's Mate on board a man of war for upwards of 20 years, and has a pension from Chatham Chest. When waked at midnight, by the beadle of the street, covered with snow, she cried, "Where the Devil would you have me sleep?" She has generally slept in this way, and dresses like a man; and is so hardy at a very advanced age, that she never catches cold.'[206]

If a navy sailor had been killed and he left a widow, then that lady would receive the equivalent of one year of his pay. Every warship and vessel in commission officially had 'Widow's Men' as part of their complements. These were permitted, fictitious, men 'directed by Act of Parliament…[to be] borne on her Books as able seamen, the produce of whose wages and the value of whose provisions are applied to the relief of poor widows of Commissioned and Warrant Officers in the Royal Navy.'[207] Any sailor who deserted after the taking of a prize, before prize money was given out did not receive his share. Together with shares not demanded within six years they were given to Greenwich Hospital.[208]

Sailors eagerly sought prizes. A string of them could net a man enough money to set him up for life after sea service, so an unknown sail upon the horizon instantly caught everyone's attention. As the crew gathered on the weather deck to consider the potential worth of the prize, they would have known that their fellow seamen and officers would fight alongside them. The possibility of their proving 'shy' was dealt with in the Articles of War.[209] Officers had another motivation. On 14 March 1757 Admiral Byng had been executed on the quarterdeck of HMS *Monarch* (74 guns) over the loss of Minorca. His death sent a powerful message to the fleets. Ineptitude, or the perception of an officer not doing his 'utmost', would not be tolerated. Voltaire included Byng's death in *Candide*, where Martin (a self-confessed pessimist) opined how 'in this country it is found requisite, now and then, to put one admiral to death in order to spirit up the others

---

206 *The Sporting Magazine or Monthly Calendar* (1808) Vol 30, 11. Also reported in the *Naval Chronicle*, but the veracity of the name Tom Bowling is questionable as it was a common epithet given to sailors and was used by Smollett in *Roderick Random*.
207 Falconer (1830), 630. Also part of the Regulations and Instructions.
208 Mortimer, *ibid*. As to non-demanded shares these could be later overturned.
209 Which is not to say men did not baulk in combat.

to fight.'[210] All commissioned officers and midshipmen assumed roles of leadership with the expectation that they would lead by example. From a seaman's perspective, 'His officer is the first to advance, the foremost to encounter, the last to hesitate, and the most willing to take more than his share of danger and of suffering; and this inspires the men with an emulation to do likewise.'[211]

Despite what many thought to be adequate care and rewards for seamen, in 1797 the Royal Navy suffered serious mutinies at Spithead, Plymouth and the Nore. Similar, isolated, incidents followed. After four years of continuous warfare common seamen had had enough. The nature of naval recruitment had brought onboard their warships and vessels 'a number of outraged individuals',[212] and the intermingling of impressed and quota men with volunteers had hardened some minds. Seamen resented how much they were paid, and the amount of leave they received. Victuals often turned their stomachs, and what was doled out always fell short of the mark, for salting added bulk to casks but lessened the amount of actual flesh inside. In a pound weight of sixteen ounces the purser withheld two ounces for waste.[213]

Enmity broke out amongst the Channel Fleet at a perilous time for Great Britain. The French then threatened invasion, the Bank of England faced the prospect of insolvency, and Ireland suffered insurrection. The nation 'trembled on the pivot of her destiny,'[214] as Lord Howe began to receive letters, and unsigned petitions, from seamen who had served under him when he had commanded the Channel Fleet. To express their grievances the seamen knowingly sidestepped their own ship's captains. Seamen asked him, as the 'sailor's friend',[215] to help answer their complaints. On closer inspection some letters appeared to be written by the same hand,[216] but all were respectful. The Channel Fleet then patrolled off Brest, under Lord Bridport, but most ships moored at Spithead during March and April 1797. Seamen had expected an answer to their letters before they returned to sea, unless a convoy was required or the enemy ventured out of port. 'The greatest loyalty to the king was professed, with the greatest zeal and

---

210 Voltaire (1806) Vol II, 98.
211 Gilly (1851), xxv.
212 Neale (1842), 3.
213 Smyth (1867), 550.
214 Accredited to Curran, as mentioned in Blunt (1860), 2.
215 *Beeton's Brave Tales* (1872), 946.
216 James, *Naval History* (1826), 34.

attachment to their country.'[217] Howe had pondered the letters and consulted with Rear Admiral Lord Seymour, who dismissed them as a few discontents intent on scandal. Howe had not been so sure, but he neglected to answer them promptly. As seamen heard nothing they became disgruntled with what they took to be inaction. According to Neale, 'the expectation of the enemy's fleet putting out to sea, and the ardour of men upon the eve of engagement, were supposed to offer a sufficient check for the prevention of any serious demand for immediate redress.'[218] Ships at Spithead lay quietly at anchor for two weeks, and no news arrived.

By 13 April the port admiral had gained intelligence of discontent over wages, especially on board *Queen Charlotte* (100) and *Royal Sovereign* (100). On 15 April it was particularly tense, with ship's boats scurrying to and fro throughout the fleet. The Admiralty received details of seamen's ill-feeling and considered it best to send the ships back to sea as soon as possible. Ships received the signal to proceed to sea on 15 April, but sailors on board *Queen Charlotte* ignored it. This apparently came as a complete surprise to her officers, who must have stood on the quarterdeck in some alarm. The shock would have coursed throughout the fleet.

Everything came to a head the next day, Easter Sunday, when seamen took control of their ships. Admiral Bridport had to invite two delegates from each warship to meet in *Queen Charlotte*'s great cabin. That would have been a sacrosanct place some seamen had never entered before. The sailor's committee arrived, and they wrote out two separate petitions. One was for Parliament, and the other for the Admiralty. The petition for Parliament began, 'Humbly showeth, That your petitioners, relying on the candour and justice of your honourable house, make bold to lay their grievances before you, hoping, that when you reflect on them, you will please to give redress, as far as your wisdom shall deem necessary.'[219] It laid out how seamen's pay had been settled in the time of Charles II, when necessaries had been thirty per cent cheaper 'than at the present time', and therefore requested their lordships to review their pay and make amendments. Howe was mentioned as their advocate, a man who had left them 'unprotected'. Expressions of their zeal and loyalty followed, and they mentioned their 'jealousy' of the increase in the pay and pensions of the army and militia while theirs had remained

217 *The New Annual Register* (1798), 77; and *The Universal Magazine of Knowledge* (1797) Vol C, 302.
218 Neale, *ibid*, 10.
219 *The Scots Magazine* (1797), 356.

neglected. The petition to the Admiralty argued their 'worth and good services' in the American war, this present war, 'and laborious industry in defence of their country'.

The first grievance was with seamen's wages. These 'ought to be raised, that we might be better able to support our wives and families.' They asked that 'provisions should be raised to the weight of sixteen ounces to the pound and be of a better quality',[220] the same as in the merchant service. They no longer wanted flour while in port, but vegetables. They desired better care and provision for sick sailors with an end to embezzlement of 'necessaries' in times of sickness, better shore leave after a long cruise, and if any seaman was wounded his pay should continue until he was either cured or discharged. They added their names to the petitions.[221]

News reached shore and people gathered in the streets. What had happened, they enquired? Why had sailors refused to sail? The wife of a petty officer on board one of the ships rushed from her workplace to look out across Spithead. She could not see her husband but she desperately tried to connect with him. Over the next few days snippets of news reached her, and her family, and they all went through a range of emotions from surprise to exultation, anger, pride and embarrassment, despair and hope. This was an event of national and historical importance. The wife only wanted her husband to be safe and in her arms. Some crews put their officers ashore. A ship's crew was like a pyramid, with the larger bottom comprised of common seamen and the top the captain. Petty officers were part of the thin end, and not prone to throw away their positions and perks lightly.

This would not be a bloody revolt in the mode of the French Revolution. These were men of an armed service, so ropes were reeved high[222] on every ship. Respect and order were maintained. Sailors and marines stood on their weather decks and took an oath. Thereafter, each ship's crew made cheer every day, as a vocal and visible sign of their continued adherence to the mutiny. The first time they did so it would have rolled like a broadside

---

220 *The Scots Magazine*, 356.
221 *The New Annual Register ibid.*, 78. Two delegates from each ship: the 100s *Royal George*, *Queen Charlotte*, *Royal Sovereign*, and *Glory* (98), the 90s *London* and *Duke*, the 74s *Défense*, *Defiance*, *l'Impetueux*, *Mars*, *Marlborough*, *Minotaur*, *Pompée*, *Ramillies*, *Robust* and *Terrible*. The names of delegates were typically British-Irish: Joyce, Morris, Glynn, Richardson, Ruly, Green, Harding, Dugan, Bethell, Adams, Anderson, Blithe, Clear, Porter *et al*. There was also a John Vassia.
222 A sign of hanging.

across the fleet. The wife, if she heard it, would have been moved to tears. Soon afterwards sick sailors confined to Haslar hoisted handkerchiefs out of their windows as a sign of sympathy. However, Spithead remained open to traffic, and warships set for convoy, the vital protection of the lifeblood of the nation, were allowed to depart.

Authorities had to respond so Rear Admiral Charles Pole took chaise to London.[223] En route his mind must have been in turmoil. At the Admiralty the porter could think of no reason to delay him, so Pole met with the commissioners the next day to inform them of the mutiny. Within a short time the admiral returned to Portsmouth accompanied by the First Lord, Earl Spencer, Lord Arden, Admiral Young and Mr Marsden the Second Secretary. Upon their arrival they met with admirals Lord Bridport, Gardner and Colpoys at a Portsmouth inn. The wife of the petty officer had tried desperately to get a peek at them. Their combined presence indicated to the whole town the seriousness of events. *Oh no*, the wife had thought, *my husband is in for it now*. The commissioners and admirals would have been conscious that all eyes were upon them. Correspondence with the seamen's committee was opened and conducted by way of officers, for men of such high standing did not consort with common seamen.

Lord Bridport was the fleet commander so the admiralty board members gave him their answer. They replied that after consideration of the 'price of the necessities of life' they had resolved to place their recommendation in front of the king to increase seamen's wages. They laid out a table of increases for petty officers, able seamen, ordinary seamen and landmen. Seamen wounded in service would be paid until healed, or declared 'unserviceable', whence they would receive either a pension or be admitted to Greenwich Hospital. It was hoped by the Admiralty that seamen would return to sea to 'meet the enemy of the country'.[224]

Next day, 19 April, the seamen's committee made a polite reply. They objected to the term 'landmen', and the omission of marines. They proposed their own pay scale, an increase in their pension to £10 per annum extended to include seamen of the East India Company, and an increase in their monthly dues for their pensions. Seamen's demand for improved victuals, what they called an end to 'leakage', was restated and they vowed to 'not lift an anchor' until such demands had been met.[225]

---

223 Neale, *ibid.*, 14.
224 *The European Magazine* (1797), 335.
225 Herbert (1876), 150.

Admiralty board members returned to London to meet with the Duke of Portland, Lord Greville, Mr Dundas and Lord Walsingham. As they left Portsmouth many in the town must have wondered what was going on. In London the commissioners met for three hours, after which time the cabinet members travelled to Windsor to meet with the king. Another council was held, in His Majesty's presence, that resulted in sailors' wages increased, and their demands for allowance of victuals met in full. Wounded seamen would henceforth receive full pay, until healed or declared incurable, when they would receive a pension. A full pardon was given. Business thereby concluded, 'near ten o'clock at night', and a messenger immediately dispatched to Portsmouth with the news. It became a rush to nip things in the bud, for the mutiny had widened to ships at Plymouth.[226]

The mutiny became the topic of the moment. What did it mean for Britain that her 'wooden wall' had revolted? Some thought that naval discipline had been poor, and the navy was run on 'unsound' principles. Some questioned the language of sailor's petitions, and wondered whether any sailor could actually have written them.[227] Had the fleet been infested with agents of insurrection?

On 21 April the fleet commander was 'required' by the Admiralty to communicate their acceptance with each ship's captain, who then had to tell their crews they should be sensible to what had been offered, but if they persisted to disobey they would not receive 'smart money', pensions from the chest at Chatham, nor admittance to any royal hospital. The king's pardon had been given, but only for those seamen and marines who returned to their duty and ceased 'intercourse' with anyone who remained disobedient. Seamen had to comply within one hour of receipt of the communication. When Lord Bridport repaired onboard the *Royal George* to inform his captains, the petty officer's wife had said to herself, *please say yes!* Captains went back to their own ships to read out the royal message. Seamen considered what they heard and replied that they could not settle independently of their committee, and two of their members were then ashore. These were eventually found and returned to their ships.

The wife was beside herself with agitation. Everything seemed to take so long! The seamen's committee met, replied with sincere gratitude, but stated they would persist until their demands for vegetables, augmentation

---

226 These were the *Atlas* (98), and the 74s *Edgar*, *Majestic* and *Saturn*.
227 Out of work, and in debt, attorneys, clerks, teachers and barristers had joined the navy.

of pensions, the passing of an act to settle their demands and His Majesty's pardon confirmed everything. Until then the fleet would remain at Spithead. They ended with a curt, 'this is the total and final answer'.[228] That would not have gone down well with admirals, as those august men were not used to that level of insolence, especially after the king had already answered them. Admirals Gardner, Colpoys and Pole boarded the *Queen Charlotte* in hopes that a discussion with the seamen's committee might end the situation. Seamen stood guard at the great cabin, instead of the customary marines, and common sailors held 'court' inside. The admirals had to be ushered into their own place of authority. The meeting was tense. The seamen's committee remained adamant, so much so that Admiral Gardner became angry and grabbed a sailor by the collar and threatened him with the noose, 'together with every fifth man in the fleet'.[229] That ended the meeting. When news reached other warships a red flag was raised aboard the *Royal George,* and sailors took to their guns with lighted matches. When the tide of gossip reached shore the wife went white with shock and fell to her knees.

On 23 April Lord Bridport repaired to the *Royal George*, hoisted his flag and made a speech saying that all demands had been met. The red flag was lowered and everyone involved considered the matter ended.[230]

Although she hadn't seen her husband through the whole ordeal the wife cried with love and pride. She waved to the fleet and choked on her emotions, as slowly, and with great relief, the ships moved down from Spithead to St Helens. With fair winds they would sail from there – but the winds were not fair.

In London the First Lord dismissed comments about naval disaffection in the House of Lords. The House of Commons dragged its heels over seamen's wages. On 1 May the Admiralty issued an order for captains and commanders of His Majesty's ships to be attentive and 'on the first appearance of mutiny, to use the most vigorous means to suppress it, and to bring the ringleaders to punishment,' and 'from the disposition lately shown by the seamen belonging to several of his Majesty's ships, it had become highly necessary that the strictest attention should be paid by all officers...to ensure a proper subordination and discipline, and to prevent, as far as may be, all discontent among the seamen.'[231]

---

228 *The New Annual Register, ibid.*, 84.
229 *The Universal Magazine of Knowledge and Pleasure* (1797) Vol C, 377.
230 Grimshaw (1852) Vol I, 213.
231 Barrow, *Howe* (1838), 329.

The delay of the fleet in sailing allowed the news from Parliament and the Admiralty to reach the ears of seamen and their loved ones ashore. The wife became too distracted by it to work – it was supposed to have ended! *Good God*, she prayed, *would they agree to sail when the time came? Would Britain be defended?* The signal to sail was given on Sunday, 7 May, but sailors once more refused to work their ships. A second mutiny commenced.[232]

Vice Admiral Sir John Colpoys was onboard the *London* (90) when seamen's delegates took boats to meet with him. When they arrived off the ship the admiral refused them access. He drew up his marines on deck and opened the gun ports against them. His crew demanded the delegates be allowed onboard. The request was refused, and the seamen were sent belowdecks. They complied, but managed to keep an eye on events through the open ports. The delegates tried to board so the *London*'s marines were ordered to fire into the boats.[233] Three delegates fell dead. Upon the ship one seaman, no doubt in a fury, unlashed a gun and turned it aft. He was shot by an officer. Angered to a rage the crew turned more guns inwards. Some took up arms. Open insurrection broke out. Dozens rushed on deck with bloody revenge in mind. There they met and told the marines, men they messed with, to throw down their arms. Their officers were soon restrained. Lieutenant Simons, of the marines, was wounded. Seamen grabbed their first lieutenant and made preparations to hang him, until Colpoys let them know that that officer had acted upon his orders. That saved him. So all officers were placed under arrest in their cabins and marines taken captive. The situation remained volatile.

The town of Portsmouth, and the nearby coast, became unsettled. The petty officer's wife was so distraught she fell into a swoon. Sympathy mainly lay with the seamen. Orders were given to strengthen the garrison and cover possible landing places with field-pieces. Days passed, the wife slowly recovered, and tempers cooled. The sailors, 'having lost three of their comrades, in consequence of the resistance made to their going on board the London...wished to bring them to Kingston church yard, and to carry them in procession through the town of Portsmouth.'[234] They received permission and hundreds turned out to give their respects. The wife had feared the worst, and felt ashamed when she learned her husband would not be one of those buried.

---

232 *Ibid*, 330.
233 Herbert, 158.
234 *The Monthly Magazine* (1808) Vol XXV, 566.

Panic spread to the capital. Many thought the king should personally visit the fleet to try to mollify the mutineers. Pitt, in Parliament, asked members to forgive him in asking for monies to help raise seamen's pay, while not offering the normal considerations. He said, 'I feel it my duty to ask, and entreat the silent judgment of the committee on the proposition which I shall make... . For advance of pay £351,000; for additional allowance of provisions £185,000. Making a total of £536,000.' Fox replied that present difficulties were due to silence, not discussion. He said, 'This House should not have been the confidants of the minister, and remained silent so long upon this subject. Had this House interposed upon the commencement of this matter, instead of indulging the ministers with the scandalous delay of a fortnight, I verily believe we should not have heard anything of the misfortunes which have recently happened.'[235] He warned that what had happened at Spithead could happen again.

The Admiralty had to make a final settlement. The commissioners met with Lord Howe and dispatched him to Portsmouth on 11 May, with full powers to negotiate with the seamen's committee. Upon his arrival he informed them of the total compliance with all their original demands. He offered details of the 9 May 1797 Seamen's Additional Pay Bill,[236] together with the king's pardon 'to all who should immediately return to their duty'. He did a round robin of every ship over three successive days, and persuaded most crews to return to their duty. It would have been a laborious task for an old and frail man, and perhaps the most important duty he carried out for his nation. When it was obvious everything was to be made right the wife became ecstatic. Delegates continued to demand the removal of officers they considered to be 'obnoxious', and the *Duke* (90) and *Mars* (74) carried on with the mutiny until threatened by other ships to desist, but on 15 May delegates went ashore to the Governor's House to collect Lord Howe and escorted him in honour for a final visit of the fleet. It became a festive event. With flowers in hand, and in her hair, the wife joined the crowds.

Signalled to put to sea, on 16 May, ships managed to do so the next day. Other ships joined them mid-Channel so that twenty-one ships of the line

---

235 Neale, 67 & 68.
236 The full title was, *An Act carrying into Execution His Majesty's Order in Council of the Third Day of May 1797, for an Increase of Pay and Provisions to the Seamen and Marines serving in His Majesty's navy; and to amend so much of an Act made in the 35th Year of the Reign of His present Majesty, as enables Petty Officers and Seamen, Non-commissioned Officers of Marines, and Marines, to allot Part of their Pay for the Maintenance of their Wives, Children, or Mothers.*

and accompanying frigates left and sailed for Brest. All along the coast men and women would have borrowed spyglasses to see them sail off. After weeks of uncertainty and fear, Spithead and St Helens must have seemed empty. For the petty officer's wife, and many others, their ordeal ended, but it had not ended for all.

The Nore then acted as a naval anchorage, where the Thames meets the North Sea. Unlike ships at Spithead, Nore ships were not so unified. Some of them belonged to the North Sea Fleet at Yarmouth so sailors were not familiar with those on most other ships. On 12 May the seamen on board the *Sandwich* (90) mutinied. Ships at the Nore[237] had a large proportion of crews made up of quota men, some real hard cases, and they were less likely to be civil in open insurrection. Richard Parker became their president. He had served on his ship only six weeks, but had been recognized as 'a man of good natural parts'.[238] Order was maintained at first, but seamen revelled in their new-found authority. Some observers wondered whether this mutiny had any connection with radical elements rampant throughout the kingdom. It had a different feel about it.

After meetings ashore, in various pubs, the mutineers of this 'floating republic'[239] made their complaints known. They wrote up eight articles by which they laid out how they wanted those 'indulgences' given to sailors at Spithead applied to them plus better liberty given while in port, all arrears of pay to be paid prior to sailing, men taken off a ship not to be reemployed on the same ship without seamen's consent, pressed men to receive two months advance of pay to buy 'necessaries', deserters to be declared safe before joining a ship, better distribution of prize money to be organized, an amendment made to the Articles of War and some articles abolished. They also stated how the mutiny would continue until their demands had been 'ratified' by the Lords Commissioners of the Admiralty.[240] On 23 May the seamen's committee received a reply from the Admiralty that said nothing beyond the agreement made at Spithead.

Angered, the mutineers took hold of a number of gunboats and moved them off shore. The next day, ships moored at the Little Nore received orders

---

237 Including the 64s *Director* and *Inflexible*, *St. Fiorenzo* (40, that had just arrived), the 38s *Clyde* and *Espion*, the 32s *Iris* and *Niger*, the *Brilliant* (28), the *Champion* (24), the armed *en flûte* stores ship *Grampus*, the floating battery *Firm* (24) and the *Swan* (16).
238 *The Annual Register or a view of the History, Politics and Literature for the year 1797* (1807), 214.
239 Chambers, *Book Of Days* (1879), 780.
240 Cunningham (1829), 23-5.

to move further out to the Great Nore. Their intention was to blockade the Medway and interfere with shipping along the Thames, but the crew of the *Clyde* (32) appeared to deliberately delay their compliance. On 27 May, an incredible seventeen days after the mutiny commenced, the Admiralty finally sent the same delegation that had visited Portsmouth. They arrived the next morning and once more opened proceedings by way of intermediaries. Parker and other delegates attended a meeting in Sheerness where 'their behaviour was so audacious, that the lords of the admiralty returned to town without the least success,'[241] although the *Clyde*, *St Fiorenzo* (32) and *Director* (64) showed signs of wavering. Attitudes of local authorities hardened, and seamen were stopped from coming ashore. In return *Inflexible* (64) had to threaten the *Clyde* with a full broadside to make her remain loyal to the mutiny.

At dawn on 30 May the *Clyde* cut her cables, drifted away upon the tide, and sailed into harbour. Next day the *St Fiorenzo* did the same, managed to reach the Essex shore, and thence proceeded to Portsmouth. The mutiny unravelled towards the end of May, despite seven ships of the North Sea Fleet appearing unexpectedly,[242] and seven more on 6 June 1797. These ships had deserted their stations off an enemy coast, the Batavian Republic, something no other mutiny ship had done. That fact posed the troubling prospect that 'the Love of Country and the Spirit of National Enterprise, which upon all occasions had animated every Individual in our Fleets to banish private feelings whenever an Enemy or other obstacle was mentioned, were now in danger of being lost.'[243] But public opinion was firmly against them. When mutineers landed at Gravesend to persuade warships there to join with them, local townsfolk attempted to have them arrested. They escaped, later returned, and were only stopped by the guns of Tilbury fort. The *Lancaster* (64) joined their cause.

When mutineers began to tar and feather some of their captives, flog their own and punish some for disrespect to their delegates, it was obvious the mutiny had entered its end phase. A public demonstration was made, to prod those who wavered, to break away. Two store ships slipped their cables and returned to harbour. On 6 June 1797 Parliament passed two bills, the Incitement to Mutiny Act 'for the better Prevention and Punishment of Attempts to seduce Persons serving in His Majesty's Forces by Sea or Land from their Duty and

---

241 *The Annual Register* (1807), 215.
242 The *Montague* (74), the 64s *Agamemnon, Ardent, Belliqueux, Lion, Monmouth, Nassau, Repulse* and *Standard*, the 50s *Isis* and *Leopard*, *Inspector* (20), and the 18s *Ranger* and *Pylades*. *Annual Register, ibid.*, 214.
243 Cunningham, 55.

Allegiance to His Majesty, or to incite them to Mutiny or Disobedience', and 'An Act for more effectually restraining Intercourse with the Crews of certain of His Majesty's Ships now in a State of Mutiny and Rebellion, and for the more effectual Suppression of such Mutiny and Rebellion.'[244] Many mutineers lost heart. Two other ships slipped their cables and fled. 'The Ships now by degrees withdrew from the Mutinous Confederacy, some through the exertions of the Officers, but the greater part of them voluntarily.'[245] After a few more days it was over. Parker was arrested, sent to jail, placed on trial and swung from the yard of the *Sandwich* on 29 June.

Mutinies ended around the British coast, but seamen showed discontent off Cadiz, on board the *Hermione* (38) off Puerto Rico, and at the Cape. Afterwards many asked themselves what lessons had been learned. The British government could put to sea the grandest fleet imaginable, but without motivated and supportive crews they were worthless. Crews remained obedient until 1797, but discontent had simmered. The fact seamen's pleas to Lord Howe had initially been ignored prompted detractors to say that this could not be tolerated again. Neale later wrote, 'it was hoped that the whole affair would be an awful warning to ministers, how they presumed to trifle with the petitions of an aggrieved people.'[246] Seamen did not complain about discipline, impressment, or flogging. They simply wanted better pay, pensions, victuals, and leave. In successive years, after the mutiny, the Royal Navy continued to make improvements to conditions of the average sailor, so that by 1838 John Barrow argued how 'A man-of-war's man is better fed, better lodged, better and cheaper clothed, and, in sickness, better taken care of, than any class of labouring men; and when he has completed twenty-one years' service, he may retire, if he wishes it, with a pension for life.'[247] These were more reasons why the Royal Navy was becoming, by 1800, a true 'superpower'.

---

244 *The Statutes at Large* (1798), 556 & 7.
245 Cunningham, 79.
246 Neale, *Narrative* (1861), 47.
247 Barrow, *Howe*, 355.

Chapter 6

Steady, Boys, Steady

The Îles Saint-Marcouf lie three miles off the coast of Normandy. Two specks upon the sea. Ordinarily uninhabited, their height barely exceeded the freeboard of a first rate.[248] War had made them an ideal observation post for the British.[249] Taken possession of in 1795, blockhouses accommodated a garrison of marines, seamen invalids and artillerymen. They were fewer in number than the crew of a third rate.[250] The main rock, crescent-shaped Île de Terre, supported a small garden but the garrison had to be supplied by ship. Two 4-gun vessels, *Badger* and *Sandfly,* provided protection and they carried horrendously powerful 32-pounder carronades, enough to make any enemy vessel think twice.[251] Three British warships occasionally stood in to make their presence known and harass local sea trade. The *Adamant* (50), *Eurydice* (24), and *Orestes* (18) lurked somewhere over the horizon. However, with such fine and calm May weather it seemed unlikely they would beat up in time to join the defence of the islands. An enemy fleet of flat-boats, that had recently cluttered the mouth of the Orne river, had crawled along the coast to La Hogue in preparation of an all-out assault. The French wanted to regain the islands.

On Île de Terre the garrison's unpopular commander, Lieutenant Papps Price, lowered his glass and muttered something droll to his ever-present female companion.[252] A marine stood watch close by his shoulder, ramrod straight with fixed bayonet, so after the lieutenant and his sweetheart had returned to their quarters gossip raced through the camp. 'Papps reckons there'll be trouble.' 'The Frenchies will pay us a visit, mark my words.' 'Buff your belt buckles, boys, the time has come!'

---

248 The height of a ship's hull above the waterline.
249 Long (1895), 92.
250 James, C., (1810), under 'Marcouf'.
251 James, W. (1837) Vol I, 114.
252 A woman of Portsmouth.

Another marine private stood idle beside the camp's flagpole, as a seaman friend limped over to pass the time and share a pipe. The sailor had a spyglass and with great eagerness, not asking where his friend had got it from, the marine took it and put it to his right eye. La Hogue's Vauban tower came into hazy view. Underneath its dark shadow, dotted along the shore, were dozens of *bateaux à la Muskein*.[253] Hundreds of men, all in long lines, poured into the flat-boats from a camp. At this distance they resembled a nest of ants. He concluded their objective would be the Île de Terre.

'See 'em?' asked the invalid.

'I see 'em.'

He gave back the glass and thoughtfully looked along the fringe of the isle. Some long 24- pounders and one of the two 32-pounder carronades faced towards the peninsula and the enemy. Those guns would do cruel damage against mere floating tinder-boxes, but there would be many boats, so some could break through.

'Didn't the *Diamond* and *Hydra* try to stop them?' he asked.[254]

'Guess they didn't. Just like the fleet didn't stop the Frenchies at Fishguard.'[255]

The French were active, and they had made an attempt against Ireland. His home. The private had been thinking a lot about that, and about his grandfather. That kindly man had joined the marines in 1757, after Parliament paid for more than 11,000 men to serve.[256] He grew up in awe of him. A similar draft had been made in 1795, and he had been pleased to receive his grandfather's blessing after he took the bounty. What would his grandfather think of him now? Here he was with white-trimmed black bicorn, red jacket with white facing, white waistcoat and trousers, black gaiters, two crossed leathers and bright-finish sea service musket. He looked smart but had a sense of anxiety. This would be his first action and he hoped to make his grandfather proud.

The sailor looked up at the bright blue sky. 'There'll be no moon tonight. The French will make the most of it.'

The marine's stomach tightened. Tonight? He made a silent prayer.

---

253 boats named after the man who organized them for an invasion.

254 Low (1890), 184. In April 1798 a flotilla of French flat-boats tried to attack the two islands and were driven off by two British frigates, *Diamond* (38) and *Hydra* (38). The boats had to stand into the Orne river to make repairs. They were joined by seven heavy gun-brigs and armed fishing vessels.

255 In February 1797 three French warships and a lugger landed 1,200 men, but no cannon. A local militia had repulsed the invasion.

256 *The Universal Magazine of Knowledge* (1757) Vol XX, 15.

'And they know these waters well.'

Evening approached so they shook hands in respect of the work to come and departed to their duties.

That night it was indeed dark. Men throughout the camp talked in low whispers. By midnight the French made their approach. The *Badger* and *Sandfly* sent up dozens of flares to light them. The eyes of the garrison strained to see the enemy. They could make out more than fifty boats with two French brigs. Yet the flotilla held off and waited until dawn. When daylight finally crept in no British warships, apart from the two gunboats, could be seen. They were alone.

The French flotilla broke up into three separate divisions. Their heavy brigs remained between the islands and the mainland. Half of the flats moved towards Île du Large while the rest moved towards Île de Terre. Each flatboat had a long 18-pounder in the bow and a 6-pounder in the stern. It was obvious they would try to convene between the two islands. With deep booms they began to fire on the garrison.

The tide pushed the northern division towards Île du Large, so that their crews had to take to the oars in a messy attempt to remain in formation. The same tide carried the southern division towards the Île de Terre. The old sailor and his fellow gunners feverishly fired upon them. The marine was ordered to stand along the cliff top and fire on any boat that came within range. Under a warm and graceful sun he witnessed the whole action unfold.

Both islands brought to bear seventeen guns. Their loud reports stunned and rippled the water underneath their muzzles. A boatswain on Île de Terre roared out orders for the 4- and 6- pounders to load with canister.[257] Most guns focused on what seemed to be the French commodore's boat. They peppered it mercilessly. With shouts of glee the British witnessed it take repeated hits, break up and sink. Debris and men floundered but were soon taken away by tide and wave. For two hours the guns blazed out; as they grew hot, water had to be constantly thrown over them. The French brigs maintained a distance no closer than 300 yards, so their heavy guns fired to little effect. Eventually some flats came within musket shot, and the marine private could fire off a few rounds. Whether he hit anything he was unable to say. Below, he observed the boats scatter, collide and struggle to keep order. A silent part within him seemed to stand as a mere observer. He barely heard the noise. Shouts, shrieks and the moans of drowning men did not register. From the other island he saw

---

257 James, W., *ibid*.

black balls fly in strange arcs to fall amongst the enemy, gunsmoke from their guns trailing off towards the north-west.

Seven enemy boats were destroyed. They splintered to pieces. A few seemed to explode in gushes of water when hit. One upturned, threw everyone into the sea, and floated off. The men in the water disappeared as though pulled down by some unseen force. The tide, the guns, and utter destruction began to force the flotilla back. Not one Frenchman managed to land on either rock. When the *Sandfly* approached, to fire her two carronades, the enemy scattered for good. Dispirited, they turned and headed back to La Hogue. With immense pride the garrison stood and shouted in one voice, 'Huzza! Huzza! Huzza!'

Handshakes and hearty embraces followed. Bottles of spirits appeared. There was a slight lull after the announcement of the butcher's bill was made, with one marine dead and two sailors wounded, but gaiety soon returned. Liquor softened the blow. That is, until they inspected an upturned flat named number thirteen. When someone translated the papers found onboard the garrison fell into silence. That boat had carried 144 men, most of the *2e bataillon Boulogne*, and every one of them had drowned.[258] At that rate the French lost more than 900 men.

By late afternoon the old seaman and the young marine managed to meet again at their customary spot. They offered their own take on the day. The gunner remained deeply satisfied, while the marine was confused. He had fired a few shots but he could not believe so many Frenchmen had died. It seemed unfair.

'Divvin' give it a thought, marra. It's the way of things. If they had landed it's likely none of us would have lived. If we had, a French prison don't bear thinking about.'

They had given a good account of themselves. The marine thought his grandfather would be proud, as the rocks remained British. Later, he saw the commander and his companion take their customary evening stroll. No doubt the lieutenant would receive a long-overdue promotion and a way off this rock, this Island of Earth. As the sailor had said, it is the way of things.

The Battle of Îles Saint-Marcouf took place on 7 May 1798. Afterwards Lieutenant Papps Price received a promotion as a reward. These small islands remained in British hands and formed a small part of one theatre[259]

---

258 Edmonds (1890), 184.
259 The term 'theatre of war' has an uncertain etymology, but a book printed in 1793 was titled *A Tour Through The Theatre of War in the months of November and December 1792 etc,* London, J. Bew.

of war. By being close to Britain this theatre was considered the most important. From 1793 until 1795 it comprised the North Sea, both sides of the English Channel, the coasts of Ireland and Brittany, and the long western coast of France and the Atlantic. After France overran Holland and captured the Dutch fleet on 17 January 1795,[260] the theatre widened to give greater protection throughout the North Sea with a blockade placed upon the main Dutch naval arsenal, Den Helder, and the Texel roads. After Spain declared war on Britain on 11 October 1796,[261] northern Spain and Portugal became a greater part of this same theatre. The English Channel and the Thames estuary were the origin and confluence of much of Britain's sea trade, and thereby the most important part of the region. To emerge victorious against revolutionary France and her allies the Channel Fleet had to maintain a 'wooden wall' at all times. That required naval strength, dominance of the seas, disruption of enemy sea commerce and the threat and ability to land troops on enemy soil.

In early 1793 France had the advantage and her warships were often superior in sailing qualities, but she suffered indiscipline. She was also hampered by her geography and the situation of her naval officers[262]. With both an Atlantic and Mediterranean coastline her two major arsenals had to be separated at some distance by land and sea.[263] Almost half of the French fleet lay far from Britain in the Mediterranean. Her manpower also suffered division, and many of her naval officers had either refused to take an oath in favour of the revolutionary government or had abandoned their posts. Yet France still managed to score early successes. From 1793 until 1795 French privateers captured close to 3,000 British 'craft of all sizes and rigs'.[264] Many were simple colliers and small craft, but some were plump Indiamen with full cargoes. Sea commerce was the lifeblood of Britain. It pulsed through sea-lanes like blood through arteries. A few well-appointed French privateers had persistently ranged out from numerous French ports to sever and worry those arteries.

In response Britain had had to work up her fleet, while at the same time help her allies on the continent. She did not have a large army that

---

260 The winter of 1794/5 was severe and rivers and canals froze solid enabling the French to cross them with ease.
261 Spain signed the Treaty of Ildefonso with France on 19 August 1796.
262 Many French naval officers were either forced out of office for not taking the new republican oath, or they voluntarily left due to persecution.
263 Brest was on the western coast, Toulon in the Mediterranean.
264 Norman (1887), 377. The metaphor of arteries is Norman's; Mahan also mentions this number.

could land and sweep through France to Paris. Some of her few regiments were sent to the Dutch Republic, under command of the king's son,[265] to coordinate with Austrian, Prussian, Dutch, French émigré and some Germanic small-states' troops. Combined they presented a coalition against the revolutionaries. There was 'strategy' involved, but the word did not then have the same connotations it later gained. It required Carl von Clausewitz to formalize military 'strategy' in his posthumous book *On War*, published after 1835[266] and Alfred Thayer Mahan to formalize 'naval strategy' in the latter years of the nineteenth century. In these years 'strategy' was thought to be the art of bringing together troops under the direction of a general, or ships under the direction of an admiral. Between 1793 and 1800 it was the 'policy' of Great Britain to have her Royal Navy dominate the seas. Regiments were sent abroad, but the navy had to transport them and safeguard the nation.

The Channel Fleet covered home waters, and thereby many of her sailors had families at close quarters. The wife of the petty officer had an uncle, an old sailor long pensioned off after his right leg had been shot away from the thigh down, whose own son served with the Channel Fleet. From the vantage point of 1800 the old sailor considered what had been an extraordinary time. He remembered vividly when Lord Howe had arrived at Portsmouth, on 27 May 1793, to hoist his flag on board the *Queen Charlotte*.[267] He had guessed then what that admiral's initial instructions had been. To achieve victory he knew it would be necessary to blockade France's main regional arsenal, Brest, to push the 'front' away from Britain and bottle up in port the French fleet so it could not molest British shipping. He realized then that if the French fleet had put to sea then battle would have been sought in hopes of weakening the enemy through wreck or capture to a point where it would struggle to pose a threat. All the while preserving British warships and vessels. With the enemy in port it only required a few ships to maintain a blockade, so the majority of the fleet would be able to lie safely at a roadstead.

The old sailor knew that the cautious policy of Admiral Lord Howe perfectly suited that man, under whom he had served in 1777, and it certainly suited the nature of the region. Often the seas around Britain are tempestuous, even in summer, and storms in the Channel could make it difficult for ships to make their way westwards. His journal reminded him

---

265 Prince Frederick, Duke of York.
266 *Vom Kriege* in German.
267 Barrow, *Howe* (1838), 211. The author sets out what the admiral's instructions were.

how, on 14 July 1793, a fleet had sailed from Spithead. Fifteen ships of the line and six frigates then headed for the Atlantic, and four days later were off the Lizard[268] when a heavy squall descended and caused the *Majestic* (74) to collide with the *Bellerophon* (74).[269] She had to be towed into Plymouth, and did not put to sea again until 11 August. Another time, in November 1793, another fleet had made several attempts to sail beyond the Lizard but they could not. Ships suffered sprung yards and much wear and tear. He had wondered whether those warships had been ill fitted, navigation had been poor, or it was just folly to keep ships and vessels at sea during stormy months.[270] He knew that warships had to remain at sea, but the damage incurred could be severe.

Storms wearied crews. The old sailor knew that all too well. The worst prospect for any sailor had to be a lee shore, a stretch of coast on the leeward side of a ship upon which the wind blows from the sea with a prospect of pushing a ship onto rocks, reefs, shoals or a beach battered by waves. William Hutchinson wrote in 1791 that 'most people pity seamen when in a gale of wind, but none so much as those who know from experience the hardships they go through in cold weather, long dark winter nights, dangerous situations, and near a lee shore, especially if it is a rocky one; when the waves run high it is most to be dreaded, and the utmost endeavours should be used to keep from it, because it gives little or no chance of saving either the ship or the lives of even the best of swimmers.'[271] The whole coast of Brittany, and the long western reach of France, faces the full brunt of the Atlantic. To maintain a blockade on Brest and other ports thereabouts required ships to suffer the perpetual prospect of a lee shore. A ship could easily become embayed, with little or no room to move, with winds high enough to cause problems if she ever did miss stays. He had once carved a model ship just to demonstrate to his son how dangerous miss stays could be. He placed the model in a puddle and told him, *when a ship fails in her attempt to turn into the wind, she loses headway. If very violent the wind could push her towards a nearby shore.* To sail near Brest, with her unforgiving coast of rocks and shoals and a high wind and surf pounding the shore, was a prospect best not to think about. So Lord Howe had adopted a policy of keeping his fleet at moorings for as long as possible. During

---

268 Britain's most southerly point.
269 *The United Service Magazine* (1840) Part II, 361. It says: 'fell athwart hawse the Bellerophon.'
270 Barrow, 216.
271 Hutchinson (1791), 261.

winter months, unless the risk of invasion ran high, only a few warships and vessels maintained watch upon that coast.

Whatever the season, risks always resided at sea. Between 1793 and 1800 the Royal Navy lost ninety-eight ships (of three masts) and other vessels (of one or two) to shipwreck. Fifty-two were lost in British waters and off the coasts of France, Spain and Portugal. For the first two years of the war no ships were lost to wreck in any of those waters, but in 1795 there were two and in 1796 there were ten. From 1797 until 1800 at least eight ships were lost each year throughout the region. The worst year was 1799 with fourteen losses.[272] Not every wreck was due to a lee shore, as ships either struck shoals, sands or reefs, foundered, burned, blew up or were sunk after battle, because life at sea had more dangers than the wind. The old salt had kept notes of some of those losses. The *Boyne* (98) burned at Spithead on 1 May 1795. *Amphion* (32) blew up in the Hamoaze, Plymouth on 22 September 1796. *Amazon* (32) ran ashore south of Brest on 14 January 1797 after chasing the *Droits des Hommes*. The *Lutine* (32)[273] sank off Vlieland on 9 October 1799. The largest group of losses were with unrated vessels. With such a prolonged blockade of Brest, five went down in waters close by, but the North Sea[274] and the English Channel accounted for the largest group of wrecks. December and January were the two months of most losses: fourteen were lost in those months between 1793 and 1800. Most wrecks resulted in few deaths but the majority of the 215 crew aboard the *Amphion* died, as did all ninety souls of the *Curlew* (16), lost somewhere in the North Sea.

Warships that sailed towards Brest, and into the Atlantic, often found prevalent winds prolonged their passage. Sailors were resigned to how winds often doubled sailing distances with the need to work against them. Blockade therefore proved to be an arduous, tedious and wearisome activity. It took a real toll on ships and men. The longer the time on blockade the more ships deteriorated. Weakened, they would then face a French fleet made equal, or stronger, than their own. Lord Howe doggedly pursued his policy of loose blockade and had urged caution and the persistent pursuit of the preservation of the fleet.[275]

---

272 All figures found in Gilly (1857), 372-86.
273 A French-built ship.
274 Specifically off Holland and the Elbe.
275 Mahan believed that consequent wear and tear, and the strenuous effort required to maintain a blockade off French Atlantic ports, actually improved the effectiveness of British sailors: 'Good men with poor ships are better than poor men with good ships.' Due to general inaction the French found themselves to have good ships, with poor men. Mahan, *French Revolution* (1892) Vol I, 102.

CAPTURE OF THE FRENCH "REUNION" BY THE "CRESCENT," 1793.
"CRESCENT," Frigate, 888 Tons. Launched Bursledon, 1784. Heaviest Gun, 18 Pdr.

The promise of a major French prize lay somewhere over the horizon. Frigates, like the *Crescent* and *Nymphe*, became mainstays of the era. These 'eyes of the fleet' kept watch upon enemy ports and were often on detached and independent cruises. (title: 'Crescent – "Reunion". Date: 1793', from archivist, fotolia)

He pulled more than a few ropes. Dozens of them, all rearing up amongst the sails and masts. Stays. Braces. He struggled to name and comprehend them all. A ship of the era required a large amount of rope and rigging. Upon first boarding a ship a landman would have 'been all at sea', until he 'learned the ropes'. (title: 'masts', from Pawel Nawrot, fotolia)

A man who could work high above the deck, while a ship pitched and rolled on rough seas, and deal with sails when winds howled all around was a precious resource. Seamen often had a perilous job, with the need to climb up masts to reef and shake out sails. (title: 'Up the mast' by RTimages, fotolia)

Thomas Rowlandson.   GROG ON BOARD A SHIP   1785.

What about the drunkenness of sailors? Half a pint of spirits every day to every sailor regardless of their age. In an era when freshwater at sea was sparse, grog and other alcohol had been a norm of life at sea. (title: 'Sailors Drink - Rowlandson. Date: 1789', by archivist, fotolia)

'*Encouragement of Seamen employed in the royal navy, and for establishing a regular method for the punctual, frequent, and certain payment of their wages*' *had brought certain improvements, but wages remained static.* Sailors not only contributed their labour, blood and lives, they also contributed their earnings to help fund the war. (title: 'Sailors Contributing. Date: 1798', from archivist, fotolia)

Admiral Bridport had to invite two delegates from each warship to meet in Queen Charlotte's great cabin. That would have been a sacrosanct place some seamen had never entered before. Warships were not just for war but were a means to assert authority and project British might.

The wife of a petty officer on board one of the ships rushed from her workplace to look out across Spithead. Many sailors of the navy had family ashore, all around the country, including mothers, sisters, wives and girlfriends. These women would have sought out any news or gossip of events at sea. (title: 'Working Class Dress 1795. Date: 1795', from archivist, fotolia)

The old sailor knew that the cautious policy of Admiral Lord Howe perfectly suited that man. With long experience Howe pursued a policy of preservation of the Channel Fleet as much as possible. He commanded the British fleet at the Battle of the Glorious First of June, 1794. (title: 'Officer Richard Howe Medallion Bust in Greenwich', by chrisdorney, fotolia)

NAVAL OFFICERS AND SEAMEN, EIGHTEENTH CENTURY.

Apart from their different uniforms, both marines and seamen shared similar stories and backgrounds. Naval officers adopted epaulettes in 1795, and uniforms changed over the years. Seamen had no defined uniform until after the fall of Napoléon. (title: '18th century Naval Uniform', by archivist, fotolia)

For more than three weeks the deficiency of numbers, opposed to what the Spanish could command, would have forced a more timid commander to harbour. Not John Jervis; he was too resolute for that. A disciplinarian and accomplished naval administrator, Jervis helped the Mediterranean Fleet achieve dominance. (title: 'John Jervis, 1st Earl of St Vincent', by Georgios Kollidas, fotolia)

The resultant fire turned night into day. It 'laid open to view, by its light, all who were aiding… . The enemy, having now distinct objects to point at, opened his batteries from every quarter; when, suddenly, a tremendous explosion, unexpected by all, awed into silence both the besiegers and the attacked.' The Siege of Toulon ended in evacuation and the burning of French ships. (title: 'Burning Ships - Incendie de la Flotte - end 18th century', by Erica Guilane-Nachez, fotolia)

Cutting out expeditions, raids and landings made the navy a flexible force, and helped project its strength ashore. Men became famous through such actions. HMS *Hermione* suffered a mutiny in 1797. The mutineers sailed her to join the Spanish, and she was 'cut out' and taken back into the British service in 1799. She was renamed HMS *Retaliation*. (title: 'Hermione Captured. Date: October 1799', from archivist, fotolia)

Above: The Battle of Cape St Vincent commenced a period during which the British navy 'struck all Europe with astonishment'. After the victory there were various ways by which Britain signified the win, including pennies. This particular version shows Britannia, a naval ship and the sea. (title: 'British Cartwheel Penny', by Steve Lovegrove, fotolia)

Right: 'We are but few, but of the right sort.' Nelson came to fame in this era, with his actions at sea and on land. His commanded the fleet that brought the French to battle at Aboukir. (title: 'Horatio Nelson, 1st Viscount Nelson', by Georgios Kollidas, fotolia)

Nelson himself 'passed from the fore chains of his own ship into the Enemy's quarter gallery, and thence through the cabin to the quarter deck, where he arrived in time to receive the sword of the dying Commander, who was mortally wounded by the boarders.' The captured *San José* was taken in to the British service and renamed *San Josef.* (title: 'An engraved illustration image of Nelson boarding the San Josef at the Battle of St Vincent from a vintage Victorian book dated 1886 that is no longer in copyright,' by Tony Baggett, fotolia)

About ten o'clock the l'Orient exploded. Ships had done so before, would do so again, but the sound of this one was so great it caused an instant pause, a death-like sullen silence, for at least three minutes. This battle allowed the Royal Navy to regain dominance throughout the Mediterranean. (title: 'An engraved illustration image of the Battle of The Nile, from a vintage Victorian book dated 1886 that is no longer in copyright,' by Tony Baggett, fotolia)

In their wake, supply ships crept up the coast. There had been one corvette and nine gun-vessels, all prizes for the taking. Small craft, often of less than 8-guns, were gadflies that harassed and annoyed the enemy. (title: 'HMS Berbice - Modelbauschiff ohne Segel', by ExQuisine, fotolia)

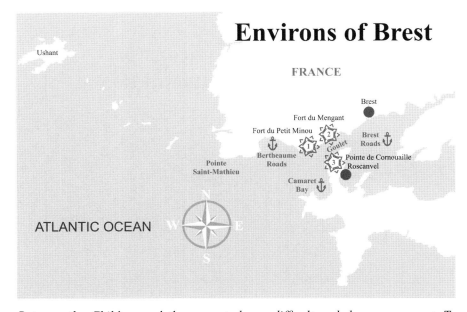

Between the Childers and those masts lay a difficult and dangerous coast. To larboard were the rocks and shoals of Pointe Saint-Mathieu, and the Bertheaume roadstead. To starboard lay the iron hard Roscanvel peninsula, and the Camaret roadstead. This part of the French coast became a focus for the whole Channel Fleet. (Map by the author)

France is visible from Dover, and the English Channel has always been vital to Britain's welfare. Risk of invasion required this congested seaway to be highly protected. This whole region was vital to British merchant interests. Likewise the North Sea, after the Batavian Republic became a French client state. (Map by the author)

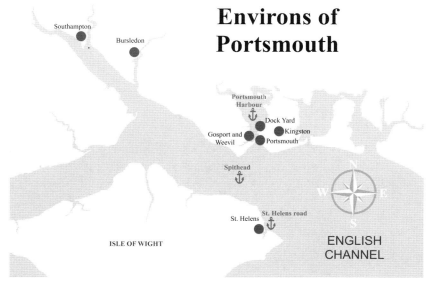

Residents of Portsmouth, and other south coast towns, were aware of how close the enemy lay. Portsmouth was Britain's largest naval arsenal, and together with Spithead witnessed thousands of merchant ships and ships of war arrive and sail off between 1793 and 1800. (Map by the author)

Environs of Toulon

Ollioules

Mont Faron

Fort Malbousquet

Toulon *Fort Lamalgue*

Fort Sainte-Marguerite

inner road

La Seyne

Grosse Tour

outer road

Fort Mulgrave

Fort de Balaguier

Cepet peninsula

Hyères Roads

Îles d' Hyères

MEDITERRANEAN SEA

N E S W

Toulon had two long moles, basins, magazines, an armoury and victualling office that were impressive. One writer had explained how there were 'huge pyramids of cannon balls, and the vast ranges of storehouses, in which are deposited every species of hostile weapons, and also the different yards, stocks, bakehouses, &c.' Toulon was France's main naval arsenal in the Mediterranean. (Map by the author)

The Mediterranean contained strong foreign fleets that could fall from a favourable alliance, status as a neutral, or join with France and thereby menace shipping. With two major enemy fleets in the region, the Royal Navy had to cover a large expanse and needed supportive small states to maintain a presence. (Map by the author)

The **Eastern** Mediterranean

The Mediterranean was only one theatre but the significance of the Battle of the Nile lay in the fact that it destroyed more than a third of France's naval force, and stranded Bonaparte in Egypt. The Battle of the Nile allowed the Royal Navy to regain dominance of the entire region. (Map by the author)

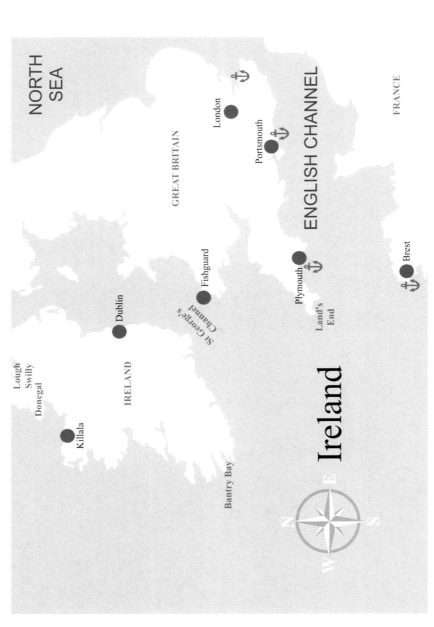

The Channel Fleet had had to provide a strong 'wooden wall' at all times, and project force where needed. That had required a defensive and offensive ability. Defensively, to have sufficient strength to dominate seas around Britain and Ireland. Ireland had been the 'weak link' of the whole region. (Map by the author)

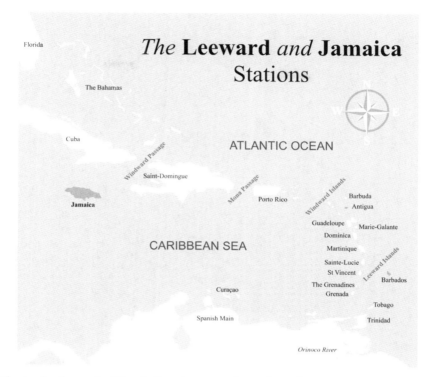

The trader knew the West Indies theatre to be wide and extensive, with scattered islands throughout. It had always been difficult to gain a naval presence everywhere. The whole region was also renowned for its 'sickly season'. (Map by the author)

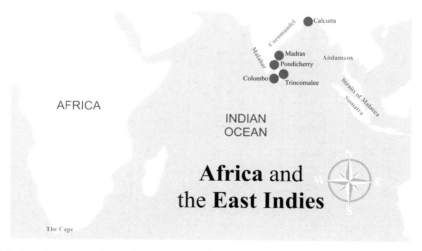

Britain's factories along the coasts of Coromandel and Malabar, the Andamans, interests in the straits of Malacca and upon Sumatra. Some were more than five weeks sailing from one another. This was a vast area from which Britain had increasingly important interests. (Map by the author)

Saint-Domingue remained their main concern. France could not furnish a proper fleet to protect the colony, and internal struggles permitted pirates to harass merchants upon the Windward Passage, that is the exit of the West Indies between Cap-Haïtien and Cuba. An attempt was made to control this troubled region, but the British had to quit in 1798. (Map by the author)

From Brest the nearest British naval dockyard able to maintain and replenish warships was Plymouth. With extensive dockyard facilities and a large roadstead, where ships 'may have gone through a course of repair or refitment, or those new from the stocks, may assemble and complete their final equipment for sea,'[276] she was too open to the wind, and with no breakwater could not be extensively used.[277] Spithead had been considered the best roadstead to station the majority of the fleet, despite its distance from Brest. It had access to a major dockyard, Britain's main naval arsenal, and a harbour that could accommodate the largest warship. Either side of that port, between Land's End and St Margaret's Bay, numerous roadsteads and harbours accommodated groups of smaller warships and vessels, and some allowed for more than one squadron. Falmouth had 'permanently stationed...two squadrons of frigates, one under the command of Sir Edward Pellew...the other under the command of Sir John Borlase Warren... Each squadron consisted of five frigates... and, in addition to these, there were continually arriving and departing from Carrick Roads, the outer anchorage of Falmouth, line-of-battle ships, and smaller vessels of war.'[278] The Channel Fleet therefore divided to cover enemy harbours and anchorages. Squadrons mostly worked out of Plymouth, Torbay and Spithead. When health forced Lord Howe to retire, his policy of loose blockade was maintained by his successor Lord Bridport. In 1800 command of the Channel Fleet devolved to Admiral John Jervis, Earl of St Vincent, who introduced a policy of continual blockade. That resulted in widespread wear and tear of ships, vessels and men; Jervis expected his ships to conduct repairs while on station.

Both the old sailor and his son knew that to beat the French, and their allies' fleets, the Royal Navy had to coax them out of port.[279] One spur to do so was to molest their sea commerce. 'An order of the 8th of June, 1793 [had been] issued from the cabinet, by virtue of which "all vessels loaded wholly, or in part, with corn, flour, or meal, bound to any port in France, or any port occupied by the armies of France," were required forcibly into England, and the cargoes were either to be sold there, or security was to be given, that they should only be sold in the ports of a country in amity with his Britannic Majesty.'[280] The issue of seizing

---

276 Knight, *Mechanics Magazine* (1821) Vol I, 18.
277 Construction on the breakwater did not commence until 1811.
278 *Navy and Army Illustrated* (1894) Vol VI, 17. The two squadrons were stationed there 1794-6.
279 Mahan, 99.
280 Dallas (1871), 303.

French and neutral ships,[281] that transported goods to France, became a passion of his son's. While on leave he had once said, *Father, do you remember in 1780*[282] *an armed neutrality had been made between Russia, Denmark, Sweden, Prussia, Austria, Portugal, the two Sicilies, Spain and Holland? They had argued that their neutral ships should be considered as carrying free goods, that ought to have passed free of search. They believed their flags of neutrality enough to make their cargoes free of contraband.*[283] *Well, two further armed neutralities have been made in this war. One between Sweden and Denmark, in 1794, and another between Russia, Sweden, Denmark and Prussia in 1800. I believe that while we are at war we have the right to seize contraband found in the bottoms of any neutral, even if they attempt to enter a port we have put under blockade*[284] *and have no warships offshore.*[285] The son talked and talked until he fell asleep. The old man had stoked the fire, placed a blanket over his boy, and quietly retired.

Residents of Portsmouth, and other south coast towns, were aware of how close the enemy lay. France is visible from Dover, and the English Channel has always been vital to Britain's welfare. Risk of invasion required this congested seaway to be highly protected. Portsmouth was very important in this regard, and the old sailor knew the town through and through. From The Point to her dockyard the streets were a constant cacophony of sound. He loved the energy of the place. When larger ships passed by they dwarfed town buildings and he stood transfixed. He often sat outside the dockyard, hoping to sell one of his carvings, and simply enjoy the bustle of the world's largest naval arsenal. The dockyard had 'the appearance of a town, from the number of its dwelling-houses, storehouses, offices, and other edifices erected for the purpose of carrying on the various employments of the yard.'[286] Some 5,000 men and women were employed there. They traipsed in and out every day to work the docks, rope house, blacksmith's shop, stores and naval college. It was a continual hive of activity.

France commanded a number of ports and anchorages along her own Channel coast and beyond. Some regional French ports had protected one

---

281 One source, *Niles' Weekly Register* (1820) Vol XVIII, 89, talks of a neutral as being those *who do not, by treaty, owe any thing to either party; for if they do, they are federates, or confederates, and not simply friends.*

282 *Colburn's United Service Magazine* (1871) Part I, 126. This source argued that *the Armed Neutrality of 1780 was mostly a protest.*

283 Tytler (1823), 368: '...sufficient pledge and security that...cargoes were not contraband of war.'

284 Deane (1870), 15.

285 Or a 'paper blockade'.

286 Allen, *Portsmouth* (1817), 160.

or two warships, and permitted the gathering of parts of an invasion flotilla. Dunkerque, Boulogne, and Le Havre de Grâce[287] supported gun vessels, vessels of war, frigates and privateers that caused havoc. Cherbourg, at the top end of the Cotentin Peninsula and close to Portsmouth, was a naval arsenal with a huge breakwater, basin and docks that could have accommodated many ships of the line. Just outside the chops of the Channel,[288] Saint-Malo offered French privateers an ideal harbour to work from.

Southwards, Ushant (Île d'Ouessant) became the focus of the Brest blockade. Just over four miles long by two miles wide its rocks and rapid tides had to be avoided at all costs. By 1796 British sailors had talked of this place so much that even civilians knew of it. The song *Spanish Ladies*[289] became popular. The old man often sang it while he carved away.

> *We'll rant and we'll roar, like true British sailors,*
> *We'll rant and we'll roar across the salt seas,*
> *Until we strike soundings,*
> *In the Channel of old England,*
> *From Ushant to Scilly is thirty-five leagues.*

Between Ushant and Spain, the long French Atlantic coast had offered numerous harbours and roadsteads where the enemy fitted out ships and vessels to make adventures upon the West Indies and Ireland. Hidden rocks, reefs and shoals often meant that larger warships struggled to maintain station, with long swells, tides, enemy batteries and their top hamper.[290]

With a map of France and northern Spain to hand, the old sailor ran his finger down the line that represented the French coast below Brest. There had been so much turmoil there! That whole region had been the centre of a civil war that had kept France distracted from 1793 until 1799. For Britain, that proved useful as it meant the enemy's coast had been open to invasion, or at the very least, a union with French royalists. After Spain declared war on 11 October 1796, events there had hindered the enemy becoming one whole united front. With Iberia jutting far out into the Atlantic, the Royal Navy only had to cast a loose net of frigates and vessels towards

---

287 In 1804 some 1,800 gun-boats, gun-vessels, and small craft had been gathered in Boulogne and along that stretch of coast. Colomb (1895), 175.
288 The entrance and exit from the Channel and the Atlantic.
289 From 1793 until that time British ships had helped supply Spain for her war effort.
290 The weight and amount of sails, yards, and rigging above a ship's deck.

the north to provide a watch. Any French privateer or warship from ports south of Brest had to sail across the Bay of Biscay and into the Atlantic before they reached busy sea lanes. When they had, they had come out of Lorient, Quiberon Bay, and Belle-Île-en-Mer (Belle Isle) in the north; Saint-Nazaire, Nantes, and Rochefort in the centre; Bordeaux and Bayonne in the south.

The French Brest fleet had often gathered at Quiberon. The old sailor had been there a few times. It was a long, rocky peninsula connected to the mainland by a narrow neck of land that at high tide, and amid storms, was covered with water. Fort Penthièvre guarded the land approach, while the lee of the peninsula offered a roadstead. He remembered how, in 1795, émigrés in conjunction with a squadron of British ships had made an attempt to take the place. His finger touched the map at Belle Isle, an island nine nautical miles in length, that also offered a roadstead. In September 1793 the French fleet had mutinied there, for her *matelots* were ill provisioned and suffered scurvy.[291] They had forced their ships to sail for Brest. Further south, across the Bay of Biscay, the Spanish had a naval arsenal at Ferrol that could have supported a substantial number of ships. Thankfully, their fleet had mostly lain in the Mediterranean. He remembered how people in town had considered Spain's navy to be formidable, but he had known that had only been on paper. An abstract of the time showed Spain had 76 ships of the line and 105 'under-line' vessels. The threat of a combination of three major fleets – French, Batavian and Spanish – would have been a serious threat if they had united. His son had then thought the enemy incapable of such an effort, although they had tried. At least Portugal remained an ally, and although she could only put to sea some six ships of the line and a few frigates[292] the old sailor had raised a glass of port in her favour.

The British policy of loose blockade lessened wear and tear but in late winter and early spring months the Channel Fleet, and her detached squadrons, had often been delayed in leaving their roadsteads. Two examples during the early years of the war proved this point. From the middle of 1794 France had successfully repulsed coalition land forces on her borders. British regiments had to fall back into the Austrian Netherlands and the Dutch Republic. France was suffering shortages[293] and had had to look to the United States of America and the West Indies for supplies. When these

---

291 James, W., 83 and 84.
292 James, 55.
293 Taine (1885) Vol III, 377-9.

had been secured they required shipment across the Atlantic. The French revolutionary government then believed it controlled a navy similar to one that had humbled Britain in the previous war, so they had ordered the Brest fleet to sail, meet the grain convoy mid Atlantic, and escort it back to France. The French had dreaded the prospect of famine, so this enterprise commanded immense importance.

Before the French fleet had put to sea on 17 May 1794,[294] Jean-Bon Saint-André and Jean-Jacques Bréard arrived in Brest to publicly embolden the *matelots*. These two Convention delegates assumed the British Channel Fleet was then in British waters, but fourteen days beforehand it had sailed from St Helens with thirty-four ships of the line, numerous frigates and some unrated vessels.[295] A squadron soon separated to escort, as far as Cape Finisterre, 400 British merchantmen, so reduced the fleet to twenty-six ships of the line and six frigates. The British knew that a French convoy had been due, and they had desperately wanted something to celebrate. Apart from numerous small actions no decisive sea battle had occurred since the war commenced. That had irritated the old sailor who, like everyone else he knew, wanted to savour a victory.

Lord Howe had made for Ushant, but a fog of unusual thickness meant his ships sailed for days with nothing in sight. Throughout, 'bells and drums, which his own ships kept sounding as fog-signals, were distinctly heard by the Frenchmen'[296] who sailed, unbeknown to the British, close by. On 19 May the British reconnoitered Brest to find the enemy fleet had already put to sea, under command of *contre-amiral* Louis-Thomas Villaret Joyeuse. The French had been strengthened by the *Patriote* (74)

---

294 The Brest fleet was the *Montagne* (120), the 110s *Révolutionnaire, Républicain,* and *Terrible,* the 80s *Indomptable, Jacobin, Juste,* and *Scipion,* the 74s *Achille, America, Convention, Entreprenant, Eole, Gasparin, Jemappes, Impétueux, Montagnard, Mont-Blanc, Mucius, Neptune, Northumberland, Pelletier, Tourville, Tyrannicide,* and *Vengeur.* The Rochefort fleet was *Sans-Pareil* (80), the 74s *Audacieux, Patriote, Téméraire* and *Trajan.* From James, W., 141. James calls the *Convention* the *Conception.*

295 These were (ships of the line): the 100s *Queen Charlotte, Royal George* and *Sovereign,* the 90s *Barfleur, Glory, Impregnable* and *Queen,* the 80s *Caesar* and *Gibraltar,* 74s *Alfred, Audacious, Bellerophon, Brunswick, Culloden, Defence, Invincible, Leviathan, Majestic, Marlborough, Montagu, Orion, Ramillies, Russell, Thunderer, Tremendous* and *Valiant;* (frigates) 38s *Latona and Phaëton,* 36s *Aquilon* and *Southampton, Niger* (32), and *Pegasus* (28), the fire ship *Comet* and the hospital ship *Charon.* The convoy squadron comprised the 74s *Alexander, Arrogant, Bellona, Ganges, Hector,* and *Theseus;* (frigates) *Hebe* (38), *Venus* (36), and the 28s *Circe* and *Pallas.* From James, 138-40.

296 Yonge (1863) Vol I, 435.

from the Rochefort squadron. Oblivious to all of that the British had sailed westwards in hopes of either detecting the enemy, or joining with a British squadron to offer aide if the French convoy should pass. They stumbled upon French captures, that had been part of a Lisbon convoy, and when repossessed learned the whereabouts of the enemy. Howe immediately set course for where he assumed the French fleet to be. On 28 May, amid heavy seas, 'lookout frigates'[297] sighted strange sail to windward.[298] Howe's weathermost division of 74s, *Bellerophon*, *Marlborough*, *Russell* and *Thunderer*, were sent to reconnoitre. They soon found the enemy fleet, twenty-six ships of the line and five frigates, heading their way.

Combined, the French had the advantage with men, guns and broadside weight of metal. Aggregate tonnage of British warships that would face them stood just shy of 47,000 tonnes to the French fleet's 52,000. There were 18,200 British sailors[299] opposed to 19,900 French *matelots*, 1,087 British broadside guns to 1,107 French broadside cannons, and 23,000 lbs of British broadside weight of metal to the French 28,000 lbs. Tactics of line of battle required a great amount of work for ships to remain in position. If a ship's mast, or yard, broke it would cause a ship to lose headway. A ship behind then ran the risk of collision, or be forced to take evasive measures. If signals were ignored, not seen or misinterpreted it could be hazardous. At this early stage of the war the Royal Navy struggled to demonstrate exactness of line discipline. Officers were as yet untested, with crews comprised of many newly recruited seamen. Mistakes were to be made on both sides. Yet it became clear as the two fleets converged that the French suffered from indifferent seamanship.

The French had formed line ahead, while the British formed up in two columns, altered tack, and conducted a general chase. The *Bellerophon* soon engaged the rearmost enemy ship, the *Révolutionnaire* (110), until her main-topmast was lost. The *Leviathan* and *Audacious* joined in. It was, however, left to *Audacious* to fight on until late into the night. Other ships could only watch and some observers thought the French ship might have struck her colours. Lord Howe signalled the *Thunderer* to take possession of the *Révolutionnaire*, *Audacious* by then being dismasted, but confusion followed and the French ship slipped away under cover of darkness. Badly damaged, with large loss of life, the French ship had had to return

---

297 William James's term.
298 Long, 33.
299 James, after subtracting supernumeraries and widow's men, gave 17,241. *Ibid*, 141.

to Rochefort under tow. The *Audacious* was also heavily damaged, and had had to make her way to Plymouth.[300]

Next day, 29 May, the British fleet formed line of battle. Nine ships sailed ahead of the flagship, *Queen Charlotte*. The British van[301] fired upon the enemy rear, so the French line had had to turn in succession to provide support. As the enemy van approached the British centre, Lord Howe had ordered his ships to tack, cut the enemy line, and tack again to gain the weather gage. Gun smoke no doubt hid his signals as not all his ships fully complied. Besides, the lead ship *Caesar* (80) had already been damaged, likewise the *Queen* (98). The British line was put in disarray, the flagship forced to leeward, and a limited engagement followed. The *Orion* (74) expelled two broadsides into the *Indomptable* (80). Other ships took heavy damage. The French line suffered misunderstandings with their own flag's signals, but they did manage to come to the aid of their discomfited ships. As evening deepened both fleets separated to draw breath and repair. It had been the first fleet engagement between the two belligerents, but not a full battle. Fog descended to such an extent that no ship could see another, so for the next two days no further engagement had been possible. For the revolutionaries the imperative had been to lead the British away from their convoy, yet remain a threat strong enough to entice them to follow. On 31 May, 'it was...ascertained that M. de Nielly [from a separate French squadron] had joined [the main line]...with four fresh ships, and that, finding himself thus strengthened, Villaret Joyeuse had sent those vessels which had been most crippled back to Brest.'[302]

The fateful day, 1 June, dawned with little or no fog. It could be seen by the British that the French continued to lay to leeward so they had the weather gage.[303] Less than four miles apart Lord Howe piped his men to breakfast. A prisoner held on board a French warship, Captain Troubridge on the *Sans Pareil* (80), later wrote how this had been observed by his captors. They thought it showed timidity. He had replied, 'Don't flatter yourselves...John Bull does not like to fight on an empty stomach, but see if he does not pay you a visit after breakfast.'[304] After 8 o'clock the British

---

300 Yonge, *ibid*.

301 Lead ships.

302 Yonge, 438.

303 To the windward of another. It allowed a ship to have the benefit of moving with the wind, where the other had to work against it.

304 Yonge, 439.

bore down upon the French, with instructions to independently engage their opposite enemy number. Until they reached a distance to open fire British ships changed position in the line, to even up the oncoming confrontation. Thirteen ships then lay ahead of the flagship with eleven behind. From any of their quarterdecks it would have been a most splendid sight.

Lord Howe's plan had been to break the enemy line with the flag going astern of the enemy flagship, the *Montagne* (120). 'Between a quarter and half-past nine AM the French van opened its fire upon the British van. In about a quarter of an hour the fire of the French became general, and Lord Howe and his divisional flag officers, bearing the signal for close action at their mast heads, commenced a heavy fire in return. A few of the British ships cut through the French line and engaged their opponents to leeward; the remainder hauled up to windward, and opened their fire, some at a long, others at a shorter and more effectual distance.'[305] Those British ships that did cut the line came very close to enemy ships. In one instance flags touched enemy shrouds, and at that range broadsides would have executed great damage to ships' hulls, masts, rigging and men. After ninety minutes of hot work twenty-three British and French warships were wrecked and dismasted. Most distressed ships attempted to fish a mast[306] and move off, but remain close enough to pepper the enemy with small arms fire. The French admiral moved his own ship to protect the distressed 110s *Terrible* and *Republicain*, *Scipion* (80) and the 74s *Jemappes* and *Mucius*.

By early afternoon the main battle had in effect ended. The British secured six prizes: *Sans Pareil* and *Juste* (80), and the 74s *America*, *Impetueux*, *Northumberland* and *Achille*. After a three-hour engagement the British 74s *Brunswick* and *Ramilles* attempted to secure the crippled *Vengeur du Peuple* (74) but she sank. In total the French lost 7,000 men[307], the British lost 290 dead and 858 wounded.

Although it took years for the likes of the carver's son to admit it, 116 grain ships successfully avoided the British fleet to arrive safely in port.[308] Their arrival occasioned great delight throughout France. As for the British, Lord Howe retired his fleet and arrived back at Spithead on 13 June to the sound of bells and saluting guns. The old sailor joined in with a parade through Portsmouth, as a band played *See the conquering*

---

305 Davenport Adams (1868), 153.
306 Repair a damaged mast.
307 The French claimed it was far less.
308 They arrived at Brest on 8 June. Mivart (1892) Vol I, 30.

hero comes! News travelled horse-speed to London and the First Lord of the Admiralty, then under fire, publically proclaimed victory at the Opera, 'and the audience, roused with excitement, called loudly for "God save the king" and "Rule Britannia", which was sung by Morichelli, Morelli, and Rovedicco, opera stars of that period.'[309] On 26 June the king arrived at Portsmouth and went aboard the *Queen Charlotte* at Spithead. Portsmouth was so proud to see him. His Majesty presented Lord Howe with a diamond encrusted sword, a chain of gold, a medal, the thanks of Parliament and the epithet 'a true British sailor'. For Britain it was thereafter called the Glorious First of June; for France *la Bataille du 13 Prairial An 2*.[310] The British celebrated the battle as a 'victory quite as much for the morale effect it wrought in Europe generally, as for the immediate material injury it inflicted on the French.'[311] The usual droll heroic poems were soon printed. For instance,

> *Howe made the Frenchmen dance a tune -*
> *An admiral great and glorious;*
> *Witness for that the First of June -*
> *Lord! how he was victorious.*[312]

The French government lauded the loss of the *Vengeur du Peuple* as sinking with all colours aloft while her crew shouted *Vive la Nation!* as she went down. In memorial they suspended a ship model under an arch of their national memorial, the Panthéon.

In British taverns thereafter many argued that their sailors had wanted victory more, despite so many having been pressed. They said the battle showed everyone the worth of British ships of the line. It made people so very proud. Much later, when all had quietened down, others countered with how years of turmoil and poor treatment of naval officers had taken its toll upon the French navy. They said that many French sailors had never been to sea before, and added that the French fleet had been badly mauled but not broken. Some British naval officers later let it be known that they thought Howe should have completed the job and destroyed the French fleet. The battle had occurred, some said, partly because fog had allowed the enemy to

---

309 Chambers, *The Book of Days* (1888) Vol I, 724.
310 Based on the then newly adopted revolutionary calendar.
311 Chambers, *ibid*.
312 Adams (1885) Vol II, 84.

assemble; but also because the policy of loose blockade meant the British fleet had been too far away to stop them.

A second example showed how Howe's policy of loose blockade could be seen to be lax. On 30 May 1795 Vice Admiral Cornwallis had sailed from Spithead on his flagship *Royal Sovereign* (100). His squadron comprised the 74s *Mars*, *Triumph*, *Brunswick* and *Bellerophon*, the *Phaëton* (38), *Pallas* (32) and *Kingfisher* (18).[313] By 8 June they were off Penmarch, a headland south of Brest. They spied six French sail in company with a convoy that altered course for Belle Isle when sighted. Quick sailers they beat the British to safety, and Cornwallis had to signal his ships away from the shore batteries. He did, however, snap up eight French prizes from the convoy. Mostly these were found to carry wine and brandy. The next day, 9 June, his squadron headed north-west to weather Penmarch and Ushant and make its way towards the Channel.[314] Two days later they lay off the Isles of Scilly, and their prizes were sent into harbour. In the meantime news had reached Brest that their ships were 'blockaded' at Belle Isle. No British ships then lay off shore, and 'it was known to the more experienced among the French officers, that no blockading force could prevent Rear-admiral Vence from reaching Lorient.'[315] So nine French sail of the line and four corvettes put to sea despite being low on provisions. They sailed for Belle Isle, and when off Île de Groix joined the ships that had been penned in. They thereafter formed a fleet of twelve ships of the line, eleven frigates, and seven other vessels. Six days later, 16 June, they reached Penmarch and came across the returned British squadron en route to Belle Isle. The French squadron was far stronger, so the British turned and a general chase commenced. It became known as Cornwallis's Retreat. The *Bellerophon* and *Brunswick* happened to be overburdened and had had to cut away their anchors and throw overboard their boats, water, provisions, carronades and some shot to make themselves lighter. They still proved slow and threatened to fall behind. When the French caught them up, their ships being far better sailers, an engagement commenced. The *Mars* had soon been crippled, and the *Triumph* expelled 5,000 lbs of powder to protect her sister.[316] Cornwallis refused to abandon any of his squadron so turned to fight. He used a ruse and made a signal to unknown ships on the horizon that convinced the French the Channel Fleet must be

---

313 James, W., *ibid*, 262.
314 James, 263.
315 James, 264.
316 James, 267.

near, so they called off the chase. His rearmost ships had suffered serious damage to their sterns, but at least they reached home. Once again, the Brest fleet had been allowed to leave port as British ships had not been fully on station.

The old sailor had once sat with a friend and exchanged views about the policies their government had so far adopted in the war. One policy had been to aide French Royalist émigrés, another to make landings, or expeditions, upon enemy controlled coasts. In 1795 an amphibious operation in La Vendée had failed.[317] Parliament harboured ideas of gaining a foothold on French soil to help propel a larger force into the interior.[318] *Psshh*, his friend had snorted, as both of them knew how expeditions carried a litany of risks. Transports could be delayed, intercepted or lost en route. Landing sites might not be certain, as heavy seas could rear up or enemy troops intervene. Landing forces had to be well coordinated and planned, but petty jealousies often hampered the chain of command. Supplies might be cut off. Policy could be wishful thinking. However, Parliament had voted monies to support the *comte* d'Artois, brother of the dead French king, in his plan to land an army of émigrés along the west coast of France. They had hoped to join up with *général* François de Charette.

French sailors held prisoner in England, and émigrés found throughout England and Germany, had been recruited for the enterprise.[319] They received British rates of pay. Three British regiments added their strength and discipline to the combined landing force. Fifty transports with 2,500 men, under escort of sir John Borlase Warren's squadron,[320] departed Portsmouth 13 June. Everyone in the town had known what was up; you never could have so many ships and troops and not have gossip. The troops had been equipped with all necessary arms and artillery, and large stashes of equipment and items to arm volunteers upon arrival. So they had departed,[321] and despite an action off Île de Groix to deter a French interception out of Brest, the transports arrived at Quiberon Bay 25 June.[322] Troops landed on

---

317 The word 'amphibious' was loosely used in the era. In 1803 George Tierney (MP for Southwark) talked of marines serving in Canada, 'the soldiers employed in this amphibious kind of service'. in *The Parliamentary Debates* (1816), 376.

318 A British invasion force had been successfully landed in Holland in 1793, but the country around had not been so hostile.

319 *British Minor Expeditions 1746 to 1814* (1884), 20.

320 *The Field of Mars* (1801), under 'Quiberon'.

321 *British Minor Expeditions*, 21.

322 Massey (1865) Vol IV, 5.

the beach at Carnac two days later. Three divisions marched inland and along the coast, but the republicans managed to form a large army to oppose them. By 9 July a letter written off Belle Isle had stated, 'Our ships are daily chasing the enemy's frigates that are hovering off the entrance of Port L'Orient. Their ships sail well, for they have the impudence to come close to us, and then take to their heels.... . Sir John Warren commands the troops on shore, and Captain Thornborough the gun-boats. We now hear a very hot fire, which we suppose to be between the French batteries and Captain Thornborough's gun-boats.'[323] Troops made an assault against Fort de Penthièvre on the peninsula, and 'To assist in this attack the British Admiral sent about 300 marines and some gun-boats, and on the 30th, after seven hours' contest, the fort capitulated.'[324] Overall the expedition had lacked adequate supplies, and arguments soured émigré officers. Troops were consequently pinned down. A second British transport squadron arrived with further troops, but these were never enough to fight off the enemy. By 20 July, 4,000 British and French troops covered the peninsula but by the next day it was all over.

French prisoners recruited from English prisons were no doubt keen to leave their confinement but not so keen to fight fellow countrymen. 1,500 men were successfully taken off the peninsula but almost all of their remaining stores had to be abandoned. '10,000 stands of arms, 150,000 pairs of shoes, clothing for 40,000 men... . laden with rum, brandy, and provisions,'[325] were lost. Many émigrés could not evacuate so surrendered to the republicans. Most were executed soon afterwards. To the old man, and his friend, Quiberon had been an utter failure because transports had been delayed, the landing area suffered intervention of enemy troops, petty jealousies hampered the chain of command, supplies were inadequate, and the policy to aide French *émigrés* had been wishful thinking.

Chance could fall both ways, and other landings proved successful. The 9th Regiment resided at Norwich in July 1800 when it received orders for foreign service. They did not know their destination. On 1 August they embarked onboard the *Brailsford* transport at Southampton and sailed on 6 August. Ten days later they arrived off Quiberon, where they remained for sixteen days, until 22 August when they put to sea again. They finally arrived off Ferrol on 25 August. The regiment landed 'the same day without

---

323 *The Field of Mars, ibid.*
324 Cust (1862) Vol IV 1783-1795, 288.
325 *British Minor Expeditions*, 27.

opposition, except from a small fort, which was soon silenced'.[326] By then Britain had blockaded Spain for two years, and the policy of blockade enabled hundreds of British troops to be successfully transported and landed. The enemy fleet stood out of the way.

After 1795 French policy also helped the Royal Navy. Despite the successful repulse of British and émigré troops from Quiberon, the French fleet generally withdrew from the seas to conduct a policy of what they called *guerre de course*.[327] This remained the case until 1800. Mahan believed, 'It amounted...simply, to abandoning all attempt to control the sea.'[328] The French navy thereafter became ancillary to the French army. Harassment was key to France's naval hopes, but the threat of invasion remained from both parties.

Apart from cruises, battles, and support for landings and transports, naval warships and vessels provided protection for British and allied convoys. This was, for Great Britain, a major concern. A 1795 debate in Parliament, as to manning the Royal Navy, had Mr Pitt state, 'in order to meet the scale of exertion which it was incumbent upon the country to make in the present crisis...a great degree of inconvenience...must unavoidably be sustained.'[329] The issue was to man the 'national force', that is the Royal Navy, while the principal was 'undoubtedly...trade'. The mercantile marine had to be the first resort to provide men because 'none were more interested than the ship-owners and merchants, that the country should be able to meet the naval force of the enemy, to maintain its superiority by sea, and to supply adequate convoys.'[330] Figures for 1800, if correct, showed British shipping stood at 1,855,879 tonnes.[331] Great Britain could not afford to have her life blood drain away. It was understood that any loss of merchant ships, men, and cargoes to the enemy hindered Britain's war effort and strengthened her foes. So warships were brought together to form escorts; or one or two warships and vessels patrolled sea zones to offer protection for merchant ships that had separated from a convoy or had chosen to sail alone. The result was commercial disruption. Certain goods were conveyed in such large volumes that upon arrival at their destinations their price suffered.

---

326 Gomm (1881), 46.
327 Robinson (1894), 44.
328 Mahan, 335.
329 Credited to 'Mr Chancellor Pitt', from *The Parliamentary Register* (1795) Vol XL, 370 & 371.
330 *Ibid.*
331 Philp (1859), 377.

Many shipowners preferred the risk of dispatching their ships alone, to attain higher profits, but most ship owners preferred the convoy system. That occasioned dozens, even hundreds, of merchantmen to gather at a port or roadstead within a designated sea zone or at defined coordinates. There they awaited either one or two, a handful, or sometimes even a whole squadron of ships to escort them. It had always been the case in war. The old sailor knew, and his son came to know, that to assemble so many ships was a slow, often exasperating, process. At sea merchantmen needed to be cajoled along. Many were slow sailers, and they forced all others to assume a slower pace. Storms and fogs often separated them, and privateers always lurked upon the periphery.

After four years of war, in 1797 Parliament passed the Convoy Act.[332] After July 1798 it became illegal for any British merchant ship or vessel to sail out of convoy, or voluntarily separate from a convoy. It stated[333] that if a merchant ship pursued separation from a convoy, its insurance was made void. Each ship had to pay a bond prior to sailing, take onboard proper flags and signals, and maintain correct conduct while in convoy. The Act aimed to protect increasingly larger amounts of imports and exports. Exports declared under the Convoy Act stood over £50,000,000 in 1799, and by 1800 exceeded £55,000,000.[334]

The *Naval Chronicle* printed a letter by Captain Willis regarding his personal views of convoys. He gave an insight into certain places enemy privateers then patrolled. It argued how merchantmen, on returning to 'England', ought to 'strike Soundings in the latitude 49° 25' [North]...50 leagues to the westward of Scilly'.[335] The French, he said, patrolled close by 'in hopes of falling in with our outer and homeward-bound Convoys,' but half-a-dozen cruisers could extend southwards. 'If Cruisers, and armed Vessels, from the Firth of Forth to Scilly, were more connected, our Coast would be more effectually defended.'[336] Convoy duty necessitated a dull, perplexing, and difficult aspect of naval life; but a vital one. The home theatre had the highest concentration of departures and arrivals of merchant shipping. Without them Britain would not have sustained a long war.

---

332 Officially, *An Act for the better Protection of the Trade of this Kingdom; and for granting new and additional Duties of Customs on Goods imported and exported, and on the Tonnage of certain Ships entering Outwards or Inwards to or from foreign Parts, until the signing the Preliminary Articles of Peace.*

333 Steel (1801), 400-405.

334 Newmarch (1855), 47.

335 *The Naval Chronicle* (1804) Vol XII, 122.

336 *Ibid.*

Without the Channel Fleet the lifeblood of Britain would have fallen into enemy hands in numbers far greater than they actually did.

The old sailor and his son often talked about the weak link of the region. From the chops of the Channel a ship could sail south towards Brest, or north into the St George's Channel. From there it was possible to reach Ireland or Wales. Towards the end of 1796 the threat of an invasion rose to fever pitch. Ireland, a client state of Great Britain, had not always been in sympathy with her. Misgovernment and neglect[337] caused a high level of discontent, and before the war the society of United Irishmen had formed in Dublin. Similar to the Corresponding Society it had wanted reform of the Irish Parliament, emancipation of Catholics, and a separation from 'allegiance' to Great Britain. Brigands freely roamed the countryside, and attempts were made to create a 'national guard' clothed in green. By 1796 outright rebellion had broken out, and the United Irishmen made contact with the French government. It suited the revolutionaries to offer armed support. After two Society members, Lord Edward Fitzgerald and Arthur O'Connor, visited Paris plans had been made.

By November 1796 the British Parliament knew the French planned an invasion of Ireland. Despite the lateness of the season, 15 December, a French invasion fleet put out to sea from Brest. This *Expédition d'Irlande* comprised seventeen ships of the line, thirteen frigates and numerous transports. They shipped 15,000 troops and took with them more than 40,000 stands of arms, twenty field pieces, nine siege pieces, 61,000 barrels of powder, 7,000,000 musket cartridges and 700,000 flints. Général Hoche acted as commander, and Theobald Wolfe Tone went with them.[338] They put out in fine sunny weather, anchored in Camaret Bay to assemble the fleet, then made their way through the Raz de Sein passage to avoid the British. The *Fougueux* (74) ran foul of Wolfe Tone's ship, whose own ship nearly ran aground itself in the passage. The *Séduisant* (74) did do so, with the loss of more than 500 troops. By the time the fleet entered deep water, storms had begun to bedevil them.

En route to Bantry Bay they did not spy one Royal Navy warship or vessel. However, gales separated them and many ships suffered damage. Only half the transports caught sight of Bantry Bay and Hoche's ship failed to make the rendezvous. Wolfe Tone complained how his ship had to tack

---

337 Blunt (1860), 24.
338 Wellington later considered his legacy: 'Wolfe Tone was a most extraordinary man, and his history is the most curious history of those times.' Found in O'Brien (1893) Vol I, ix.

for hours, but hardly gained one hundred yards distance.[339] French seamen had been issued such poor clothing and provisions they were distracted by the cold; many topmen half-froze on the spars. On 23 December snow mixed with a cold wind that kept most ships offshore. Those that did manage to enter Bantry Bay were forced to wait. The Irishman wrote, 'We are here, sixteen sail, great and small, scattered up and down in a noble bay, and so dispersed that there are not two together in any spot, save one, and there they are now so close, that if it blows to-night as it did last night, they will inevitably run foul of each other, unless one of them prefers driving on shore.'[340] The forced separation of ships seriously depleted their military stores, and without their commander no clear chain of command existed. No attempt to land was made. After a week of torment their admiral, Bouvet, called it off and put back to sea. His fleet ignominiously struggled back to Brest.

By the time the French arrived home, five ships had been lost to wreck or capture. The threat of invasion had been real enough, and remained so that whole winter. On 24 February 1797 three French warships and a lugger anchored off Fishguard in Wales.[341] A small detachment of the Cardigan militia marched to intervene. Upon arrival they found 1,200 French troops already landed, but with no ordnance. When the militia approached them the French laid down what arms they had and surrendered. Their *chef de brigade*, William Tate,[342] penned a letter that explained how his men had landed at a place that 'renders it unnecessary to attempt any military operations, as they would tend only to bloodshed and pillage. The officers of the whole corps have therefore intimated their desire of entering into a negotiation, upon principles of humanity, for a surrender.'[343] Their ships had weighed and sailed off.

In 1798 a second attempt had been made against Ireland despite how in March of the same year the whole Committee of United Irishmen for Leinster, and many members in Dublin, had been arrested. This time the invasion fleet assembled at Brest and Rochefort. The Rochefort squadron put to sea on 4 August, two months after an uprising in Wexford had been put down, and reached Killala on 22 August to land more than 1,000 troops. They confused local authorities by the use of false colours. Only

---

339 O'Brien, 165.
340 O'Brien, 167.
341 *A Collection of State Papers relative to the war with France* (1798) Vol VI, 20.
342 He was an Irish American.
343 *A Collection of State Papers, ibid.*, 21.

fifty fencibles could offer resistance. The French joined up with local Irish rebels and caused disruption for seventeen days. However, there was no general uprising.[344] As to the Brest squadron, delays with payments meant it did not sail until 6 September and, 'If, according to the advice of Edward Fitzgerald, the French directory had sent a number of swift vessels to different parts of the coast, with officers, troops, arms, and ammunition, some of them very probably might have eluded the vigilance of the British cruisers.'[345]

When the French were west of the Raz passage they came across the British 38s *Boadicea* and *Ethalion,* and the *Sylph* (18).[346] The *Ethalion* had kept watch upon them, while the others sailed off to inform the nearest squadron. On 18 September the *Ethalion* was joined by the *Amelia* (38), and the day after that by the *Anson* (44). These three ships tailed the enemy squadron all the way to Ireland. On 10 October the French and British ships arrived off Tory Island on the Donegal coast. The French invasion force had intended to reach Lough Swilly in the north, but it met with other ships of Sir Warren's squadron then on patrol. These were *Foudroyant* (80), the 74s *Canada* and *Robust*, and the *Magnanime* (44). A storm intervened that damaged both the *Anson* and the French warship *Hoche* (74) and afterwards the French found themselves hemmed in by the British squadron and Donegal Bay. They formed line ahead and engaged.[347] The result was mauled French ships, and their landing having to be abandoned. Seven French ships were captured, and only two ships and one vessel ever made it back to Brest. For the British, the main prize was two Irish agents, Bartholomew Teeling and Wolfe Tone,[348] found on board the *Hoche*. Their capture, and the failed expedition, thereby ended the threat posed by France to land an invasion force in Ireland.

The final piece of the theatre had been the North Sea, that received its own squadron. The old sailor's son had often been there. Its remit stretched from the North Foreland, Kent, as far north as ships could operate. The North Sea fleet guarded against the threat of French ships rounding Scotland, to descend from the north, and enemy ships and vessels making a dash from either Cherbourg, Le Havre de Grâce, Boulogne, Dieppe or Dunkerque in the south. Perpetually busy with shipping to and from

---

344 Gordon (1803), 278 & 279.
345 *Ibid.*
346 *The Naval Chronicle* (1798), 7.
347 Maxwell, 309.
348 A third agent managed to avoid capture (Maxwell, 311).

the Baltic, and in and out of London, the region proved to be a lure for privateers. What the region benefitted from were ample roadsteads and naval arsenals, such as London, the Thames Estuary, Sheerness, Chatham, Yarmouth and ports along the whole coast of England and Scotland. After the Dutch Republic fell, in 1795, the Stadtholder[349] had fled to Britain and 'requested that Power to take possession of the Dutch colonies and hold them in trust for himself.'[350] The Dutch Republic had been overthrown in favour of a new state, the Batavian Republic, and this new nation signed an alliance with France on 16 May 1795 and thereafter acted as a client state. The Dutch fleet, nominally four 74s, five 68s, two 64s and four 56s, often lay in the Texel roads. Some considered most Dutch ships to be rotten,[351] while others thought the fleet was manned by excellent seamen.[352] Whatever the case, the Dutch fleet threatened to venture out and menace the entire eastern coast of Britain, perhaps weather the Shetlands and Orkneys to unite with a French fleet for an invasion of Ireland. A blockade of Texel was therefore necessary, and the diminution of Dutch shipping. On 19 June 1795 it became national policy to seize Dutch vessels, and more than fifty merchantmen were immediately taken as they lay in Plymouth Sound.[353]

Early August 1795 twelve Russian ships of the line and seven frigates under command of Admiral Konikoff joined with the North Sea squadron. They served as a token gesture as 'these were so defective and incomplete in every respect, as to render them unavailable for any service in action.'[354] They nevertheless helped Admiral Duncan cover the coast of Holland, the Austrian Netherlands and the French coast down to Dunkerque. The Dutch and Belgian littoral offered numerous opportunities to form an invasion flotilla, with the rivers Lek, Rhine, Waal, Meuse and Scheldt. Built separately, invasion barges could be brought together to menace England. Antwerp, on the Scheldt, was the largest port upon this littoral. Opposite the Thames estuary, under French control it had the potential to allow warships, vessels and privateers easy access to the North Sea. After years of blockade it required improvements, but after the Batavian Republic declared war on Great Britain in May 1796, the threat increased.

---

349 Ruler of the Dutch Republic.
350 Theal (1878), 141.
351 James, W. (1837) Vol I, 55. James disparaged them.
352 *The Annual Register* (1800), 99.
353 James, *ibid.*, 55. These ships were not credited as prizes.
354 Scott, A., (1853), 435 & 436.

As to the general coastline, General Sir Banastre Tarleton, in a Parliamentary debate, thought, 'The coast lying between Brest and Dunkirk, appeared to him ill calculated for a considerable enterprize; petty expeditions might be fitted out, or embarkation might be made; but as the coast in general is low, the water shallow, no large rivers except the Seine, no good ports, commodious havens, or secure harbours, great armaments could not be undertaken.'[355] Focus therefore remained upon the coastline of Holland and the Austrian Netherlands. From May 1797, until the Dutch fleet under admiral Jan Willem De Winter put to sea, the British North Sea squadron maintained a blockade. Eventually this squadron had had to return to Yarmouth, to replenish and refit, and while there received news that the Dutch fleet had sailed. They returned to their stations and soon encountered the enemy on the evening of 10 October 1797 off Kamperduin, or Camperdown, a long stretch of beach halfway between Den Helder and Amsterdam. Under cover of darkness Admiral Duncan positioned his ships to cut off a Dutch retreat. On 11 October he formed his sixteen ships of the line to place the Dutch ships closer to shore, but 'in such a position as enabled him to send a portion of his own fleet to leeward to prevent them receiving support from the coast'.[356] The British broke through the enemy line and by midday the engagement had become close action. The battle required five hours, until De Winter was forced to surrender after all his ship's masts went by the board.[357] Eight Dutch ships were captured and three Dutch admirals taken prisoner. By then ships were close inshore, and all attention had to be given to get them clear of the shallows. In a later letter, written to his brother-in-law, Duncan said he was 'rather rash' in his attack, and captured Dutch officers admitted how an invasion of Ireland had been planned but cancelled. The Dutch, he wrote, put to sea for a show; and De Winter was the only man left alive on his own quarterdeck. On both sides losses had been severe: more than 700 British seamen and marines killed or wounded,[358] but the Dutch lost more than 1,100 prime seamen they could ill afford to lose.

The threat to Britain did not abate. At the end of 1797 the French government began to gather immense amounts of materiel for an invasion. Upwards of 150,000 men assembled in camps between Den Helder and Brest. *Général* Bonaparte commanded this '*Armée d'Angleterre*'. A fleet

---

355 *The Parliamentary Register* (1797) Vol I, 211.
356 Millar (1887), 239.
357 Destroyed and fallen over the side.
358 Millar, 240. The letter is given.

of flat-bottomed boats were constructed to expedite the invasion, and it had been hoped by the French that discontents inside Ireland would rise up in support. Napoléon visited Boulogne, Calais, Dunkerque, Antwerp and Flushing[359] but soon realized the time was inappropriate. He said, 'It is too doubtful a chance, I will not risk it. I will not hazard on such a throw the Fate of France.'[360] The whole plan had to be abandoned and Bonaparte moved on to focus on Egypt. Nearly two years later, Britain returned the favour and conducted a landing with Russian troops, at Callantsoog south of Den Helder. British troops embarked on transports on 12 August 1799, but storms delayed their landing until 27 August. Vice Admiral Mitchell anchored close enough to shore 'to protect the transports, and throw a storm of shot upon the beach, while the boats, heavy with soldiers, were rowing to their landing place'.[361] The Dutch fleet, under command of Admiral Samuel Story inside the Zuiderzee, readily surrendered when the British moved to confront it. Dutch sailors refused to fight.

To emerge victorious against revolutionary France, and her allies, the Channel Fleet had had to provide a strong 'wooden wall' at all times, and project force where needed. That had required a defensive and offensive ability. Defensively, to have sufficient strength to dominate seas around Britain and Ireland, protect British and allied sea trade, and resist the landing of enemy troops on British and Irish soil; offensively, to have sufficient strength to dominate seas around France and her allies, to disrupt enemy sea trade, and to pose a constant threat and ability to land troops on enemy soil. The Channel Fleet achieved such due to luck, weather and distractions enforced upon the enemy. France could not achieve a major invasion. The need to have a superior naval presence in home waters and close by – to oppose France, Spain, and the Batavian Republic – meant the Channel Fleet was one reason why the Royal Navy became, by 1800, a true naval 'superpower'.

---

359 Blunt (1860), 16.
360 Alison (1841) Vol III, 202.
361 Bunbury (1849), 46.

Chapter 7

Drub Them Ashore as We Drub Them at Sea

What if he actually met the child and champion of Jacobinism?[362] Would he thrust his pike into his guts? No doubt he would with all the trouble that man had caused. It would be something to talk to his grandchildren about, supposing he survived this siege. And he would like to have grandchildren one day. *Imagine*, they would say, *our grandpa was the man who famously killed Napoléon Bonaparte at Saint Jean d'Acre.*

The past six months had been truly exceptional. In October he had been in Portsmouth working a dirty old collier, and never did he imagine he would one day wander down the narrow streets of an ancient city full of Turks. Turks! But a recruitment poster for the *Tigre*, then newly commissioned, had caught his attention. His sweetheart swooned when she heard about the captain; a 'sir' no less. *Not a British title,* she had said, *having been bestowed by the King of Sweden. However, a captain so gallant for having escaped a Paris prison, the very dungeon where the last French king had lived before they cut off his head.*[363] *Yes Jim*, she had told him, *take the bounty. The war will soon be over. Come back and we'll marry for sure.* So he had signed on.

Since then he had been to Gibraltar, Malta, Syracuse, Constantinople and Alexandria. Strange places, with strange people, and even stranger smells. According to the boatswain they only touched them in hopes of finding Lord Nelson. The gunner reckons Sir Sidney is none too liked by his superiors, having the ear of ministers,[364] so why the hunt took place is anyone's guess. So long as he made some prize money he couldn't care less. He has a woman to care for.

---

362 This is a quote from John Barrow's biography of Sir Sidney Smith (1848), Vol I, 232.
363 The Temple prison. Sir Sidney Smith was confined there for almost two years.
364 A form of influence

During their visit to Constantinople, a city unlike anything he could have described to people back home, the ship's crew had been told the Turks were now their friends. One man in particular, Pasha al Djezzar, was considered a new ally to stop Bonaparte; but *al Djezzar* means 'butcher'.[365] Strange bedfellows, then. Days later they were off to Alexandria, to lob bombs into that ancient port, with the *Theseus, Alliance* and two French captures[366] in company. None of his watch could fathom out why they went there, but they thought it had to be important. When Sir Sidney sent the *Theseus* off to Saint Jean d'Acre with his French engineer friend on board to ready that city's defences, they knew something would happen. Midshipman Boxer was given command of the *Marianne* prize to reconnoitre the coast, before meeting them at Caiffa,[367] and when an old salt stated that Caiffa was near Saint-Jean d'Acre they all went '*ahhhh*'.

In company with the *Alliance* they had anchored off Acre five days later. His sweetheart would like the place as it was Biblical. Caiffa lies at the southern end of a large open bay along the skirts of Mount Carmel, while the coast makes a crescent shape towards the top of the bay to where Acre sits proudly upon a promontory with two long walls facing the sea. A mole on the seaward side of Acre, with a lighthouse at the end, provides a small harbour in its lee. As part of the boat's crew he accompanied the captain ashore to meet with the French engineer and inspect the defences. As a sailor he could hand, reef, steer, fire a gun and handle a pike, but much of what those two men said had been far beyond him.[368] All he knew for certain was how the walls looked mightily shabby. Besides, he had been distracted with the heat and a sharp thirst. When they finished their tour he had returned to the launch, and eventually joined other boats off Caiffa to keep an eye out for the French. Bonaparte had been reported to be on the way.

The French appeared a few days later, and his boat had opened a brisk fire against them as they tried to make passage along the slopes of Mount Carmel. He had chuckled when they took to their heels, turned away from the coast, and marched the long way round the mountain. Those damned Jacobins still made it to the city though, from the landward side, and immediately opened trenches. The enemy put Acre under siege.

In their wake, supply ships crept up the coast. There had been one corvette and nine gun-vessels, all prizes for the taking. So the launches returned

---

365 The ruler of Acre, and the land down to Egypt.
366 The *Torride* and the *Marianne* – gun-vessels.
367 old spelling for modern day Haifa.
368 *The Annual Register* (1801), 20-9.

aboard and the squadron put to sea. After a short chase they grabbed seven of the supply ships.[369] The captain had been delighted with the captured cargo; everything needed for a long siege. There were large guns, ball and grape, and hundreds of barrels of powder. The French must have rued their loss. When a midshipman took command of one of the prize gun-vessels, he had joined the crew to work her. They anchored off shore and immediately set to harassing enemy posts.

Everyone in the service understands how each day might be their last. When the two 74s united their boat crews to cut out enemy supply boats in Caiffa, he had been saddened not to go; he still worked the gun-vessel. However, it had been fortuitous, for that expedition ended badly[370] with half a dozen killed, twenty wounded, and eight men taken prisoner.[371] One of them had been a dear friend. Little time could be given to dwell upon such sad facts, for a harsh storm had forced all the ships out to sea. They had remained offshore for more than two weeks. Up on the yards, amid that gale, his mind was kept busy.

By the time they returned to Acre the French had reached the ditch and outer wall, directly in front of the north-eastern portion of the city. A mine was already in the process of being constructed, a hazard that could easily blow up the whole wall. He had not been surprised to receive a tap on the shoulder and told to return to the *Tigre* to join a landing party tasked to destroy it. One thing he has learned these past months is that, in war, a naval life is not always spent at sea.

So here he stands, pike in hand, close to the ruins of the north-eastern tower. Around him, grim and quiet, are sailors and marines. Fatigued locals lurk amid the rubble and ruin of what was the seraglio. Colourful Albanian troops, favourites of the Pasha in their big billowy trousers, prepare to support their flanks. Their own Swedish knight consults a map with his émigré friend. Colonel Louis-Edmond Antoine Le Picard de Phélippeaux is no more than 30 years old and has spent the last few years as a spy, agitator and agent. Supposedly, as a youth he knew Bonaparte at the Military School in Paris,[372] and both men hate each other. Phélippeaux has organized Acre's defences while his old nemesis tries to capture the place. Talk about a fated

---

369 *Foudre* (8), the 6s *Négresse* and *Dangereuse*, the 4s *Vierge-de-Grâces*, *Deux-Frères*, and *Marie-Rose*, and the *Torride* (2).

370 James, W. (1826) Vol II, 288.

371 *The Tillery Journal* - JOD/28012. This journal gives an account of a sailor captured at Caiffa and beyond; found at the Caird Library, National Maritime Museum Greenwich.

372 On the examination list he came forty-first to Napoléon's forty-second.

sky. If the two ever meet again, what would they say? Would the engineer run Bonaparte through?

Lieutenant Wright[373] turns to issue orders. The men look to their weapons. His own sweaty hands grip his pike and quite unexpectedly he starts to think about his sweetheart back home. Her face even appears right there in front of him. *Grace, will I see you again?* Another face appears, the grizzled and sour face of his old schoolmaster, who looks perplexed. He no doubt wonders what his ex-student is all about. Seeking the bubble reputation, he would have said, even in the cannon's mouth.[374] How true that is.

The two faces vanish as the group of sailors and marines begin to move through a breach in the wall. The wreck of French trenches and dead bodies lies beyond. Outside, his world condenses into a cone directly in front of him. At first he hears only heavy breathing and the blood in his ears, but then there is a great noise raised by the Turkish troops. He wonders whether it is to gain the enemy's attention and distract French field pieces. Ahead of him, Lieutenant Wright's right arm jerks involuntarily, and blood sprays out in bright red droplets. The officer falls on one knee as though in prayer. Two balls have hit him in the arm, and it requires a marine to help him stand up. Their coats are wildly different colours – one navy blue, the other red – and they stand out in stark relief against the sandy brown of the covering works. Their momentum slows, and a private off the *Theseus* falls down heavily with a sigh. A vast spray of mud and debris explodes amongst the French. Clods and splinters fall like rain, with things intermingled he cares not to notice. They rally, and reach the mine entrance in good order. Pikes are lowered to skewer French guards in the way. Not by him, as he forms the rear guard. As the others enter into the works of the mine he stands ready, blessedly out of view of French muskets. The heat is horrific. Behind him, inside the shallow mine entrance, hammers and shovels appear from packs. The men begin to knock down the supports. Everything is to be destroyed, and that requires heavy work. Wood chips fly. He watches Turks attack the French in their trenches, to butcher them and collect their heads.[375]

After destruction of the mine, shouts and repeated orders are given. They depart. The wounded lieutenant has to be half-carried out. His grey face is

---

373 Of the *Tigre*.

374 *As You Like It*, Act II, Scene VII. About the seven stages of life it is the fourth stage. *Then a soldier, Full of strange oaths, and bearded like the pard, Jealous in honour, sudden and quick in quarrel, Seeking the bubble reputation, Even in the cannon's mouth.*

375 To present to the Pasha for payment.

bathed in sweat. Away from the shadows of the mine the bright light makes him squint. Tears, or sweat, stings his eyes. Sharp reports of French muskets bark behind, and sprays of dirt from ball and grape pop beside him. Another sailor falls. Blood lands upon his shirt. The breach, and safety, lies ahead.

He is tired, as his pike is cumbersome and heavy. On the verge of safety he feels the most vulnerable. They have to scale rubble, while men die all around him. He feels a sting, as of a bee, on his left leg but he ignores it. Finally back inside the city walls he stops, catches his breath, and takes a seat. They have made it back! Most of them anyway, for three marines will see no future days and twenty men have been seriously injured. Including himself. A surgeon's mate attends him and only then does he realize he has taken a bullet to the lower leg. It is a most wicked cut. Fear strikes him. Fever is already rampant in the town. With an open wound he could be next. *Grace! Grace!*

A war has so many unexpected twists and turns, with so much barbarity and waste. What would his old teacher have said? Would he have wondered whether his old student would see a fifth age? That he would not see beyond the pard?[376] That evening fever takes hold. By next morning it is all he knows. Six months previously he walked upon green fields, and had been loved. Fever-wracked, amid semi desert and heat, he is all alone. He enters a dream state, with no wreckage to cling to but fragments from his past: of school days, a wan and thin woman called Grace, and the varied moods of the sea. After four days his strength gives out and it is all over. The surgeon closes his eyes upon this world. His eternal thereafter becomes the sea, to which his remains are consigned. His epitaph might have read, *Here lies a British seaman who died in Saint Jean d'Acre in service of his country. No next of kin. Loved ones unknown.*

The Siege of Saint Jean d'Acre, or Acre, took place between 20 March and 21 May 1799. For the British there were successes and failures. Two carronades from the *Tigre* (74) were placed on sailing lighters to lob shells at the French. *Tigre*'s Midshipman Jones and one master's-mate worked a gun at a defensive earthwork. There was the sortie that destroyed the French mine. Sir Sidney Smith joined a boat's crew and ran 'armed with pikes, to the breach'.[377] Numerous sorties were made to 'impede the progress of their [the French] covering-works'. Failure came with the cutting out expedition against Caiffa. Disaster occurred on 14 May with the sudden explosion onboard the

---

376 The fourth age: Manhood.
377 *Naval Chronicle* (1799), 621.

Theseus as she lay offshore. Unexploded enemy shells had been piled upon her deck. They caught fire and detonated. Captain Miller, the schoolmaster, two midshipmen, twenty-three seamen, one boy and three marine privates instantly died. A further three marine privates and six seamen were thrown into the water and drowned. Forty men perished, and forty-seven were severely burnt. The ship's after part was wrecked beyond recognition, but the crew did manage to save the ship.[378] The French were unable to make the most of the calamity because a week before, 7 May, thirty-odd transports and Turkish corvettes had arrived from Rhodes with 7,000 reinforcements. Their arrival signalled the end of a gruelling fifty-one days.[379] The French lifted the siege and retreated. The British finally left on 12 June, but without de Phélippeaux who died shortly after the siege had ended.

Acre was one example of how squadrons and detached ships used their boats' crews and marines to cut out enemy ships and join sorties on shore. To emerge victorious against France, and her allies, the Royal Navy had to dominate theatres both at sea and ashore. Deployment of boat's crews were legion. 'These cutting-out expeditions...were then as common as pea-soup, and almost as much relished by our jolly tars.'[380] The Mediterranean theatre's diverse stretches of water gave ample opportunity to raid small harbours and roadsteads. Men like Sir Sidney Smith gained renown for their cutting-outs and raids. The most famous naval man of all, Lord Nelson, gave an account of his service in October 1797 upon receiving an annual pension of £1,000. In full he wrote, 'That during the present war, your memorialist has been in four actions with the fleets of the enemy, viz. On the 13th and 14th of March, 1795; on the 13th of July, 1795; and on the 14th of February, 1797; in three actions with frigates; in six engagements against batteries; in ten actions in boats, employed in cutting out of harbours, in destroying vessels, and in taking three towns. Your memorialist has also served on shore with the army four months, and commanded the batteries at the sieges of Bastia and Calvi. That, during the war, he has assisted at the capture of seven sail of the line, six frigates, four corvettes, and eleven privateers of different sizes; and taken and destroyed near fifty sail of merchant vessels; and your memorialist has actually been engaged against the enemy upwards of one hundred and twenty times. In which service your memorialist has lost his right eye and arm, and been severely wounded and bruised in his body. All of which services and

---

378 Douglas (1860), 287 & 288.
379 Although before they landed the French made a last determined effort to take the town.
380 Castle (1861), 75.

wounds your memorialist most humbly submits to your majesty's most gracious consideration. October, 1797.'[381]

Boats' crews allowed warships to capture prizes that sheltered in hostile harbours. For junior officers a cutting-out promised prize money, and glory if their captain mentioned them in dispatches, and potential promotion. For seamen it promised prize money and an opportunity to cause mayhem. On 9 June 1799 the *Success* (32) cruised off Cap de Creus,[382] Catalonia, when she came across a lone armed Spanish poleacre (or *polacca*).[383] She chased her into La Selva and realized no fixed shore battery existed to offer a defence. Captain Peard sent forty-two men in three boats to cut her out, under command of a naval lieutenant and a lieutenant of marines. By the time they arrived the poleacre had set up a small onshore battery. Nevertheless, *Bella-Aurora* was captured, with the loss of four seamen dead and nine wounded. Captain Peard later penned a letter to the commander in chief of the Mediterranean fleet, dated 13 June. He stated how his ship had been 'standing towards Cape Creaux[384] in pursuance of instructions I had received from Lord Keith,' when he chased a poleacre that flew Spanish colours; that he sent boats to cut her out, and those boats had 'all volunteers on this occasion'. He had not actually seen the cutting out as a point of land masked the operation, and 'gallant fellows' had died; that 'the conduct of Lieutenant Facey, my Lord, who commanded, does him, in my opinion, great honour.' He finished his letter by hoping it gave sufficient recommendation of the two lieutenants, petty officers and men who had manned the boats.[385] Included with the letter was a list of names, such as: John Grey, James Shaw, Thomas Edwards, William Robinson, Richard Hornsby, William Madden and William Lamb. On receipt of the letter Admiral Earl St Vincent had sent it with a note to Evan Nepean at the Admiralty, dated 14 June, at Port Mahon. He wrote, '[It] will, I am fully persuaded, merit the approbation of the Lords Commissioners of the Admiralty.' Soon afterwards the naval lieutenant, Stupart, had been promoted to commander, and the two letters printed in the *Naval*

---

381 Burney (1807), 415.
382 James spells it 'Creux'.
383 A three-masted square-rigged ship with a beaked prow; each mast was made from one pole.
384 His spelling.
385 A barge, a launch, and a cutter.

Chronicle.[386] Cutting out expeditions, raids and landings made the navy a flexible force, and helped project its strength ashore.

Throughout the Mediterranean there existed plenty of sea commerce to prey upon. France, Spain, and maritime Italian states considered this 'Middle Sea' vital to their own interests. France became especially interested in the north African trade after the loss of her West Indies islands, and she did much to promote positive relations with the Barbary states. By 1797 Marseilles alone had more than 300 sail of merchantmen of 'various descriptions' for the Tunis trade[387], and in return Tunis helped protect the French warship *Duquesne* (74) when chased into port by a British warship.[388]

The Barbary states complicated the whole theatre. In the west these were Fez, Algeria, Tunis, Tripoli and above all the infamous port of Salé. From that shallow Moroccan harbour corsairs had ranged far and wide for centuries. In this era the Portuguese navy had kept them contained as much as possible but from 1793 onwards their warships ventured elsewhere. Sallee rovers consequently ran free. Great Britain had previously made a treaty of peace and commerce with them, dated 8 April 1791, that had resulted in a 'Mediterranean pass'. This document, with the seal of the Admiralty and a unique scalloped top, was issued to British merchant ships and vessels that sailed anywhere near Barbary waters. The passes referred to 'treaties that have been made with the Barbary states...that the subjects of the king of Great Britain should pass the seas unmolested by the cruisers of those states'.[389] Because, although Britain then looked to the West Indies, the Baltic, Canada, India and the East Indies for the majority of her sea-commerce, she also had Turkish and Levant interests. The Mediterranean contained strong foreign fleets that could fall from a favourable alliance, status as a neutral, or join with France and thereby menace shipping. As to the risk of being made a prize, the narrowness of the Mediterranean Sea allowed merchantmen to leapfrog from port to port, under cover of darkness if wind and tide allowed, to avoid

---

386 *Naval Chronicle July to December MDCCXCIX*, 344 & 345.
387 Jackson (1806), 3. This could be a highly exaggerated number and the author himself thought it stupendous, but his source was the French consul in Tunis. If correct, that number of ships no doubt traded with other ports.
388 Schomberg (1802), 253.
389 Mortimer, *Dictionary* (1810), 'Mediterranean Pass'. British policy was to protect her sea trade – *The British Encyclopedia or Dictionary of arts and sciences* (1818), 'Commerce'.

patrolling squadrons, privateers and corsairs. However, large numbers of merchantmen were taken as prizes.

A number of French émigrés had found a safe haven in Britain. An Alsatian man had fled France in 1791 to help distribute false *assignats* in Germany, and later offered his services to the British. Fluent in both German and Italian, with good enough English, he proved ideal to aid British consuls on the Italian peninsula. As war loomed the agent had taken passage to Livorno. Eight years later, in 1801, he could look back on that journey to places of interest that afterwards became important to the Royal Navy.

The agent left Portsmouth in fine weather and arrived at Lisbon a few weeks later. Portugal remained a faithful ally to Great Britain, and one of a few states to admit British manufactures after 1796. Napoléon stated, in 1800, how possession of Portugal[390] would have countered the British in the whole Mediterranean and forced them to the peace table. If he had controlled Lisbon and Spain's regional naval arsenal, La Carraca behind Cadiz, he could have blockaded the Straits of Gibraltar and shut out the Royal Navy.

It had been dark when the agent had transited the Straits of Gibraltar, but he knew it was 'twelve leagues from Cape Spartel to Ceuta Point on the African coast, and from Cape Trafalgar to Europa Point on the coast of Spain. At the western or Atlantic entrance they are about eight leagues broad.'[391] Gibraltar, Britain's main naval arsenal in the theatre, had loomed up the next day. On a distinctive finger of land she dominates the entire eastern side of the Bay of Gibraltar. Always a vital piece of property[392] with two moles and 'trim batteries at the water's edge'[393] she had been made into a fortress. With a range of shoals and rocks in front of the town, large ships could not approach her walls; if they had, 900 pieces would have blown them out of the water. The Spanish called her 'the mouth of fire'.[394] When safely ashore he had looked up the slopes of The Rock, and seen 'small crowded edifices, looking like card-houses pasted to the naked rock... a crumbling fortress, remnant of Moorish power...higher yet, crag upon crag, - here, pierced with lines of embrasures...up to the proud old summit

---

390 France did not make an attempt until 1807.
391 Martin (1837) Vol VII, 57.
392 Mann (1870), 230. He called it a *coign of vantage for a great maritime power.*
393 Bigelow (1831), 27.
394 Martin, *ibid.* Or 'The Devil's Mouth' (*La Boca del Diabolo*).

of Mount Calpe.'[395] The signal house stood near the summit, some 1,200 feet above the waterline. It had fine views of the whole coast around, one that had often been hostile, and eight miles across the bay the Spanish port of Algeciras could easily command her sea approaches.

After a few days repose at Gibraltar he had sailed on, and soon passed Cartagena. He did not look inside, but someone told him she had an impressive arsenal, grand docks and a yard. Many considered her the 'securest [port] along the whole coast, sheltered from all dangerous winds, and well protected by nature'.[396] When Spain had become a reluctant ally of France this place gained added importance, but by then the Royal Navy had no real presence in the region. Beyond Cartagena the agent found the Mediterranean widened, and his small vessel had sailed north-east to Porto Mahón in Minorca, a fine harbour equidistant from southern France, eastern Spain and north Africa.

The agent came to appreciate Minorca's exceptionally strong fort. As to the port itself he had once read a British letter, dated 1756, that stated, 'it is excellently situated either for protecting or incommoding the Trade of all Nations in the Mediterranean, and for saving those Ships that happen to be unluckily caught in a tempestuous Levanter; and as Port-Mahon lies at the East End of the Island, there is not a safe Harbour for Ships of War in the Mediterranean, so conveniently situated for bridling the Pirates of Africa.'[397] Nelson came to consider that the island naturally belonged to the 'nation that controlled the sea'.[398] It had only been in 1798 that Great Britain had regained her.

From Minorca the agent took passage to Livorno. He sailed close to Toulon, the main focus of the whole theatre. As a younger man he had visited that port, and therefore had a good sense of her main points of interest. He knew how ships had to weather the Cepet peninsula to enter the outer road and make their way through the Eguillette channel to the inner road and the impressive arsenal. Toulon had two long moles, basins, magazines, and a victualling office that were equally impressive. One writer had explained how there were 'huge pyramids of cannon balls, and the vast ranges of storehouses, in which are deposited every species of hostile weapons, and also the different yards, stocks, bakehouses, &c.'[399] The roadsteads had a fringe of protective forts, from Balaguier to Grosse Tour, Lamalgue, Cap Brun and Sainte-Marguerite.

---

395 Bigelow, *ibid.*
396 O'Shea (1869), 103.
397 Baldwin (1756), 9.
398 Mahan, *Sea Power* (1895) Vol I, 3.
399 Beaumont (1794), 8.

In 1793 the British and her allies came to know them well. The agent had later passed by the Îles d'Hyères roads, where Vice Admiral Hood once anchored the Mediterranean fleet, and soon reached Genoa and the rugged Ligurian coast. He had marvelled at how the verdant mountains fell into the azure sea.

At Livorno, which the British called Leghorn, he had made himself comfortable and soon clandestinely met with the local British consul. He found himself employed with numerous tasks, because Great Britain needed both allies and sympathetic states to help nourish her squadrons and keep France isolated. The French desperately required foodstuffs and supplies, and if she could not procure them herself she at least had to stop others from supplying the British. As an agent his role had been to hinder their efforts for his paymasters.

Over the succeeding years he came to know intimately the 900 miles of Italian coast from Livorno southwards to the Straits of Messina and Sicily, plus the islands of Corsica and Sardinia to the west. He found the Italian west coast offered few places suitable for a large sailing ship, let alone a squadron. Politically, at first, it had been controlled by numerous small independent states: the Republic of Lucca, the Grand Duchy of Tuscany, the Papal States, and the Kingdom of Naples. Between 1793 and 1795 they were supportive of the British. Livorno, a Tuscan port, was the main naval facility in the north and was used as a depôt for stores and provisions. British warships often touched there for a refit. However, the largest naval power along the entire coast had been the Kingdom of Naples, and her Bay of Naples boasted more than twenty leagues of shoreline with good ports and anchorages. Generally supportive of the coalition she provided 6,000 troops[400] for the siege of Toulon, and her ships had cooperated with the British. The agent often found himself in a chaise, somewhere between Naples and Sicily, in efforts to secure supplies of corn.

Directly south, roughly at the midway point of the Mediterranean, the islands of Malta, Gozo, and Comino were neutral until France invaded them in 1798. The agent had taken ship there to secure seamen volunteers. He found Valletta's Grand Harbour to have a fine array of protection. Forts Saint Elmo and Ricasoli protected the entrance, and Fort Saint Angelo covered the centre, 'capable of sending to instant destruction a ship of any force that should presume to come within its reach, and one hundred pieces of very heavy cannon could be made to bear upon her.'[401] However, the town had been too dry for his tastes. The summer heat drained the life out of him.

---

400 Dyer (1877) Vol IV, 512.
401 Griffiths, *Monthly Review* (1803), 78. A second anchorage was at Marsamxett Harbour (Marsa Muschetto).

The pivot of the whole region lay west of Italy, on the islands of Sardinia and Corsica. The agent little understood the needs of a fleet, apart from food and protection in port, but a naval captain had once told him how the two islands broke up the western end of the Mediterranean into smaller seas, with less room to manoeuvre a fleet and more opportunities for ships to avoid one. The roadstead of La Maddalena, situated off the extreme north-eastern tip of Sardinia, could protect a fleet and command the Straits of Bonifacio between both islands. Nelson favoured the anchorage. As everyone then knew, the pivot of history was with Corsica, the birthplace of Napoléon.

During the agent's sojourn in Italy the Royal Navy's fortunes in the Mediterranean resembled a tide. From 1793 until 1795 it ran high, turned and ebbed from 1796 to 1798, and only after the Battle of the Nile turned again and began to flood. However, the whole extent of the theatre was seldom in play. From 1793 until 1798 the main focus of interest lay in waters where the agent could assist, around Toulon, Cartagena and Naples. To withstand the enemy threat, and menace enemy trade, it had required the presence of a strong British fleet with adequate dockyards, harbours and roadsteads. Politics and diplomacy played a part. The men whom the agent assisted, such as the consuls and ambassadors, were the ones who had dealt with both British naval flag officers and local courts. As long as France had been weak, the presence of strong British squadrons helped persuade small states to remain supportive or neutral. Small Italian states, situated in the middle of the theatre as they were, made them important to Britain's implementation of her war effort in the theatre. They could either aid, or hinder, the Royal Navy. Squadrons that worked out of Gibraltar had had to blockade Toulon, a round trip of 1,400 nautical miles regardless of the time spent on station, and for vessels with smaller holds the need for supplies became critical. He remembered with shame how, in 1796, the navy had had to evacuate Corsica, while her warships suffered a severe lack of provisions. Crews had been restricted to a third of their normal rations for the journey back to Gibraltar. He appreciated then why naval commanders continually worried about the need to secure friendly ports and harbours close to where they had to patrol. They needed to access supplies. Great Britain had wealth, and had been able to furnish allies with large subsidies and loans to keep them in the coalition; but also to gain safe ports and harbours. Austria, whose rulers could persuade Tuscany to open Livorno to the Royal Navy, had received from the British exchequer £4,600,000 in 1796, and £1,603,000 in 1797.[402] Most Italian states remained sympathetic to the Royal Navy for as long as France remained weak.

Although the agent detested what his homeland had become it pained him to admit that the French Mediterranean fleet was not fully competent, or capable, to wage a long war.[403] When Britain entered the conflict the Toulon fleet had already fallen into difficulties. The *levée en masse* had taken away men who might have joined the fleet, and those that had been left often declined. A lack of slops, provisions, payment and discipline had wrought havoc. During what became known as the Siege of Toulon the French naval administration permitted denunciation of seamen not in favour of the revolution. The National Convention had wanted 'patriot' seamen. The agent had thought them to be fools. Many capable men thereby left the French sea service, even if they had been supportive of the regime, and in their place forceful and revengeful men had gained positions of authority. The inability to fully man the French fleet had been a direct consequence, and the partial destruction and capture of the Toulon fleet in December 1793 weakened its force even further. When republican ships and vessels had put to sea seldom did they have adequate stores or equipment, although they remained a tangible threat.[404]

As the war progressed the agent came to understand that success or failure at sea was often balanced by events on land. The elements of land and sea were not exclusive. The French fleet had been weak, but after 1794 the French army became strong. From that time onwards it gained enough victories on the field of mars to pressure neutrals throughout the Mediterranean. The agent then did everything in his power to hinder them. More than one horse fell under him as he galloped here and there. When Britain's Mediterranean allies began to desert her, the Royal Navy had had to abandon the theatre. He thereafter spent long months without any hope.

It all began at Toulon. An advance British squadron, the *St George* (98), the 74s *Captain*, *Egmont* and *Ganges*, and the *Phaëton* (38), left Spithead on 14 April 1793 under command of Rear Admiral Gell. It proved timely for the *St George* as she captured a prize off Madeira, the *St Jago* out of Lima under French colours. When condemned she netted £935,000. Gell's personal share amounted to more than £100,000.[405] A second squadron followed on 15 April. The fleet commander, Vice Admiral Lord Hood,

---

402 Hansard (1812), 21.
403 although they did have well built ships.
404 Mahan, *French Revolution* (1895) Vol I, 67.
405 Ashton (1885), 87 & 88.

arrived at Gibraltar in the middle of June 1793 to assemble twenty ships of the line, fourteen frigates, and various other vessels. He soon returned to sea and fell in with the then allied Spanish fleet[406] under Juan de Lángara y Huarte and *Almirante* Federico Carlos Gravina y Nápoli. The Spaniards had just observed the French fleet at Toulon, and although they had not been at sea long, were headed to Cartagena to replenish. This amazed the British, so the fleets separated. Ten days later Hood arrived off the French coast with nineteen ships of the line, seven frigates and associated vessels. To his satisfaction he found most of the enemy fleet in the *Grande Rade*, the outer road. His policy was to cruise offshore, observe the French, and if possible offer blockade. Nelson, then upon the *Agamemnon* (64), wrote a letter to his wife saying, 'There seems to be no French ships at sea, at least we have seen nothing like one.'[407] France had declared war, but she had not been able to put her Toulon fleet to sea.

The agent recognized how great events often required time, trouble and toil to come to fruition. It had been with utmost amazement that he heard how representatives from both Marseilles and Toulon visited Hood on his flagship, the *Victory* (104), to negotiate restoration of the French monarchy and support for their revolt. Their talks occasioned the possibility of taking possession of the Toulon fleet at little or no cost. Toulon harbour was then surrounded by royalist elements. *Exceptional!* the agent had said. *To think, the enemy's main naval strength in the region could be taken possession of in such a manner.* Of course, it had been impossible to turn down such a possibility and sailors throughout the fleet must have stood agog at the prospect. Hood issued a declaration that in part explained, if 'the Standard of Royalty is hoisted, the ships in the harbour dismantled, and the port and forts provisionally at my disposition, as to allow of the ingress and egress with safety, the people of Provence shall have all the assistance and support, his Britannic Majesty's fleet, under my command, can give.'[408] He declared how a future peace would restore to France any ships and stores the British subsequently seized. Toulon authorities replied in general agreement, 'That the Ships of War now in the Road will be disarmed according to Admiral Hood's wishes.'[409] The town's citadel and associated forts were to be handed over to the

---

406 Of twenty-five sail, as found in Dundas (1805), 1. This document also considered the claim made by Hood for 'prizes' taken during the Siege of Toulon.

407 Lathom Browne (1891), 64.

408 Dundas, 2.

409 *Ibid.*

admiral, if garrisons comprised both British and French troops[410] under British command.

The French fleet had not been in full agreement. Their admiral, Jean-Honoré de Trogoff de Kerlessy, favoured events but had been ashore; his second in command, *contra-amiral* Jean René César de Saint-Julien de Chabon, remained fervently against it and made attempts to usurp command of ships he thought would offer resistance. The French had seventeen ships of the line in the roads, and a further fourteen ships building, in repairs or in ordinary.[411] It required royalists to take control ashore and seize key forts and batteries to 'overawe' the recalcitrant ships. This act alone forced the majority of revolutionaries out of the fleet, but it remained uncertain as to what the French ships would do when the British stood in. On 27 August, Hood sent in to the outer road four ships of the line, some frigates, and a detachment of marines. A French battery on the Cepet peninsula did open fire, but marines landed safely close to Fort Sainte-Marguerite. From there they marched to Fort Lamalgue; and the Spanish fleet arrived to join with the British. De Trogoff returned and hoisted his flag on the *Perle* (40). All French resistance faded, the revolutionary fleet was secured and moved into the inner road. Some 1,500 British and Spanish troops landed together with 250 British seamen to act 'as gunners'[412] for the forts. Heavy artillery was stripped from the lower decks of captured warships and placed in forts Faron, Balaguier, Lamalgue and Eguillette. On 29 August the combined fleets sailed into the harbour and landed further reinforcements, who ranged out to take up key positions. Rear Admiral Goodall became the Governor of Toulon, and *almirante* Gravina commandant of all landed troops (until Colonel Lord Mulgrave arrived on 6 September to take command of British troops and landed seamen).

It appeared then that the coalition had acquired an advantageous possession with command of sea-lanes to Sardinia, Naples, Spain and North Africa. The French then suffered great dearth, and uncertain lines of communication. 'In order to invest Toulon on the right and left side at once, it was necessary there should be two distinct blockading armies; and these could scarce communicate with each other, as a steep ridge of mountains, called Pharon, must interpose betwixt them. This gave opportunity to the besieged to combine their force, and choose the object of attack when they sallied; while, on the other hand, the two bodies of besiegers could not

---

410 As stated in the *London Gazette*, as found in Debrett (1794), 75.
411 James, Vol I, 98
412 Dundas, 5.

easily connect their operations, either for attack or defence.'[413] Perhaps the coalition should have considered how Toulon was not an island remote from the mainland, and that the French were highly resilient. Marseilles, further down the coast, had been subdued; and the *Armée d'Italie* could afford to send troops, at first under *général* Jean Baptiste François Carteaux, to intercede.

The French advance guard reached Ollioules west of Toulon, within sight of the harbour, on 30 August. Within two weeks they had managed to surround Toulon upon both flanks of Mont Faron behind the town. The French brought together 14,000 men,[414] just as the coalition started to bicker. Later, after the siege ended, the agent had met with a British lieutenant who explained how small expeditions with national seamen was one thing, but full amphibious operations with foreign nationals another. Operations, he told him, required planning, coordination, clear judgement, vim, vigour and adequate lines of communications to succeed. Coalition forces at Toulon had comprised five different nationalities 'and languages...[so] no common object of interest held them together.'[415] National jealousies, even outright contempt, surfaced to cause problems. The British account of the siege was scathing of 'foreign' troops, something that annoyed the agent to read, and some British naval commanders had considered Spanish sailors to be poor seamen. He knew nothing of that, but he came to believe that many commanders at Toulon lacked experience in this 'species' of war. He wondered whether the appreciation of the needs of troops, versus sailors, had been lacking; the needs of the separate coalition members often ran counter to each other. Spain had the largest presence there, in both ships and men, and her troops had by far the greater experience. The Spanish royal family had close links with the French royal family, so no doubt believed they had the better claim to command. Admiral Hood refused to hand over his authority.

At the time of the Toulon siege the agent had wondered as to its purpose. Had it been to maintain an occupation and link up with Austrian forces? Or had it merely been a prolonged raid? Either way coalition forces remained inactive. When details reached London, Parliament assumed that Toulon had been made 'safe'. So they had sent out as many troops as possible. Major General Dundas arrived on 25 October, General O'Hara the next

---

413 Sir Walter Scott (1833) Vol VII, 148.
414 Dundas, 7: 'Their Army towards the end of the month amounted to near 7000 men in each quarter.'
415 Dundas, 10.

day, and Sir Gilbert Elliott shortly thereafter. All forces ashore were put under the command of General O'Hara. 'The French, Piedmontese, and Neapolitans paid, or subsidized by Britain, acknowledged his full authority; but the Spaniards did not.'[416] The coalition command structure became strained, whereas the command of French artillery became coordinated to a high degree under a young Corsican then unknown to the outside world. Napoléon Bonaparte requisitioned powerful coastal pieces and placed them in thirteen newly constructed batteries to pepper the allied fleet. Ships had had to move out of their range, away from the western end of the inner road, and thereby isolated the wooden and earthen redoubt the coalition had constructed near to La Seyne, that they called Fort Mulgrave.[417] Toulon became a stalemate.

The agent's naval colleague later told him that further down the coast there had been no stalemate. Left to themselves the Royal Navy remained aggressive. The French ship *Modeste* (36) had entered Genoa in company with two armed tartans,[418] while at La Spezia the *Impérieuse* (38) lay dormant under the loom of Fort Santa-Maria. A small British naval detachment had been sent to either take them as prizes or deter them from molesting supply ships out of Livorno and elsewhere. On 11 October two 74s, the *Bedford* and *Captain,* in company with the *Speedy* (14) entered the channel between the Molo Vecchio and Molo Nuovo at Genoa. They came alongside the *Modeste* as she lay inside the Molo Vecchio. The *Bedford* 'slacked her cable, hove close alongside of, and boarded the *Modeste*.'[419] Marines fired their muskets on the French, and some revolutionaries had to jump over the side. The *Speedy* seized the two tartans. Afterwards the *Captain* sailed on to La Spezia where, on 12 October, she moored near the *Impérieuse* and found her abandoned, a previous attempt to scuttle her having failed. Boarded and secured she was crewed, weighed, and sailed off to join the British fleet; both captures duly entered into the service. This type of success ran counter to events at Toulon. There the coalition had penned themselves in, with no possibility of breaking out to the landward side. If they had, where would they have gone? What use was a fleet at anchor?

---

416 Dundas, 8.
417 The French called it 'Petit Gibraltar'.
418 A commonplace French coastal vessel.
419 James, W. (1826) Vol I, 126.

Slowly the French wings approached the town and the eight outposts the coalition had to maintain[420]. Coalition forces and town residents could only be supplied by sea, and the enemy posed little threat there, but seasoned sailors worried when the weather deteriorated throughout November. Disease laid low many. With such a large number of British sailors ashore, the Royal Navy had had to secure Maltese sailors to help man the ships. The agent knew all about them, but they were late to arrive. Upon Mont Faron, where the coalition tried to keep the French wings separated, conditions turned harsh. The Toulonnaise began to lose faith. They must have perceived little unity of command, and there were bad feelings amongst the occupiers.

After 15 November the French made serious assaults against Fort Mulgrave, the heights of La Grasse and Fort Balaguier that protected the harbour. They constructed a major battery to face Fort Malbousquet, west of Toulon. The Spaniards that manned that fort decided to attack the French emplacement, in company with some British troops, to dispose of the threat. On 30 November more than 2,500 men sallied forth to overrun the French battery. They spiked (made inoperative) the guns, but foolishly ran after the fleeing revolutionaries who soon rallied, turned, and fought them back to Toulon. General O'Hara was taken prisoner. Every day thereafter the French received reinforcements. By December 1793 they commanded more than 40,000 men, opposed to no more than 11,000 effective coalition troops and seamen.[421] The siege had almost reached its culmination as Sir Sidney Smith arrived on board the *Swallow*, a tender he had secured in Turkey.

On 16 December the French commenced a great cannonade. It was rainy, cold, most miserable weather. Next day they assaulted Fort Mulgrave in force and carried the place. There followed a great slaughter. Unknown for many years afterwards a British sailor stabbed Bonaparte in the thigh and it was, by his own reckoning, the closest he ever came to being killed in action. For a while it seemed certain his leg would have to be amputated. According to the satirist George Cruikshank a British sailor later conversed with Bonaparte while on his way to Elba and talked about what had happened: 'Why,' said the veteran, 'he told us the English made a sortie, as they call it, and drove the French before them. Boney run as well as the rest, and an English seaman chased after him...gave him a shove in the stern with his bagonet, and said, "Take that, you French lubber"... . The wound

---

420 These were Cap Brun, the Fort and heights of Mont Faron, Pomet, Saint-Andre, Saint-Antoine, Malbousquet, Fort Mulgrave and Sablettes.
421 Dundas, 11.

was in his thigh.'[422] Mont Faron was assailed, and with such few troops Toulon became exposed.

The situation required a firmness of decision. 'The Town [was] declared untenable by the Engineers and Artillery Officers'[423] and it was obvious that outposts had already been lost. Coalition commanders, of many nations, met in urgent council: 'Lord Hood, Admiral Langara, Rear-admiral Gravina, Major-general Dundas, Lieutenant-general Valdez, Prince Pignatelli, Admiral Forteguerri, Sir Hyde Parker, Chevalier de Revel, and Sir Gilbert Elliot.'[424] Their only recourse was full evacuation of the fleet, together with all French ships that cooperated with them, while burning the remainder and the town magazines. Sir Sidney Smith accepted that gruesome task.

The occupation had ended, and without warning the Neapolitans departed without any recourse to other coalition members. For the remainder it was determined to embark troops off the rocky shore at Lamalgue. The sick and wounded, artillery and baggage were to be extracted by boat. The town descended into uproar. Everyone was exhausted, including the republicans, and panic reigned. By 19 December most troops had reached the ships, but much had to be left behind in the haste to quit the place. A small contingent bravely tarried to work with Sir Sidney. The fire-ship *Vulcan* (14) was placed alongside a number of French warships. At ten o'clock that night they set her alight, together with the town's magazines and warehouses. It acted as a signal for those who remained to depart. The resultant fire turned night into day. It 'laid open to view, by its light, all who were aiding.... . The enemy, having now distinct objects to point at, opened his batteries from every quarter; when, suddenly, a tremendous explosion, unexpected by all, awed into silence both the besiegers and the attacked.'[425] The Spanish had inadvertently set fire to the French hulk *Iris* whose hold had been crammed with thousands of barrels of gunpowder. When she exploded two nearby gunboats were instantly blown to pieces. Prisoners held onboard two French 74s, the *Herós* and *Thémistocle,* were released and the ships ignited. A second powder ship, *Montréal,* blew up. Parliament later reported, in 1803, that 'ten sail of French line of battle ships, and three frigates, [were] completely burnt or destroyed; and...six other sail of the line materially injured at Toulon in the year 1793; and...other French ships...taken

---

422 Cruikshank (1852), 133.
423 Dundas, 12.
424 Pettigrew (1849), 44.
425 James, 86.

possession of and brought away.'[426] The values placed upon captures brought into the British service were £236,742 for the ships, £10,421 for their ordnance, and £18,173 18s.10d. for stores.[427]

After their hot work had been completed Sir Sidney Smith's men rowed back to the fleet in total exhaustion, as the recaptured forts Balaguier and Eguillette peppered them with shot. That would have been something they talked about long afterwards. More than 14,000 Toulonnais men, women and children escaped. The *Princess Royal* (90) took onboard more than 4,000 evacuees.[428] Yet many were left behind. Distraught, some attempted to swim to ships and either drowned, fell to artillery barrage, or were forced back on shore. Some stoically remained in the town, but after the coalition had sailed off to Hyères the republicans took possession and took their revenge.

Soon after the evacuation the agent had written in his diary about this failed enterprise. He had asked, *should the coalition have succeeded? They made every effort to keep the place.* Later commentators, especially William James, argued that 'The port should have been entered by force of arms...the captured ships should have been manned and sent to England; the town garrisoned by troops upon whom a reliance could be placed; and such of the ships and stores as could not be brought away at the final abandonment of the port should have been wholly, not partially, destroyed.'[429] The British argued that petty jealousies got in the way, the Spanish and Neapolitans could not be relied upon, there were too few men, too wide an expanse to defend, and Austria had shied away from assistance. Yet Spanish troops proved more than dependable along the Pyrenées, and with a more thoughtful plan the Neapolitans might have stood firm. The agent noted how the British seemed to cast no opprobrium upon the conduct of their own sailors.

After Toulon, the British fleet had plenty of captures but lacked sufficient weight of guns to achieve long term success in the region. Lord Hood certainly thought so. Further ships of the line had to be secured, together with a harbour or set of anchorages the fleet could access. Hyères was not tenable after the French took command of the coast. Genoa remained neutral. Leghorn happened to be friendly but store ships had to sail too close to hostile France. Naples might be a possibility, likewise Port Mahon and Alicante. The distance to Gibraltar was too great. A solution presented itself directly southwards of Toulon – Corsica, that fulcrum of history. That island

---

426 *The Parliamentary Debates from the Year 1803 to the Present Time* (1812), 1169.
427 *Ibid.*
428 *Ibid.*
429 James, 84.

had rebelled against France and, as the British naval presence then 'rode triumphant in the Mediterranean',[430] her authorities naturally sought help from the British fleet to help expel French garrisons from Bastia and Calvi. For the Mediterranean Fleet the bay of Saint-Florent, or San Fiorenzo, could be a favourable place to reside. Whereas the evacuation of Toulon had upset the general situation, it had also released forces to help expedite matters on the island. Therefore, some sixty sail soon[431] proceeded there from Hyères.

A fierce storm separated them, but troops under Major General Dundas managed to land at San Fiorenzo, on 7 February 1794. An unusual tower they found at Mortella did severe damage to the *Fortitude* (74) and thereby caught the attention of British engineers who later adopted its design with 'Martello' towers. After San Fiorenzo had been secured, the naval commander could not persuade the army commander to march on and besiege Bastia. Dundas argued he must wait for reinforcements. Therefore Hood decided he would go and do the job himself. Captain Nelson went with him. Up until that point Nelson's service record showed how the British fleet covered the whole of this western part of the theatre. In June 1793 he had been at Gibraltar, in August off Toulon, September off Leghorn and at Naples (to give news of the occupation of Toulon and organize Neapolitan troops), October at Tunis and November off Genoa. At Corsica he landed twice in company of seamen, first at Macinaggio and then outside Bastia. In a letter to his wife, dated 6 April 1794, he stated how 'our batteries opened on the 11th, and apparently have done great execution... . We are but few, but of the right sort.'[432] On land his sailors had had to drag heavy guns up precipitous heights to become 'attached to the batteries' and fire upon the enemy. It would have been hot and exhausting work. The siege of Bastia required forty-one days to force the town to surrender. Heartened by the result Corsican deputies convened at their capital, Corte, and declared a new constitution with laws based upon the British model. A Parliament, similar to Ireland's, was adopted. On 19 June the island proclaimed herself released from French influence and annexed to the crown of Great Britain. She adopted the name Anglo-Corsican Kingdom, or *Regno di Corsica*[433]. Calvi, however, had held out.

---

430 Dyer (1877) Vol V, 17.
431 James, Vol I, 207
432 Lathom Browne (1891), 79.
433 Corsica was originally part of the Republic of Genoa but revolted. Genoa, unable to retake the island, ceded it to France. The French invaded and took control mere weeks before Napoleon was born. His father was part of General Paoli's court. The island, Italian in culture and language, became French. When Paoli declared the island aligned with Britain in 1794 it (so far as I have discovered) used the Italian *Regno di Corsica* and not the French form.

Seamen were landed at Calvi, together with 1,450 troops.[434] Hood stripped seven guns off his own flagship for use on shore. They had to be manhandled by sailors under the hot summer sun. The terrain and lack of supplies prolonged the whole affair. On 12 July Nelson, onshore at a battery, was hit in the face by sand thrown up from a shot. He later wrote to Lord Hood how he had been 'a little hurt' but had in fact lost sight in his right eye.

Calvi finally surrendered 10 August, after fifty-one hard days. Two French frigates, the *Melpomène* (38) and *Mignonne* (32), were taken prizes, and both were put into the British service. Corsica had by then rid herself of all French authority, and with a new client-state in the region the British Mediterranean fleet gained a favourable anchorage at San Florent with access to ports at Calvi and Bastia – nothing as compared to Port Mahon, as they had no naval yard, but they were closer to France. Thereafter Corsica helped support a portion of the fleet. For a time.

During 1795 the situation remained fairly stable. Admiral Hood departed the theatre to present to the Admiralty the need to reinforce the Mediterranean fleet. Command temporarily devolved to Vice Admiral Hotham on the *Britannia* (100); but Lord Hood resigned after he failed to convince the Lord's Commissioners. The fleet then lay mostly at Livorno, and some commanders felt forgotten about. When the Neapolitan *Tancredi* (74)[435] joined with them it occasioned delight, enough to highlight the lack of ships of the line. There were simply not enough vessels to secure the Ligurian shore in support of Austria, whose army then resided in the vicinity, and not enough frigates to keep watch upon all salient points. The agent thought the British had hemmed themselves in, with troop and stores ships forced to sail far from Gibraltar and thereby expose themselves to capture. If these had been taken in large numbers their loss would have ruined the fleet. Furthermore, Corsica had not been fully sympathetic. Whereas most Corsicans detested the French, and relished the idea of release, they perceived themselves a conquered people under British occupiers.[436] A fact the agent could appreciate. So Corsicans had been ripe for insurrection; and it did not take long for the backcountry to become uncertain.

Emboldened by the situation the French fleet at Toulon, now seventeen ships of the line, put to sea with the potential to menace Corsica. It had been

---

434 Pettigrew, 57. The loss of Nelson's eye is mentioned
435 James, 337.
436 Allen, *Nelson* (1853), 48.

obvious, even to the agent, that a full engagement had to take place, but only two lesser engagements followed. The first, 14 March 1795, and the second 13 July. In themselves they were ineffective, but they did keep Corsica in British hands. If anything they were 'incomplete, and the arrival at Toulon of six sail of the line, two frigates, and two cutters from Brest, gave the French a superiority which, had they known how to use it, would materially have endangered the British Mediterranean fleet.'[437] The Royal Navy had not been able to deter passage of the enemy through the Straits of Gibraltar nor their arrival at Toulon, but the French had not taken advantage.

By his actions Hotham had been considered far too careful. He no doubt feared a loss of ships and vessels, but for some in the service he lacked aggression. As Lord Hood had resigned, his replacement, Sir John Jervis, duly arrived and took over command. Recently returned from the West Indies with yellow fever, Jervis was a strict taskmaster. On arrival in the Mediterranean he hoisted his flag on board the *Victory*, and his tenure became fortuitous because French national fortunes had by then improved. There commenced, for Great Britain, the slow erosion of friends and allies along the entire Italian peninsula. It became a torrid time for the agent. The Kingdom of Sardinia abandoned the coalition on 15 May 1796. Alarmed by Austrian defeats in Italy, Naples declared an armistice and forbade her ships to cooperate with the British. 'To the great surprise of politicians... the grand duke of Tuscany, first acknowledged the French republic, concluded peace...and, by a formal treaty, breaking his engagement with the coalition, promised in future to observe the strictest neutrality.'[438] Early June 1796 Genoa was invested with French arms. On 27 June French troops entered Livorno and forced out the British;[439] the agent fled for his life, and a great amount of naval stores had to be abandoned.

Deprived of Livorno's harbour the British fleet had no regional yard, and no fleet could remain operative without regular repair, refit, replenishment and reinforcements. Napoléon had been behind all of these events, and by dint of being Corsican had desired to rid his birthplace of the British. Corsica became exposed. During that whole summer a pro-French faction made attempts to retake Bastia. In August, Spain declared war upon Great Britain. It then seemed everything conspired against the Mediterranean Fleet. Yet many sailors, something the agent could not quite fathom, considered such events as a great opportunity to secure their own fortunes.

437 Southey, *Nelson* (1831), 84.
438 Bisset (1811) Vol IV, 214.
439 *The Debates and Proceedings in the Congress of the United States* (1849), 2249.

One Jervis biographer later wrote, 'Nothing could have been more grateful to our seamen; they coveted Spain for an enemy, on account of her wealth, and despised her for her want of skill.'[440] Prize money. Ever prize money! And Jervis happened to be the man who would face the odds.

The British garrison on Corsica could not withstand the new-found threat. Parliament ordered the navy to evacuate the island and pull out of the Mediterranean. The evacuation had mostly been completed by 19 October,[441] after the majority of British personnel were temporarily placed on Elba. As to abandoning the Mediterranean, Nelson considered it dishonorable. 'I lament our present orders in sackcloth and ashes.'[442] He believed the British fleet more than capable of withstanding the combined Spanish and French fleets. By 2 November the island had no further British presence. Ships pulled back to Gibraltar and, together with the loss of Corsica, lessened British influence in the theatre. The whole western Mediterranean came under the dominion of other navies.

After Spain had declared war her navy needed to be accounted for. It was numerous, but not considered powerful. At worse it would be an 'awkward embarrassment'.[443] Nelson was probably not untypical of British officers who considered Spanish shipwrights very good, but the average Spanish sailor very poor.[444] Spain then had seventy-six ships of the line.[445] Not all of them could be put to sea in a good condition. Indolence infected her crews, mostly ex-prisoners and men taken off the streets. But combined with a French fleet it would be a serious threat. Gibraltar had to be considered an obvious target for investment, but it had been assumed Spain would try to unite her fleets with the French for an invasion of Britain. That required the Cartagena fleet to pass through the Straits. Therefore it could be intercepted off Gibraltar. However, it had been preferable to gain sea-room, so on 16 December 1796 Jervis ordered the fleet from The Rock to stations off Portugal.

As they put out the weather had been terrible. The *Gibraltar* (80) ran aground.[446] Three 74s were soon wrecked: *Courageux* off Morocco, *Zealous* on a rock off Tangiers, and *Bombay Castle* while entering Lisbon.[447]

---

440 Codrington (1846), 460.
441 Southey, *Nelson*, 81.
442 *Ibid*, 82.
443 Mahan's words in *The Influence of Sea Power Upon the French Revolution and Empire*, 82.
444 Codrington, 460.
445 James, Vol I, 72. This number is stated for 1793.
446 *The Graphic* (1884) Vol 30, 294.
447 James, 354.

Damaged and depleted, the fleet had to lay at moorings in the Tejo river, Lisbon, until 18 January 1797. When it did return to sea, the *St George* (98) ran ashore at the bar of the Tejo. That left but ten ships of the line fit for sea-service. These were the *Victory* and *Britannia*, the 98's *Barfleur* and *Blenheim*, the 74s *Captain*, *Culloden*, *Egmont*, *Excellent* and *Goliath*, and the *Diadem* (64).[448] For more than three weeks the deficiency of numbers compared to the Spanish would have forced a more timid commander to harbour. Not John Jervis; he was too resolute for that. Besides, the situation with regards to Britain had been tense and invasion fears ran high. The admiral had doggedly remained at sea.

On 6 February reinforcements from the Channel Fleet arrived. *Prince George* (98), *Namur* (90), and the 74s *Colossus*, *Irresistible* and *Orion*[449] made up numbers but they did not strengthen the fleet. On 12 February the *Culloden* collided with the *Colossus*, took damage, but her crew managed to effect repairs. Observation of the Straits continued, the normal array of frigates and vessels ranged out to watch for the enemy, and it was Commodore Nelson who brought intelligence on board *Minerve* (38)[450] that the Spanish fleet had entered the Straits.

Almirante Don José de Córdoba y Ramos no doubt had gained intelligence of British ships at Lisbon, but he could not have known of recent arrivals. He probably assumed he had superior numbers, with twenty-seven ships of the line that included the world's largest warship, *Nuestra Señora de la Santísima Trinidad* (136),[451] six 112s, two 80s, eighteen 74s, ten frigates, some vessels and seventy transports. Their ultimate destination had been Brest, but were then on passage to Cadiz. Throughout the night of 13 February the British heard their signal guns.[452] Next morning, Valentine's Day, dawned with a haze but the wind had veered to allow the Spanish to head for port. When they spied the British they assumed them to be a convoy.

The British formed two divisions, and six ships gave chase. When the haze fully cleared the Spanish realized what really confronted them, but they were scattered. In effect the Spanish comprised two separate groups and wind conditions meant they struggled to 'effect a junction'.[453] The agent

---

448 Shippen (1894), 247.
449 *Ibid.*, 248.
450 He later joined the *Captain* as Commodore; the ship remained under command of Captain Miller.
451 As given in the *Annual Register* (1823), 223.
452 Shippen, 249.
453 *Ibid*, 249.

later read an eyewitness account of events, made by an officer then onboard the *Lively* (32),[454] and other reports. It seemed to him that the Spanish lacked prime seamen, and most Spanish crews would have been new to the sea with 'scarcely sixty to eighty seamen in each ship-of-the-line'.[455] Jervis meanwhile formed line ahead. The *Culloden* was his lead ship, despite her recent knock, and they approached under a press of sail. Alerted, the main Spanish group, centred upon their own flagship, began to wear.

Before noon the *Culloden* opened fire, and the British admiral 'communicated his intention to pass through the enemy's line, hoisting his large flag and ensign; and soon after the signal was made to engage.'[456] The rearmost Spanish ships, the 112s *Conde de Regla* and *Príncipe de Asturias*, and the *Oriente* (74), came together to confront the *Prince George*. The *Colossus* took such a battering that she lost forward motion and became vulnerable to raking fire. The *Orion*, aware of that awful prospect, moved to cover her and thereby deterred the Spanish. Jervis's plan to cut the enemy groups in two succeeded, so he turned attention to their main body and the enemy flag. He wished to break their line, as the Spaniards continued with their attempts to unite. Nelson was instrumental in resisting that union. In the rear of the British line he approached the Spanish flag, that partial four-decker, and despite disparity of ordnance engaged her and others in an act that seemed to 'stagger the Spanish Admiral'.[457] Amongst the British cohort it caused open admiration, despite how Nelson had disobeyed his admiral's orders, and prompted other ships to offer him support. The British gained the advantage and it seemed, to the observer at least, they would win the day. Their rate of fire seemed far superior; more consistent and effective.

Enemy shrouds, sails and masts took heavy damage. 'The *Culloden*, captain Trowbridge, expended 170 barrels of powder.'[458] The *Blenheim* expended more than 180 barrels. British guns fired so rapidly that the Spanish ship *Oriente* became shrouded in smoke when she had to 'run the gauntlet' along the British line.

The *Excellent* poured a heavy broadside into the Spanish ship *San Nicolás* (80), then collided with the *San José* (112). That caused the *San José* to run

---

454 Anonymous, *A Narrative of The Proceedings of the British Fleet etc off Cape St. Vincent* (1797), throughout.

455 Mahan, *French Revolution* (1895) Vol I, 76.

456 *A Narrative of The Proceedings of the British Fleet etc off Cape St. Vincent*, ibid.

457 *Ibid.*

458 *Annual Register* (1823), 223.

foul of the *San Nicolás*. The *Captain*, so damaged she seemed dead in the water, came alongside the *San Nicolás*. Lieutenant Berry commanded the boarding party, with soldiers acting as marines, and quickly secured the Spanish ship. Nelson himself 'passed from the fore-chains of his own ship into the Enemy's quarter gallery, and thence through the cabin to the quarter deck, where he arrived in time to receive the sword of the dying Commander, who was mortally wounded by the boarders.'[459] The *San José* harassed the British with musket fire, and ordinarily a party might have retreated to secure just the one prize, but Nelson opted to secure the second one. He collected eager seamen and boarded the larger ship. His sheer audacity cowed the Spanish, who had lost many men, and their commander dropped to one knee to offer his sword. Uncertain as to whether this might be a ruse, Nelson gathered the Spanish officers together and made them all surrender their swords. His coxswain tucked them under his arm. It formed a great scene, and one long remembered. Nelson thereby captured two ships of the line in a matter of minutes, but the British had to deal with fires on board the *San Nicolás* before they could celebrate.

As night approached British ships had crowded together to secure four Spanish prizes.[460] They hove to (that is, allowed their ships to discontinue the battle and pursuit) and no doubt doled out some grog in recognition of the win. Whereas the Spanish expended a few more broadsides they shied away from further close action and took the opportunity to depart. Several Spanish ships urgently needed to reach the safety of Cadiz. At this, the Battle of Cape St Vincent, the British suffered 300 casualties and thereafter blockaded, and bombarded, Cadiz to keep the Spanish contained within. The *Lively* was dispatched to England with the good news.

The French agent knew at the time that this victory would have a decisive effect upon British public opinion and morale. It lessened the threat of invasion and permitted the war to continue, despite the heavy burden. At the start of 1797 the Royal Navy had not been in command of the Mediterranean, and many considered her inferior to the combined fleets of Spain, France and the Batavian Republic (the triple alliance), but he had thought that if she could keep them apart she was equal to, or better, than any one individual fleet. All of Europe watched with keen interest to see whether Great Britain's navy could withstand them. The Battle of Cape St Vincent commenced a period during which the British navy 'struck all

---

459 *A Narrative of The Proceedings of the British Fleet etc off Cape St. Vincent,* ibid.
460 All taken into the British service, *San Josef* (114), *Salvador del Mundo* (112), *San Nicolas* (80), and *San Ysidro* (74).

Europe with astonishment'.[461] Some said the Spanish had been 'impressed into a service for which they were unqualified, and against a nation with which they had not reason to quarrel',[462] and had felt compelled to join the French. The Dutch soon received their turn at Camperdown. To signify national gratitude, not felt since the Glorious First of June, Sir John Jervis received a peerage. Nelson was knighted, and promoted to Rear Admiral of the blue.

France continued to land further political and military blows. The Venetian Republic fell in late 1797, and her estates along the Adriatic and Ionian Islands went the way of other Italian states. Austria signed a peace with France on 18 October. As a Frenchman the agent had asked himself, how could France defeat Great Britain? He thought the ruination of Britain's commerce could be one means, but French privateers would never achieve that end alone. Another means was to close European ports to British commerce. British manufactures to the Batavian Republic had already been forbidden when France imposed 'this new system of hostilities' upon the greater part of Europe. 'The English manufactures found no entrance into any port from the Elbe to the Adriatic, save those of Portugal. Spain...had entered partly into the plan... . Genoa was compelled to yield.'[463] The Papal States, forced to leave the coalition in 1797, Tuscany and Corsica all complied.

Another means to beat Great Britain was to molest her and her possessions. By 1798 the French tried to convince Europe she would invade England, while secretly she planned to land troops in Egypt. Bonaparte had hoped 'the ports of Italy, of Corfu, Malta, and Alexandria, and the Mediterranean would become a French lake',[464] and thereby cut off British trade through the Levant to India. To molest the British the Toulon fleet would, like the Spanish before, have to pass through the Straits if it intended to combine at Brest and make England a target. British fleets therefore had to wait, and keep watch upon ports where France could amass such a fleet. That included Toulon. Intelligence remained active in the region, and the Livorno consul provided information that 40,000 men had gathered at Toulon with 400 sail. He wrote, 'their destinations are daily circulated and varied, so that no certainty can be obtained,'[465] but he was convinced it would first be Malta, for an invasion of Sicily 'in order to secure that granary', then

---

461 *The Annual Register* (1800), 95.
462 *Ibid.*
463 *The Annual Register* (1797), 62.
464 Barrow, *Sidney Smith* (1848) Vol I, 234.
465 Allen, *Nelson* (1853), 89.

Naples, and ultimately Alexandria, Cairo and Suez. His report was one of many. There had also been the possibility that the French would land troops on the Spanish coast to march against Portugal, or force the Straits for an invasion of Ireland.[466] Admiral Jervis had had to consider all possibilities, but he formed a detached squadron to observe Toulon. He gave command to Nelson, newly recovered and returned from England after he had lost his right arm in a raid against Tenerife, on board the *Vanguard* (74).[467] Nelson went to Gibraltar and collected the 74s *Orion* and *Alexander*, the *Emerald* (36), *Terpsichore* (32) and *Bonne Citoyenne* (20). By 9 May he was back at sea but unaware that Bonaparte and the French fleet, under *contra-amiral* François-Paul Brueys d'Aigalliers, had departed Toulon on 19 May with thirteen ships of the line, two 64s from the Venice fleet, seven frigates, twenty-four vessels and hundreds of transports. It had been an immense French endeavour.

Nelson's squadron would have met the French off Corsica, but a gale kept the fleets apart. His frigates separated, did not return, and the admiral had to seek urgent repairs at Isola di San Pietro off the island of Sardinia. When he returned to sea he sailed to Toulon and found it empty. The *Mutine* (16) joined him on 5 June, with updated orders that gave him full reign to deal with the French anywhere within the Mediterranean, Adriatic, the Greek islands and the Black Sea. A rendezvous was given to collect fresh reinforcements. Meanwhile the French had arrived at Malta, which Bonaparte needed to secure to allow lines of communication towards the east. Gozo fell, as did the southern portion of Malta, and Valletta capitulated two days later. Far to the north-west Nelson kept his rendezvous and increased his squadron to include his flagship (*Vanguard*), the *Orion* and *Alexander*, plus the 74s *Culloden, Bellerophon, Minotaur, Defence, Zealous, Audacious, Goliath, Majestic, Swiftsure* and *Theseus,* and the *Leander* (50). It had been hoped these ships would be sufficient to take, sink, burn or destroy the enemy. Thereafter a race commenced to ascertain where the French had gone. However, naval commanders knew regional winds well and they correctly surmised that the enemy must have gone east.

---

466 James, W. (1826) Vol II, 171.

467 This upset two more senior officers. It was noted in *The Athenaeum* Issues 793-844 of 1843 (p.1087) that whereas St. Vincent approved the promotion 'it naturally gave umbrage to the senior Flag officers, and especially to Sir John Orde' who argued so loudly he was sent home, and in pique printed the correspondence (the Admiralty censored St. Vincent). A duel between the two was offered. If Nelson had not won at The Nile, St. Vincent might well have faced a court martial. The other overlooked officer was Sir William Parker.

Nelson sailed his squadron down the west coast of Italy, speaking with merchant ships and the British ambassador at Naples for any news. At Valletta the French deposited a garrison and their fleet departed on 19 June. The next day Nelson reached the Straits of Messina and finally received news of events on Malta. On the way there, a foreign brig told him how the French had already sailed east. Any ships the republicans came across were destroyed so they could not give their whereabouts. On 30 June the republicans sighted Candia (Crete), far to the north of Egypt. That proved fortuitous because Nelson arrived off Alexandria two days earlier, to find it empty of any French ships. Confounded, Nelson had put back to sea. Both adversaries missed each other, and the French arrived at Alexandria on 1 July. There they were told they had only just avoided the British. Bonaparte commenced immediate disembarkation of his troops, fearful all the while that the British would arrive to ruin his hopes. Nelson wandered aimlessly until he entered Syracuse on 19 July for water and provisions. The usual intelligence from local fishermen, traders, and observant people told him that the French had not passed their way so they must remain over towards the Levant. So Nelson sailed back the way he had come. On passage, at times of calm, he gathered his captains in his cabin to discuss the modes of attack suitable to where they might sail, general tactics for a battle at sea, and a plan if the enemy happened to be found at anchor. The marine sentries who stood outside his cabin must have eavesdropped as much as possible to later tell their mess-mates. Everyone in the fleet would have been eager to know what was up. Off the Morea, that is southern Greece, Nelson learned that the French had been sighted at Candia and had sailed south. The French had to be at Alexandria.

What occurred thereafter changed affairs throughout the theatre and history. Nelson touched Alexandria on 1 August and found it darkened with 'a wood of masts',[468] and French flags flying. Standing upon his quarterdeck Nelson's face must have tightened. The ships sighted were mostly transports and a few Venetians. It fell to the *Zealous* to find the true enemy, at anchor in a bay called Aboukir east of the town. Seventeen ships lay at anchor unaware of the British. There was *l'Orient* (120), three 80s, nine 74s, two 40s and two 36s. Nelson immediately made his way there and gave signal to 'prepare for battle'.[469] The plan to attack the enemy found at anchor was

---

468 James's words.
469 *The Naval Chronicle* (1799) Vol I, 52.

understood by all his captains. The thrill of excitement upon every British warship would have been immense. Finally, the main chance had come.

The British formed a line of battle and as 'all the officers were totally unacquainted with Aboukir Bay, each ship kept sounding as she stood in.'[470] Unfortunately the *Culloden* ran aground. As they approached, the British could see that the French had anchored in line of battle as close to the shore as possible, with shoals, gunboats and four frigates on their flank. A shore battery had been set up on a small island just ahead of their line. They therefore thought themselves secure. However, seasoned British commanders standing on their quarterdecks knew instantly that a ship had to swing upon her cables, so there had to be deep water between the French ships and the shore. Nelson's plan could therefore unfold, and the French would never expect the British to send ships inside their line.

As evening approached the British arrived from the north-west, so that rearmost French ships could not open fire. British seamen had to work their ships, sails, braces and anchors as well as man their guns, while French *matelots* only had to wait and account for their cannons. The *Naval Chronicle* later emphasized French marine artillery, 'their superior skill in the use of which the French so much pride themselves, and to which indeed their splendid series of land victories was in general chiefly to be imputed.'[471] The *Goliath*, *Zealous*, *Audacious*, *Orion* and *Theseus* moved out of line and manoeuvred around the French van and down the enemy's larboard flank. Behind them the *Vanguard* ignored the first two French ships, *Guerrier* and *Conquérant*, and moved down the starboard flank of the French, to stop within pistol shot of the *Spartiate*, their third in line. Remaining British ships successively moved to positions further down the French line until the *Majestic* reached the furthest French ship to be engaged, the *Mercure*. Three French ships remained unmolested. The *Goliath* and *Zealous* had to take the brunt of initial French fire, but all British ships withstood broadsides on their bows until most 'anchored by the stern'.[472] The *Leander* went between the *Peuple Souverain* and the *Franklin*, raked the latter, and hit the *l'Orient* beyond.

Night fell and observers onshore could only marvel as gunfire flared out at ragged intervals. The rage of the guns proved devastating. Within twelve minutes the *Guerrier* had been completely dismasted. Within two hours

---

470 *Naval Chronicle, ibid.*; sounding was the method of dropping a lead weighted line overboard to ascertain the depth of water.
471 *Naval Chronicle, ibid.*
472 *Ibid.*

the *l'Aquilon* and *Peuple Souverain* had been boarded and taken. Other French ships struck their colours. At ten minutes after nine the event this battle has always been remembered for commenced. On fire the *l'Orient* appeared discomfited enough for Nelson, then below with a head wound, to be informed. No sailor liked to see another ship burn, for the prospects were terrible. So Nelson sent over a boat, and other British ships did the same. Seventy *matelots* were taken off, and so strong was the inferno it lit up the whole bay. Sailors moved under a bright, eerie, flickering light. About ten o'clock the *l'Orient* exploded. Ships had done so before, would do so again, but the sound of this one was so great it caused an instant pause, a death-like sullen silence, for at least three minutes. The 'wreck of the masts, yards, &c. &c. which had been carried to a vast height, fell down into the water and on board the surrounding ships.'[473] It was an appalling, awesome and long remembered event. Seamen and officers would have stood smeared in sweat, grease and blood, wide-eyed at what had happened. Some might have crossed themselves, perhaps even shed tears. A later poem pictured the end of the l'Orient:

> *The vast fabric, leaping from the sea,*
> *Rent with her throes of death-straught agony,*
> *High through the air upheaves her giant frame,*
> *And falls in thousand wrecks, a cataract of flame!*[474]

Then realisation would have seeped back that there remained a battle to be won, so orders, pushes and back to work. For another twenty minutes it had raged, a brief pause, then continuance until three in the morning. Hours and hours of hot work.

By dawn of the next day only two French ships had their colours aloft. *L'Artemise* (32) was deliberately set alight, rather than surrender. Another French frigate had sunk. The *Bellerophon* drifted away, dismasted, but later received assistance. Four French ships cut their cables and made their ponderous way to sea. The whole of the second day the victorious British took possession of various French ships. On the third day the *Timoleon* was burnt, and the *Tonnant* towed off the shore. As prizes had been secured exhaustion would have set in. It was a major victory, and all those concerned appreciated its importance. What efforts had been made! The French sent

---

473 *Ibid.* According to other sources, some men taken off the l'Orient were saved after the explosion.
474 Brereton (1863), 6.

ashore more than 3,000 men, and suffered 5,225 deaths; the British suffered 895 killed and wounded.[475] Thereafter it was called the Battle of the Nile by the British, the *Bataille d'Aboukir* by the French. Nelson retained a few ships on blockade off Alexandria, but quitted Egypt soon after. 'He was received in triumph, and every mark of honour at Naples.'[476] When the agent heard he had been outside and literally jumped for joy, screamed, and sent a donkey into fits. The Royal Navy had successfully regained the Mediterranean!

The agent grasped the fact that to emerge victorious against France and her allies the Royal Navy had to dominate all theatres both at sea and on shore. The Mediterranean was only one theatre but the significance of the Battle of the Nile lay in the fact that it destroyed more than a third of France's naval force, and stranded Bonaparte in Egypt. In Parliament, 20 November, Sir John Sinclair stood up and said there had never been such a naval victory in Britain's maritime history; 'in the battle of the Nile, it is well known that the French fleet was superior in number of men, in the number of guns, and in weight of metal: that they were anchored in a bay full of shoals, and protected by every contrivance that ingenuity could invent.'[477] He said it was the 'uncommon talents' of naval skill, discipline, courage and firmness that had brought victory. He also excoriated ministers for delays in the creation of a fleet to invest Malta; that Nelson had not been furnished with frigates, so that when *Leander* had been sent home with the news she had been captured; that transports in Alexandria had not been destroyed; that the destruction of the French fleet had only been occasioned by happenstance, as the French flagship had been too big for Alexandria's harbour so had anchored at Aboukir.

Nothing became easier by the result, but overall it opened up the eastern part of the theatre and restored esteem and dominance to the Royal Navy throughout the region. Britain and her allies thereby began to reassert their influence in that quarter. French Levantine commerce was eventually annihilated. Small Mediterranean states gained hope. With Bonaparte contained within Egypt, the largest regional power, the Ottoman Empire, became central to affairs. Ostensibly the whole Mediterranean coast of North Africa, the Levant, Greece and her islands, the Balkans and Turkey formed part of this Empire. In reality it had become a fractured and unruly affair. The whole Barbary coast comprised independent states. The British

---

475 *The New American Cyclopaedia of General Knowledge* (1869) Vol I, 38
476 Hazlitt (1803) Vol I, 123.
477 *The Parliamentary Register* (1799) Vol VII, 43 & 44.

knew their own interests depended upon the goodwill, if not alliance, of the Turks, so had sent Sidney Smith on a secret mission to join his brother at the Sublime Porte in Constantinople. It proved fruitful. After the Battle of the Nile the Annual Register of 1798 wrote in incredulous tones about Napoléon's bold attempt. 'It was believed that his object was to penetrate either by the isthmus of Suez, or by the Red Sea, to the Indian Ocean, to embark his troops, and, by a co-operation with Tippoo sultan, to endeavour the overthrow of the British empire in the East. To us it appears probable, that the directory in this wild undertaking had no definite, and certainly no rational object.'[478] A later edition added that 'Buonaparte had strengthened his army by the wrecks of the navy, and by recruits of different nations in Egypt',[479] and had tried to offer peace to the Turks. However, Aboukir emboldened the Porte to ally with Britain and Russia, and attack the French by way of Syria. Napoléon realized the threat to his venture, so had marched into Syria in advance of a combination. Many years later, while confined on St Helena, he talked about Sidney Smith and his men. He thought the Englishman to be '*mezzo pazzo*', or half-crazy, but his seamen had given the Turks a 'great advantage', and had shown them how to defend the walls.[480]

By the end of 1798 an uprising had broken out on Malta, that caused the French to retreat to Valletta. On 18 September the Portuguese fleet appeared offshore, later joined by part of the British fleet[481] returning from Egypt, and they supplied the Maltese with arms and ammunition. Thus commenced a long blockade. In December 1799 British and Neapolitan troops landed on the island.[482] On 4 September 1800 the French surrendered. Events were mirrored at Genoa and Corfu, and Minorca in 1798.

The British Mediterranean fleet became the dominant naval power in the region. That had been achieved through endeavours both at sea and on shore, with her fleet and those who had assisted her. It was one reason why the Royal Navy became, by 1800, a naval 'superpower'.

---

478 *The Annual Register* (1799), 313.
479 *Ibid.* (1801), 20.
480 Bourrienne (1885), 182.
481 This comprised the 74s *Northumberland* and *Généreux*, the troopship *Stately* (64), *Charon* (44), *Princess Charlotte* (40), *Pallas* (38), *Penelope* (36), the 32s *Success* and *Niger*, *Champion* (24), *Bonne Citoyenne*, the 16s *Port Mahon* and *Vincelo*, *Minorca* (14) and the bomb vessel S*trombolo*.
482 Sears (1848), 463. The Neapolitans were stated as 'Sicilian troops'.

Chapter 8

'Tis to Glory We Steer

The gunner calls it warlike practice. Practice. Practice. Practice. Seldom live fire, for the ship cannot afford to expend too much gunpowder. Hot work nonetheless. Running in. Running out. Physically moving forty-two hundredweight of metal, wood and heavy rope on a moving deck in tropical heat is hard work. Practice makes perfect, so gunnery practice takes place almost every day. Cuts, bruises, pulled muscles and jarred limbs are guaranteed. The rare times there is a rolling broadside it excites the blood. Fourteen long 18s and six long 9s shake the timbers and rattle the teeth. Gunpowder tingles nostrils.

His gun crew practises because the enemy always lies somewhere over the horizon. About to enter the Mona Passage, rumour has it the *Vengeance*[483] sails these waters and she is a thumping great 40-gun frigate. A difficult adversary for sure, but his ship also has long guns.

The long 18-pounder he crews, *Harsh Justice*, would certainly give it to the enemy and that makes his heart sing, as it does the rest of the gun crew from the lieutenant[484] of their division to the powder monkey[485].

With long experience he should have been gun captain, but his eyes are no longer what they used to be. Standing behind the gun, lanyard in hand, he would struggle to see beyond the barrel. So he acts as loader. The powder handler is new, a replacement of an older hand who died of yellow fever. They are one crew of fourteen guns a side. Fully manned the frigate heels under their weight.

The marine drummer stands ready, until the order is given, then makes a relentless thrumming rat-a-tat-tat. Cabin partitions and useless lumber disappear, and with a delighted confusion the men rush down hatchways to

---

483   She shipped twenty-eight long 18-pounders, sixteen long 8-pounders, and eight 36-pounder carronades.
484   Lieutenant George Milne was killed in action against the French ship.
485   Often a ship's boy.

stand by their guns. Ordnance is manhandled to face the gunports. Then an expectant silence.

The man at the rear right of the gun makes a check and shouts out *Clear!* It is his turn, so he takes hold of a long wormer and reaches forward to carefully place it in the barrel and ram it down. A few deft turns then he withdraws the wormer, certain no detritus is present from the previous firing, then stands aside to hand the wormer to the man behind him at the rear left of the gun. The man at the rear right places a thumb stall over the touch-hole, before the front right loader reaches forward and rams a wet sponge of lambskin down the barrel. When withdrawn the sponge is reversed to show a ram-head. The gun is ready to load.

The powder monkey has brought the cartridge from below. The powder handler takes it, moves forward and hands the cartridge over to him. He takes it and places it deftly into the barrel. The other loader follows with the rammer, and pushes the cartridge down to the bottom of the barrel. The gun-captain takes his pricker and jams it down the touch-hole, to confirm the cartridge is indeed home. *Home!* he shouts, and stands back. The lieutenant waits for all crews to reach the same point then barks out the command, *Shot your guns!*

The powder handler collects a cannon ball, the shot, and hands it over. When he has it in both hands he reaches forward, his back strained, to push it down the barrel. He takes a wad from the man at rear left and places it in the barrel. The right front loader rams it all home. Everyone stands back from the gun.

Run out your guns! Grunts and bunching back muscles as the dead weight of the gun is heaved forward by tackles. The barrel of the gun reaches through the gun port. *Train your guns!* The two rear men, and the powder handler, take hold of long handspikes[486] and place them under the gun to heave it slightly to the right. The two rear men place their spikes underneath the barrel, raise it slightly, and the powder handler puts a wooden wedge under the barrel. *Prime your guns!* The gun captain takes hold of his horn of powder and shakes some onto the touch hole. With lanyard in hand he crouches, this newfangled gunlock an 'innovation' not universally liked by the men, and looks down the barrel to the deep blue sea beyond. He raises his hand when happy with the sighting.

All gun captains' hands are soon raised. *Fire!* Lanyards are pulled back with a jerk and the guns 'fire'. In this case not so, as no powder has been

---

486 Long wooden paddles.

used. The men have to artificially run back their guns to pretend a recoil has taken place. More grunts, more effort, and more strained muscles. A stubbed toe and a muffled curse. Sweat on the brow. Allowance is given for the time needed to heave the guns, as the ship's roll makes it difficult. *Serve your vents!* The captain closes the touch-hole, and the process starts all over again.

They want to achieve one terrible, full-throated broadside to shock and overawe the enemy. Then three minutes to fire again, with the fervent hope of three salvoes in five minutes. That is the benchmark they ceaselessly practice for. It could bring them victory. However, they are seldom fully manned, and heat and fatigue often slow them down. Practice, practice, practice, nonetheless.

In one past action, when he served on board the *Pique*[487], he had caught a kind of red fever. It had been as though the heat of the guns penetrated his very skin, and the deck, men, gun, gun-port and sea had all taken on a red glow.[488] It had worried him at first. There happened to have been a red sunset the night before, so it must have been a portent of what had happened. Since that time all other engagements have made him wonder whether the red fever would return. It has not so far, but then most engagements have been short.

Evening practice is over, so they clear away their buckets, rams and sponges and lash the guns to the ship's side. Everything is inspected. Finally, a ladle of precious water is doled out to sip, and wipe the brow. The new powder handler is pleased with himself. Normal routine returns. Just over the horizon a French frigate sails on unawares.

The *Seine* (38), a previous capture, entered the Mona Passage between Hispaniola and Puerto Rico on 19 August 1800. She sighted the *Vengeance* (40) on 20 August, out of Curaçao[489] and bound for France. A chase immediately commenced. By midnight the British ship had to fall back with damaged rigging, but quick repairs had allowed her to continue the chase. On the morning of 25 August the *Seine* brought the *Vengeance* 'to close action.'[490] For the next ninety minutes she fired her guns in utmost anger, to dismast the *Vengeance* and wreck her enough she had to strike her colours.

---

487 The *Pique* captured the *Seine*, but had to be abandoned. Her crew then became the crew of HMS *Seine*.

488 These words mirror Goethe's account of 'cannon-fever', that he personally observed at the Battle of Valmy in 1792. From Goethe (1884), 116.

489 A Dutch colony.

490 As written by the ship's commander, Captain Milne, in a letter to Lord H. Seymour. As found in Southey, *West Indies* (1827) Vol III, 176 & 177. The casualty figures are from this source.

The *Seine* certainly suffered in return, one lieutenant and twelve seamen killed and twenty-nine wounded.

Military glory inferred honour, praise, fame and renown, but 'the paths of Glory lead but to the grave.' After this era ended the pursuit of glory was often seen as folly. Sir Charles Napier bemoaned how France, of the late 1840s, still teemed with it but 'the love of military glory is a strong disease in all countries.'[491] In that same decade the pursuit of glory was denigrated by Frederick Augustus Farley when he wrote, 'And this is Glory! Methought, as the funeral procession passed near my residence.... . As that brilliant cortege defiled through the city...and the plaintive wail of those fine bands rose and fell...the rich and tastefully decorated coffin and the military insignia of the deceased displayed upon it...I involuntarily asked myself, is this the reward of so much sacrifice? A young man - in the freshness of his strength - exchanges a peaceful and happy home for a camp. Why?'[492] During the war occasioned by the French Revolution the pursuit of glory had been extolled. Pride, pomp, and circumstance[493] all had their place. Countless cutting-outs, raids, engagements and sea battles showed reckless courage and bravado. The simple sailor, cutlass in hand, who jumped onto a burning deck probably had 'glory' in some part of his mind, as well as survival and prize money.

No British naval school of gunnery existed at this time.[494] Effective gunnery had been down to individual captains. 'Many ships...were brought into admirable fighting order by dint of the spontaneous exertions of their commanders.'[495] It had been a haphazard affair. Some captains' main concerns were to man their ships, put to sea, attend to navigation and maintain blockade or patrol against a mostly passive enemy. If the weather turned foul gunnery practice suffered, and even in good weather it required time to learn and improve efficiency. Seldom did weather remain settled for long, and as men died, deserted or fell sick other men had to take their place.

The French, with their mania for *égalité*, ruinously rid themselves of their elite marine gunners[496] even before Great Britain entered the war. The revolutionary government had considered it 'patriotic' not to have an

---

491 Napier (1850), 24.
492 Farley (1848), 3 & 4. Farley was an American pastor talking about the Mexican War.
493 The words of Major Jackson in 1851.
494 One was created in 1830, onboard the hulk *Excellent,* at the top of Portsmouth harbour in Fareham Creek, and later moved to Whale Island.
495 Hall, B., *Fragments of Voyages* (1841), 127.
496 Their *corps royal cannoniers-matelots* was disbanded in 1792 in favour of *corps d'artillerie et d'infanterie de marine,* that was itself disbanded in 1793.

exclusive corps of gun crews on their warships. They argued that any true 'Frenchman' should be allowed to work a cannon. It had been deemed their right, and French gunnery suffered. Throughout the war actions at sea show British gunnery being more effective than their enemy's, although the *Seine* showed that the French always posed a danger.

From 1793 until 1800 abstracts and returns show the size of the British navy in any one year. The first one, 'An abstract of the ships and vessels belonging to the British Navy at the commencement of the year 1793'[497] set out all the ships and vessels then in commission, in ordinary, building or so ordered, but not their names. It stated their 'class' and armament carried. They were all floating gun batteries. The only first rate in commission at the end of 1792 typically carried the heaviest ordnance on her lower gun deck, with each successive deck above carrying smaller calibre guns: twenty-eight 32 pounder guns on the lower gun deck, twenty-eight 24 pounder guns on the middle gun deck, twenty-eight 12 pounders on the upper gun deck, twelve 12 pounders on the quarterdeck and four 12 pounders on the fo'c'sle. In total she carried one hundred guns that could throw a broadside weight of 1,048 lbs of metal, assuming she was fully manned with a fit and competent crew.

Naval guns fired round shot, double-headed, chain, canister and grapeshot. Round shot were hefty round balls used to batter a ship's hull. Double-headed shot, or bar shot, were two 'rounds' joined together by a bar used to destroy masts and disable a ship. Chain-shot consisted of two hollow balls, or hemispheres, joined by a short chain. When fired, the two balls separated to the length of the chain. Used to hit and disable enemy rigging, there were occasions when chain-shot cut a sail from the yard. A canister-shot was 'a metallic cylinder about one caliber in length, filled with balls and closed at both ends with wooden or metal disks.'[498] Upon discharge from a gun, the case was destroyed that forced fragments to move independently of each other within a short frontal cone. They had limited opportunity for use as they only covered a distance of 300 yards. The British Mariner's Vocabulary of 1801 stated that 'case shot, or canister shot…are principally used when very near to clear the decks of the enemy. Besides these there are others of a more pernicious kind, used by privateers, pirates, &c.; such as langrage shot, star shot, fire-arrows, &c.'[499] In a primitive form, case shot had also been called 'langridge', and small stones, nails, bits of

---

497 Actually printed later.
498 Moore, *The British Mariner's Vocabulary* (1801): 'shot'.
499 Moore, *ibid.*

metal and anything heavy that could be propelled were used. Grapeshot was a projectile of small balls or metal pieces, even bullets, clumped in small quilted canvas bags. In appearance they resembled a bag of large 'grapes'.

At the start of the war most belligerents controlled overseas colonies.[500] For economic, and strategic purposes Africa, India, North America and the West Indies were vitally important to Great Britain. The West Indies originated close to a fifth of all British imports.[501] The East Indies and India were increasingly a major contributor to her wealth. Africa offered a few scattered waystations to help with the long passage between Europe and the East Indies, and continued to be a source of the slave trade. Canada was important for both her fisheries and timber. Within the West Indies Britain controlled numerous islands including Barbados, Antigua, that had a dockyard, and Jamaica that also had a dockyard. Her colonies had to be protected, and the war furnished hopes of adding further islands to Britain's control. Many ships sailed between them. Despite the war, and serious losses incurred by privateers, some ship owners managed to expand their fleets and increase their wealth. They made the most of the gains Britain made, from 1793 until the peace of 1802.

Captured islands had to be supplied, and their produce sent to market. One ship's master, a lone trader, worked the Leeward Islands and Halifax, and later added some captured islands to his routes. He therefore came to know the movements of the Royal Navy's Leeward and Jamaica squadrons very well. As soon as Britain entered the war the battered Leeward flagship, *Trusty* (50), had been superseded by larger and more powerful ships. The first time the trader came across a fleet, as it approached Barbados, he had been taken aback by their number. To have a ship of the line off his beam, row upon row of gunports high above his own deck, with distant faces looking down and some wit making comment, masts and sails far, far above his own, was enough to make him gulp in awe. His crew quivered in fright.

The trader knew the West Indies theatre to be wide and extensive, with scattered islands throughout. It had always been difficult to gain a naval presence everywhere. The general direction of the wind blows east to west,[502] from the Atlantic towards the Caribbean Sea, and that made sailing times quicker *to* islands than away. That was why the navy had divided itself into two main 'stations', one station centred upon Jamaica, and the other on the Leeward Islands. The Leeward Station, in the east, covered the fringe

---

500 Including Denmark, not then at war.
501 Around 20% in 1793, increasing to 28% by 1800.
502 The hurricane season was always a major concern.

of islands that trends in a crescent shape southwards from Puerto Rico to Trinidad. The navy only had to control a few select islands there to help control the remainder. In 1793 the French owned Guadeloupe, Martinique, Sainte-Lucie, petty Saint-Martin and nearby Tobago. They became obvious targets. The trader had once spent time on Martinique, so he knew it to be strongly defended. It did not surprise him when it had, at first, been ignored. 'On February 10, 1793, a few days only after notice had been received of the French declaration of war, directions were transmitted to Major General Cuyler, the commander in chief of the British troops in the Windward Islands, and to Sir John Laforey, who commanded in the naval department, to attempt the reduction of Tobago.'[503]

Laforey and Cuyler had been resident on Barbados, and needed to collect troops from other islands. A friend of the trader's offered his vessel to transport some of them. Once collected they moved briskly to avoid the 'sickly' season, roughly July to October, although most islands admitted sick troops to hospitals between October and February too.[504] On 12 April they set sail, the *Trusty* accompanied by the *Nautilus* (16) and the *Hind* (10). Two days later they had anchored in Great Courland Bay on the west coast of Tobago. Some 470 troops, thirty-two of them marines, landed and marched across the island to take the fort at Scarborough. The trader later read how it had been an easy and useful acquisition, and two French royalist ships were found to reside there. The *Ferme* (74) and *Calypso* (36)[505] willingly joined the British in a later attempt to take Martinique.

The war had arrived. Such things were all new to him, for he had missed the last one, but what he came to understand was the almost annual alteration of naval commanders on the Leeward Station. When he returned from business on another island he found Laforey had already been relieved by Vice Admiral Gardner. A whole new fleet had come with him. There had been the *Queen* (98), *Duke* (90), the 74s *Hannibal, Hector, Monarch* and *Orion*, the 32s *Heroine* and *Iphigenia*, the *Rattlesnake* (14), and various transports, with 1,100 troops and 800 armed French sympathisers.[506] They were imposing, but their attempt to take Martinico failed. Troops landed

---

503 Thompson, G.A., *Dictionary of America and the West Indies* (1815) Vol V, 286.

504 Shown in tables prepared from the Army Medical Department and War Office returns, as laid out in *Statistical Report on the Sickness, Mortality, and Invaliding among the troops of the West Indies* (1838), appendix pages. The years covered are 1817 to 1836 and obviously do not include wounds from war.

505 They later sailed off and joined with the Spanish on Trinidad. The '470' troops stated in James, Vol I, 127.

506 James, 127.

on 14 and 15 May, to attack the main town, but French royalists fired upon themselves. The British were forced to withdraw, and so quit the island. Later, British newspapers arrived that informed how Lord Wycombe in Parliament had argued for an investigation into this expedition. His lordship had said that by its failure 'Jamaica was left unprotected', and the French allowed to prey upon trade routes. He added, 'But for the insubordination of the French crews, Newfoundland, Halifax, and our other possessions in that part of the world, would most probably have fallen a sacrifice to the force which was fitted out against them.'[507] The trader had made another journey, and when he returned the *Hannibal* and *Hector* had been sent to Jamaica and Gardner had returned home. So ended the first regional campaign of the war.

During the sickly season the trader much preferred to sail far north to Nova Scotia. When he returned in early 1794 Vice Admiral Sir John Jervis had arrived with expectations to deal with a whole range of islands.[508] He brought with him another fleet of ships, the *Boyne* (98), the 74s *Vengeance* and *Irresistible*, the 64s *Asia* and *Veteran*, the 44s *Assurance* and *Ulysses*, the *Beaulieu* (40), *Santa-Margarita* (36), the 32s *Blanche*, *Ceres*, *Solebay*, *Terpsichore*, *Quebec* and *Winchelsea*, the 28s *Blonde* and *Rose*, the 16s *Avenger*, *Nautilus*, *Seaflower*, *Rattlesnake* and *Zebra*, the bomb ship *Vesuvius* (8), the hospital ship *Roebuck*, and store-ships *Dromedary* and *Woolwich*. General Sir Charles Grey commanded the embarked regiments.[509]

Later on he read how Lord Wycombe – by then he could almost see him in his mind's eye – had considered the attached naval commanders to have 'known abilities', but 'their force had been so maimed and curtailed previous to their final departure, that he doubted if ministers themselves could entertain any very sanguine hopes of their exertions.'[510] However Jervis and Grey were determined men. The trader had been in port when Martinique fell on 22 March, after forts Bourbon and Royal capitulated. A cutting out expedition took the *Bienvenu* (20) 'under a smart fire of grapeshot and musketry from ramparts and parapet of the fort';[511] and he was at sea when St Lucie fell on 4 April, after a three-days conflict.

507 *An Impartial Report of the Debates That Occur in the Two Houses of Parliament* (1794) Vol I, 61.
508 Norie (1842), 247. The islands were Martinique, Sainte Lucie, Les Îles des Saintes, Marie-Galante, and La Désirade island off Guadeloupe.
509 James, 240.
510 *An Impartial Report of the Debates That Occur in the Two Houses of Parliament,* Vol I, 61.
511 Norie, *ibid.*, 247. She was renamed HMS *Undaunted*.

Guadeloupe, an island shaped like a butterfly, fell on 12 April. Other islands were 'secured' by 20 April. However, the speed they were taken meant only small garrisons were landed. Some people later argued that the loss to France was of a higher importance than the gain to Britain, so the revolutionaries had far more determination to take them back. When French reinforcements arrived on 3 June to recapture Guadeloupe they succeeded. The British fleet had dispersed by then, and traders like himself had to sail elsewhere to avoid the conflict. Jervis collected what men he could and landed them on the eastern 'wing' of Guadeloupe on 19 June; but from then until 10 December that island was ceaselessly defended until the British had to concede defeat. Jervis quit the station with yellow fever.

When the trader arrived back from a trip to Halifax he found another commander had been appointed. The gossip in town ran with how Vice Admiral Caldwell had taken part in the Battle of the Glorious First of June, but since then had not been happy. According to some his name had not been put forward for a gold medal. He never did see the admiral, who left the station within six months to return home and ignore any further dealings with the Admiralty[512]. Lo and behold, Laforey returned on 9 May 1795 as his relief.

With his second tenure Laforey hoisted his flag on board the *Majestic* (74). With the fall of the Dutch Republic her islands and colonies became targets. Everyone whom the trader knew, planters and ship owners alike, became excited at the prospect of new trade routes. Berbice, Curaçao, Demerara, Essequibo and Suriname were often topics of conversation. The French, though, were never idle and successfully sponsored slave revolts on St Vincent, Grenada and Dominica. They happened to be British islands. The situation on Sainte Lucie turned sour and had to be evacuated. British hands were then full.

Back at sea the trader lost all sense of time, and he always had to read later about events. Laforey worked alongside General Sir Ralph Abercromby, but the rain and sickly season forced them to wait. A vast number of troops were ordered from Britain, their transports placed under Rear Admiral Sir Hugh Cloberry Christian, with '200 sail of transports and West Indiamen, on board of which were embarked upwards of 16,000 troops.'[513] Their story became something all sailors could appreciate. They sailed as expected, late in the year, on 16 November.

---

512 James, B., *Journal of Rear-Admiral Bartholomew James 1752-1828* (1896), 263.
513 The fleet is laid out in Steel's *Naval Chronologist.*

They were due to arrive in the West Indies after the sickly season. However, Britain and the Atlantic in deep winter are places of mighty storms. The trader himself had been off Halifax and ran into a terrible gale. When he limped back home, his rigging and sails in serious need of repair, he learned how the transports sent from Britain had had a torrid time of it. In the English Channel the whole fleet had to scatter before the wind. Some ships managed to reach Torbay, Portland and Portsmouth, but some were wrecked and 200 bodies were washed ashore south of Bridport. Reconstituted, the fleet put out again on 9 December: the 98s *Glory* and *Impregnable*, the 74s *Colossus, Alfred* and *Irresistible*, the 64s *Trident, Dictator* and *Lion, Abergavenny* (54), the 50s *Hindostan, Grampus* and *Malabar*, the *Alcmene* (32), and *Babet* (24).[514] This 'ill-fated' fleet had also been hit by storms. After seven weeks' utmost misery the *Glory, Impregnable, Colossus, Irresistible, Trident, Lion, Alcmene* and fifty transports and merchantmen crawled back to Spithead. Many did manage to arrive in the West Indies, but the rest foundered or were taken as prizes. Christian had to rehoist his flag on the *Thunderer* (74), gather as many ships as he could, and sail for a third time on 20 March. He finally arrived at Barbados one month later.

In the West Indies disease never distinguished between class, nor the time of year. Admiral Laforey contracted yellow fever and had to resign his post on 24 April, in favour of newly arrived Admiral Christian. Laforey returned home and died on passage. The troops sent out from Britain, together with some seamen, were landed on Sainte Lucie, and that island finally surrendered 25 May 1796. Sir Abercrombie wrote in his dispatches, 'Rear-admiral Sir Hugh Christian, and the royal navy, have never ceased to show the utmost alacrity in forwarding the public service. To their skill and unremitting labour the success which has attended his majesty's arms is in a great measure due. By their efforts alone the artillery was advanced to the batteries, and every co-operation, which could possibly be expected or desired, had been afforded in the fullest manner.'[515]

---

514 *Naval Chronicle* XXI, page 181, and Moore, A.W., The Manx Note Book (1885), 100.
515 Moore, *ibid.* According to the *Naval Chronicle* Vol XXI (p.183) the ships that managed to take part in the reduction of the island comprised 74s *Alfred, Canada, Ganges, Minotaur, Thunderer,* and *Vengeance,* the 54s *Abergavenny, Charon, Hindostan, Madras,* the *Woolwich* (44), *Beaulieu* (40), the 38s *Arethusa* and *Hebe, Undaunted* (36) the *Astrea* (32) the *Laurel* (28), *Tourterelle* (20), *Beaver, Bull Dog, Fury,* and *Pelican* (16) *Victorieuse* (14), and the *Terror* (8).

Christian's tenure had been unexpected, and so he only had to hold the post until another relief appeared on station. Rear Admiral Harvey arrived on board *Prince of Wales* (98), but Christian remained on station until October 1796. Demerara, Essequibo and Berbice were soon afterwards secured by the *Scipio* (64), *Malabar* (54), the 40s *Undaunted* and *Pique*, and the *Babet*.[516] The trader heard how Dutch commanders readily joined with the British, and even helped to repulse a Spanish incursion made across the Orinoco river region. That must have been hot and difficult work. Soon afterwards British squadrons had sailed to deal with the revolts on St Vincent and Grenada.

By then the British government had become concerned with the seeming decline in their West Indies trade. The war had allowed privateers and pirates to take their toll. An account made after the war laid out the types of vessels captured, or recaptured, and their various cargoes. They were vessels such as the brig *Patty*, taken off Antigua, laden with American produce; the brigantine *Despatch*, taken off Saint-Domingue, laden with lumber and provisions; the schooner *Active*, captured off Barbados, laden with rum and sugar[517] – small craft involved in a very lucrative trade. Stated imports from the West Indies to Great Britain stood at £4,128,047 in 1792, £5,294,742 in 1794, £4,645,972 in 1795, and £4,541,217 in 1796.[518] From a peak in 1794 imports sharply declined, and a perturbed Parliament made approaches to France for a possible peace. The British had offered to return to France her lost Caribbean colonies but the French were then in no mood to negotiate. Nothing came of it and the war continued.

For the 1797 campaign it was planned to capture both Trinidad and Porto Rico.[519] Troops embarked on 12 February from Fort Royal on Martinique, aboard transports that rendezvoused with other ships off the Grenadines. That fleet sighted Trinidad on 16 February.[520] A local Spanish squadron then lay at anchor, in Chaguaramas Bay, at the north western tip of the island.[521] There were four Spanish ships of the line and one frigate and all but one were eventually burned. Troops landed on 17 February and the

---

516 Dalton (1855) Vol I, 244. This source does not mention the *Scipio*.
517 *American State Papers* (1859) Vol VI, 563-6.
518 In 1798 it stood at £6,390,658. from Edwards (1819) Vol II, 596.
519 Accounts of the time do not appear to use 'Puerto Rico'.
520 The *Prince of Wales* (98), the 74s *Bellona, Invincible, Scipio, Vengeance; Arethusa* (38), *Alarm* (32), *Zebra* (18), *Favourite* (16), the 14s *Thorn* and *Victorieuse, Zephyr* (10), the bomb *Terror*.
521 Marshall, J., *Royal Naval Biography* (1823) Vol I, 112. This account gives the bay as 'Shagaramus'.

island 'surrendered' the next day, but fighting seemingly continued for days afterwards. Porto Rico proved to be a very different proposition. The expedition for that island assembled, and sailed from Martinico on 8 April. It rendezvoused off St Kitts, took pilots and guides on board, and sighted San Juan on 17 April. Later dispatches by General Abercrombie described how the fleet struggled to find an entrance. 'The whole of the North side of this island is bounded by a reef, and it was with much difficulty that a narrow channel was discovered.'[522] Smaller vessels made the passage, and troops could be landed the next day, but the local castle commanded their approach. To reach that fortification required the passage of a lagoon with enemy gunboats en route. General Abercrombie bombarded the town for a while but decided to withdraw. Troops re-embarked on the night of 30 April and inevitably some ordnance had to be left behind. Again, the general mentioned the good conduct of naval seamen, some 300 of them who had been landed, and the good organisation of transports. The fleet thereby departed.

There were no major expeditions for 1798, as by then the whole region, apart from Suriname, had been pacified. Only trade and the pursuit of privateers continued. The trader spent weeks at sea, his holds mostly full, with all the eyes of his crew on the horizon for any strange sail. That year an incredible ninety-nine privateers were taken throughout the West Indies, 'eighty-nine French, eight Spanish, and two Dutch'.[523]

Vice Admiral Lord Seymour arrived on the Leeward Station in 1799 and remained until June 1800. He hoisted his flag on board the *Prince of Wales*. The trader had actually heard of him, for that admiral had made the news by championing the use of epaulettes. By then the Royal Navy controlled the Leeward and Windward islands. Any small, and isolated, foreign colony would surrender as soon as a British squadron arrived offshore. Suriname[524] was taken after one small squadron, the *Prince of Wales* and *Invincible* (74) with five frigates and two small vessels, sailed from St Lucia and Martinique on 31 July 1799. They sighted the Suriname river on 11 August but could not anchor for five days. On 19 August the frigates and small vessels moved up the river for a demonstration, while troops took possession of Braam's Point at the mouth of the river. It was more than enough to convince the governor at Paramaribo to peacefully surrender the next day.

---

522 *The Field of Mars* (1801), under 'POR'.
523 Southey, T., *West Indies* (1827) Vol III, 149. This happened to be the peak year.
524 The British spelled it as 'Surinam'. The British fleet found in Southey, 163.

Seymour resigned his position to take up command of the Jamaica station and his relief, yet another, had been Rear Admiral Sir John Duckworth who served until 1801. On 22 July 1800 the French managed to occupy the western part of Dutch controlled Curaçao. When the *Néréide* (36) appeared off the island on 10 September, the governor much preferred 'British to French protection, [so] took an opportunity of informing captain Watkins of the Nereide, that he would permit the English to garrison the forts which commanded the capital, if they would assist him in the expulsion of the French.'[525] The French withdrew and the *Néréide* took possession on 23 September. Forty-four ships were found to be in the harbour. Soon afterwards the trader sailed there to open up negotiations for commerce. Merchantmen were never far behind.

The trader purchased a second vessel, despite the fact that costs had increased, and with pride gave his son command. He therefore became interested in the western range of the theatre where the Jamaica Station had remit within the western Caribbean Sea, the Gulf of Mexico, and the Gulf of Honduras. He knew that this station had not had as high a rate of removal of commanders as the Leeward Station had. Saint-Domingue remained their main concern. France could not furnish a proper fleet to protect the colony, and internal struggles permitted pirates to harass merchants on the Windward Passage, that is the exit of the West Indies between Cap-Haïtien and Cuba. He remembered how some owners had long complained about that situation. French royalists fled to various islands, including Jamaica, and had asked for British help as early as 1791. When intelligence came that a small port called Môle-Saint Nicolas, that commanded the narrowest part of the Windward Passage, was ripe for seizure it had been thought a British reduction could be made.

The French, so desperate to retain their island, had proclaimed an end to slavery[526] with hopes that freed slaves would resist the British. Some released slaves stayed on their plantations but a vast number fled into the interior. White settlers were few, and a large proportion were said to be 'desperate adventurers who had nothing to lose, and everything to gain, by confusion and anarchy...but a very small number were cordially attached to the English.'[527] The first British troops for Saint-Domingue sailed from Jamaica on 9 September 1793, on transports in company with *Europa* (50)

---

525 Smollett, *The Critical Review* (1800) Vol XIII, 579.
526 Burke (1806), 109.
527 Edwards (1819) Vol II, 153.

and the 32s *Penelope, Iphigenia* and *Hermione*.[528] They had navigated for the long finger of land called the Tiburon peninsula. The frigates dispersed early to seize ten merchantmen on the southern end of the finger of land, while *Europa* sailed to Jérémie upon the northern coast of the peninsula. She arrived there on 19 September. Troops were so warmly greeted[529] it was decided to leave them and sail north to seize Môle-Saint Nicolas. Assured of a quiet coast the *Europa* anchored off that town on 21 September. To fend off the enemy, Commodore Ford could only muster his marines and seamen, and they had to provide the garrison until 12 October. The town proved useful,[530] but the small force had been woefully inadequate, and yellow fever ran rampant. To reinforce losses, troops were sent over from Jamaica, which was robbing Peter to pay Paul.[531]

In May 1794 the navy supported the assault upon Port-au-Prince, the main town of the colony, with the *Irresistible* (74), the 64s *Belliqueux* and *Sceptre*, the *Europa,* and some frigates and sloops.[532] They reached the harbour, bombarded the town, and secured the port by 4 June. Sailors must have been very grateful for the twenty-two prizes taken in the harbour. The wealthiest colony in the whole region had seemingly been taken. Yet yellow fever, 'black vomit', caused mayhem. The 1794 sickly season killed 600 British troops, while the French received a steady supply of reinforcements because the Royal Navy could not secure all ports, harbours, and roadsteads.[533] Never enough British troops were sent to fully secure the island (although 7,000 did arrive in 1795), insurgency increased and privateers roamed freely. In 1795 Spain ceded her side of Hispaniola to France, and from then until 1798 Toussaint l'Ouverture commanded the armies of Saint-Domingue. The British therefore had to abandon the interior and fall back upon Port-au-Prince.[534] Coastal supply convoys were attacked. In consequence, British influence lessened. It was a slow collapse. By April 1798 it had become obvious the colony could not be maintained, therefore the British quit.

By the time of their departure, it appeared, to Spanish colonists at least, that the British were weak. They therefore attempted a reduction

---

528 Brenton (1823) Vol III, 8.
529 James considered it one of the finest harbours in the West Indies: James, W. (1859) Vol I, 130.
530 Brenton's words. The town was backed by hills.
531 An old English expression meaning to solve one problem by making another.
532 Marshall, J., *Royal Naval Biography* (1823) Vol I, 805.
533 Two small ports especially: Jacmel and Les Cayes, on the southern coast of the Tiburon peninsula.
534 Which is not to say that L'Ouverture did not suffer setbacks.

of Saint George's Caye, off Honduras,[535] inhabited by woodcutters called 'Baymen'. A small squadron of gunboats and the *Merlin* (16) offered their only protection. Fourteen Spanish sail and a flotilla of small boats appeared offshore, but only nine small vessels could make the attempt due to difficult shoals and reefs. Over two successive days the British held them off. This event helped maintain the colony for Great Britain, and demonstrated how she did in fact control the whole region.

The trader had been vaguely aware that the West Indies theatre, during this whole period, was not a theatre of large fleet actions. It became signified by expeditions, cutting outs, small engagements and the war against privateers. Prize monies were plentiful, and losses equally so. What he did not see were the countless letters sent from commanders and resident admirals to Evan Nepean in London. They opened with the usual, 'I beg leave to acquaint you,' 'I have the honour to acquaint you, for their Lordships' information,' etc. Details were given about the capture of prizes and such like. Endings ran along the lines of, 'Your most obedient humble servant,' 'I am, Sir, &c. &c. &c.,' All were dutiful and all were respectful.

By 1800 naval commanders had achieved much throughout the theatre, and it was assumed Britain had enhanced her West Indies trade to the benefit of the nation. However, some argued that 'by conquering and improving colonies of our enemies, we have incalculably depreciated our own...that, while our manufactures and our public treasury derive an ample revenue from this branch of our commerce, the individuals immediately engaged in it experience only disappointment and loss.'[536] The trader had himself complained about a 'mistaken policy' that artificially raised British transportation prices, so that foreign bottoms could operate at half the cost of British merchants. Such were the consequences of war.

The conflict had not unduly caused the regional 'nursery of seamen' to suffer, despite the loss of seamen to disease. By 1804 there operated more than 800 merchant ships to the West Indies with 17,000 merchant seamen.[537] The theatre was close enough to European waters that those very seamen could be subsumed into the navy if needed, and upon arrival in the West Indies they helped replenish naval crews decimated by disease. Dysentery and yellow fever were recurring problems. Few people so afflicted, if they survived, ever returned to fighting condition, and both killed hundreds of men and women. James Anderson, a doctor, wrote in 1798 that the region

---

535 Modern day Belize.
536 Lowe (1808), xiii.
537 Lowe, 7.

appeared to have two 'species' of disease 'indiscriminately called Yellow Fever'.[538]

Hurricanes and gales also sowed destruction. Notable hurricanes of the era were August 1793 along the northern Antilles, August 1794 at Cuba, August 1795 at Antigua, and October 1796 at the Bahamas.[539]

Yet the West Indies trade, long steeped in literature and folklore, maintained high wages and an allure few places could ever manage. It encouraged young men to take to the sea. Gains made in the theatre pleased many. In Parliament Mr Pitt rose in 1801 and stated that the acquisition of Trinidad had been the 'most valuable' for protection of the Leeward Islands and as a base of operations towards South America; and such a naval port was, he said, 'our great want in that quarter'.[540]

'Our great want' could be what spurred Great Britain to maintain, and secure, places far removed from home waters. With numerous journeys to Nova Scotia the trader knew that nearby British provinces, despite a French naval presence along the coasts of the United States,[541] had enabled the continuation of their trade – timber from Lower and Upper Canada and salt fish from Newfoundland. The war could easily have destroyed those interests, but a small naval squadron kept them secure. He had smiled when he heard how Saint Pierre and Miquelon, both French possessions, had been easily secured.[542] Salt fish remained in high demand throughout the war, and British West Country fishermen who had traditionally sailed across the Atlantic to fish those waters either suffered, or had to settle in the region. 'Want' created large social changes and not just with Britain.

There had been much uncertainty, and in March 1793 Nova Scotia made preparation for 'calling out the internal force of the province',[543] to offer resistance to any French invasion, but the French had poured most of her resources into her army; her navy duly suffered and could not press the issue. Britain made the most of the vacuum thereby created.

The trader circulated within a group of people never remote from the outside world. They voraciously read newspapers, books and pamphlets for any news of events far and wide. They shared news and gossip. Whereas

---

538 Anderson (1798).
539 Schomburgk (1847), 692.
540 *The Parliamentary History of England* (1820) Vol XXXVI, 64.
541 Woodfall (1794), 223. In 1794 it was reported this comprised the frigate *Ambuscade*, the 22s *Marseillois* and *Perdrix*, *Good Intent* (16) and the 10s *Astrea* and *Cerf*.
542 In 1793.
543 Woodfall, 219.

Canada, Africa and India might have been a long way off in terms of distance, the constant arrival of ships and vessels from those places telescoped them into their homes. Ships' crews told of isolated forts and stations dotted along the coast of western Africa, of remote islands like St Helena, and British factories in India.

The trader had a brother long resident in India, and he received five letters from him between 1793 and 1800. In one letter his brother had written of Britain's factories along the coasts of Coromandel and Malabar, the Andamans, interests in the straits of Malacca and upon Sumatra. Some were more than five weeks sailing from one another,[544] and the monsoon season significantly lengthened that time. At the start of the war the Royal Navy had but a very small naval force in the whole region. At Madras there had only been the *Crown* (64),[545] and at Calcutta a few frigates and sloops. However, the war gave an urge to seize other colonies. British warships sailed forth from Britain and over successive years accumulated numerous sites. Pondicherry succumbed in 1793, the Cape of Good Hope and Trincomalee in 1795, Colombo, Amboyna, Banda and Foul Point in 1796. Britain had a determination to benefit by the conflict.

Colonists, settlers, plantation owners and merchants all came to know of, and appreciate, the strength and reach of the Royal Navy. A squadron or fleet in local waters lessened their fears and increased their hopes. Some merchants were ruined, some struggled, and a few made great profits. Most felt pride. Some of them might have sung out loud, *'tis to glory we steer!* Men and women, such as the trader and his family, witnessed at first hand the constant arrival of ships of the line, frigates and unrated vessels upon foreign stations. Heart of oak were those ships, jolly tars were their men and they conquered again and again. Everyone of them comprehended how, between 1793 and 1800, there had been created a naval 'superpower'.

---

544 Brenton (1823) Vol I, 11.
545 James, W., 131.

EPILOGUE

Cheer Up My Lads, With One Heart Let Us Sing

Tick. Tick. Tick. Time had gone by. Eventually there were eight years of battles, actions and cutting-outs. For civilians, like the parson and the petty officer's wife, those naval feats were expressed through freedoms of the city, swords bestowed, ships made famous and heroes made. The Royal Navy both concerned and delighted them. In Portsmouth the parson had been constantly amazed with the number of ships and vessels he saw put into commission. Never before, he said, had the navy had such a fleet. *Yes, she truly is our 'wooden wall'.* The petty officer's wife disliked how warships remained longer at sea, but at least her worries about scurvy had lessened. Whenever her husband's ship had returned home it had joined dozens, if not hundreds, of craft that cluttered the harbour and Spithead. Town residents were pleased to see them, because if they had not, Britain would not have been safe for even one week.[546] Invasion or blockade would have ruined them and everyone would have starved. They all knew it.

In 1800, as people had walked the streets of Portsmouth, they came across the hubbub of a large and prosperous town. Yard workers, traders and agents jostled sailors in the streets and taverns, many with foreign accents, who talked of 'giving it to the Frenchies'. Seamen and officers loved to give accounts of their many actions, storms, Admiral Lord Howe's piercing of the French line, Cape St Vincent and the audacity of Nelson. There had been problems of course. French fleets remained a menace, Toulon, Corsica and Saint-Domingue had been lost, there had been the mutiny, the threat to Ireland had been real, and the supply of masts, spars, rigging and sails was a concern. Some argued how *ships had to be preserved and kept serviceable for as long as possible!* It had to be 'refit, repair, rebuild' rather than 'replace'. *The costs, you see. The costs! They increase every year.*

---

546 Robinson (1894), 243.

To copper, mast and rig a ship was more than £67,000 for a 100-gun ship; £44,000 for a 74; £21,000 for a 38.[547] Numbers that quite numbed the mind!

What had interested the old sailor was how recruitment bounties increased throughout the war. He wondered if those men who deserted their ships later re-joined another, under a false name, just to make some ready money. Carters and merchant sailors, who travelled far and wide, talked of hunger, unemployment, suffering, war weariness and death in other British towns and cities. Many had complained of the new income tax. Some made apologies of how the war had to be paid for somehow, and the government needed her allies. *Give thanks to Austria! They had distracted the French, and helped our navy in the Mediterranean.*

After the Battle of Cape Saint Vincent the petty officer's wife thought that people seemed less inclined to make peace.[548] The sense of terror had lessened and most people were determined to carry on. Apart from Ireland, the dark horizon of the early years had mostly cleared away. By 1800 a new generation had reached maturity, who had grown up with war in the background. Their fathers, uncles and grandfathers worked British warships, as the children of the seas, and were often unknown to them. It had become the way of things, and how things had changed! At the end of the American War Britain had been humbled. The parson had then thought that princes throughout Europe seemed gratified to see Britain laid so low. Yet after France and her revolution had caused them such havoc, they became grateful for Britain and her navy to help defend them. The Royal Navy became a 'sheet-anchor of freedom'.[549] With a new century the whiff of peace filled the air. The parson could not help but wonder *if the war was to end, would they need such a large navy?* That remained to be seen, but he and so many others were certain of one thing. The Royal Navy had become a true Neptune. She had become a 'superpower'.

---

547 Robinson, 44.

548 Baynes, *Encyclopedia Britannica* (1888) Vol VIII, 362. He wrote, *The attempt at invasion had roused the national spirit to stubborn resistance; whilst the Government itself...freed from the blind terror which had made it violent during the first years of the war, was able to devote its energies unreservedly to carrying on hostilities.*

549 Brenton (1823) Vol I, 3.

Bibliography

Adams, W.H.D., *England on the Sea; or, The Story of the British Navy Vol II* (1885) London, F. V. White & Co.

ADM/L/N 212 - The Caird Library and Archive, National Maritime Museum Greenwich.

Adolphus, J., *The Political State of the British Empire etc Vol II* (1818) London, T. Cadell and W. Davies.

Alison, A. Sir, *History of Europe from the commencement of the French Revolution in MDCCLXXXIX to the restoration of the Bourbons in MDCCCXV, Vols I & III* (1841) Paris, Baudry's European Library, and *Vol V* (1854) Edinburgh, William Blackwood and Sons.

Allen, L., *The History of Portsmouth etc* (1817) London, Hatfield and Co.

Allen, J., *Life of Lord Viscount Nelson etc* (1853) London, George Routledge and Co.

Almon, J., *The Parliamentary Register, or History of the Proceedings and Debates of the House of Commons etc Vol XXXV* (1793) London, J. Debrett.

Anderson, J., *A Few Facts and Observations on the Yellow Fever of the West Indies, by which it is shewn that there have existed two species of fever in the West-India Islands for several years past, indiscriminately called Yellow Fever, but which have proceeded from very different causes, with the success attending the method of cure* (1798) Edinburgh, William Mudie.

Archenholz, J.W., *A Picture of England containing a description of the laws, customs and manners etc* (1791) Dublin, P. Byrne.

Ashton, J., *Old Times, a picture of social life at the end of the 18th century* (1885) London, John C. Nimmo.

Baines, E., *History of the Wars of the French Revolution, from the breaking out of the war in 1792, to the restoration of a general peace, in 1815; comprehending a civil history of Great Britain and France during that period, Vol I* (1852) New York, Bangs, Brother, and Co.

Baldwin, R., *The Importance of the Island of Minorca and Harbour of Port-Mahon etc* (1756) London, R. Baldwin.

BIBLIOGRAPHY

Barrow, J., sir, *The Life of Richard Earl Howe, Admiral of the Fleet and General of Marines* (1838) London, John Murray.

Barrow, J., *The Life and Correspondence of Admiral Sir William Sidney Smith Vol I* (1848) London, Richard Bentley.

Baynes, T.S., *The Encyclopedia Britannica etc Vol VIII* (1888) Henry G. Allen.

Beaumont, A., *Select Views of the Antiquities and Harbours in the South of France etc* (1794) London, T. Bensley.

Bell, J., *Memorial concerning the present state of military and naval surgery etc* (1800) London, Messrs. Longman & Rees, and Messrs. Cadell and Davies.

Bell, C., *A System of Operative Surgery founded on the Basis of Anatomy Vol II* (1816) Hartford, George Goodwin and Sons.

Beeton, S.O., *Beeton's Brave Tales, Bold Ballads, and travels and perils by land and sea* (1872) London, Ward, Lock, and Tyler.

Biden, C. *Naval Discipline, Subordination contrasted with Insubordination etc* (1830) London, J. M. Richardson.

Bigelow, A., *Travels in Malta and Sicily with Sketches of Gibraltar in MDCCCXXVII* (1831) Boston, Carter, Hendee & Babcock.

Bisset, R., *The History of the Reign of George III etc Vol IV* (1811) Baltimore, Edward J. Coale.

Blunt, H., *Perils and Panics of Invasion in 1796-7-8, 1804-5 and at the Present Time* (1860) London, Thomas Cautley Newby.

Bourrienne, L.A.F., *Memoirs of Napoleon Bonaparte etc* (1885) London, Richard Bentley and Son.

Brenton, E.P., *The Naval History of Great Britain etc* (1823) London, C. Rice.

Brereton, J., *Battle of The Nile, a prize poem of 1844* (1863) Oxford, T. and G. Shrimpton.

Brown, J.H., *The shipmaster's guide etc* (1853) London, Bradbury & Evans.

Buddicom, R.J., (rev), *A few words in behalf of the Society for Promoting Christian Knowledge etc* (1840) Oxford, John Henry Parker.

Bunbury, H, Sir, *A Narrative of the Campaign in North Holland 1799* (1849) London, T. and W. Boone.

Burke, E., *The Annual Register for 1794* (1806) London, R. Wilks.

Burney, W., *The British Neptune: or, A History of the Achievements of the Royal Navy etc* (1807) London, Richard Phillips.

Castle, C., *John Woodburn, Royal Navy* (1861) London, Saunders, Otley, and Co.

Chambers, R., and Thomson, T., *A Biographical Dictionary of Eminent Scotsmen Vol V* (1856) Edinburgh, Blackie and Son.

Chambers, R., (edit) *The Book of Days Vol I* (1888) London, W. & R. Chambers.

Cobbett, W., Wright, J., Hansard, T.C., *The Parliamentary History of England, from the earliest period to the year 1803. From which last-mentioned epoch it is continued downwards in the work entitled "The Parliamentary Debates" Vol XXX* (1817) London, T.C. Hansard.

Codrington, H., *British Naval Biography etc* (1846) London, Adam Scott.

Collinson, A., *Smallpox and Vaccination historically and medically considered: an enquiry into the causes of the recent increase of smallpox, and the means for its prevention.* (1860) London, Hatchard and Co.

Colomb, P.H., *Naval Warfare, Its Ruling Principles and Practice etc* (1895) London, W.H. Allen & Co.

Cooper, H.C., *Annals of Cambridge Vol IV* (1852) Cambridge, Metcalfe and Palmer.

Creighton, C., *A History of Epidemics in Britain Vol II* (1894) Cambridge, University Press.

Cruikshank, G., *George Cruikshank's omnibus* (1852) London, Tilt and Bogue.

Cunningham C., *A Narrative of Occurrences that took place during the Mutiny at the Nore etc* (1829) Chatham, William Burril.

Cust, E., *Annals of the Wars of the Eighteenth Century etc Vol IV 1783-1795* (1862) London, John Murray.

Dallas, A.J., *Life and Writings of James Alexander Dallas etc* (1871) Philadelphia, J.B. Lippincott & Co.

Dalton, H.G., *The History of British Guiana etc Vol I* (1855) London, Longman, Brown, Green, and Longmans.

Davenport Adams, W.H., *Famous Ships of the British Navy - Stories of Enterprise and Daring of British Seamen* (1868) London, Virtue & Co.

Deane, H.B., *The Law of Blockade etc* (1870) London, Longmans, Green, Reader, and Dyer.

Debrett, J., *A Collection of State Papers relative to the War Against France etc* (1794) London, J. Debrett.

Dent, R.K., *Old and new Birmingham; a history of the town and its people* (1880) Houghton and Hammond.

Derrick, C., *Memoirs of the rise and progress of the Royal Navy* (1806) London, H. Teape.

Douglas, H. (Sir), *A Treatise on Naval Gunnery* (1860) London, John Murray.

Dundas, D, *Summary Account of the Proceedings of the Fleet and Army, Employed at Toulon, in 1793 etc* (1805) Brentford, P. Norbury.

Dyer, T.H., *Modern Europe: from the fall of Constantinople to the Establishment of the German Empire etc Vol IV* (1877) London, George Bell and Sons.

Edmonds, C., *Poetry of the anti-Jacobin etc* (1890) London, Sampson Low, Marston, Searle, & Rivington.

BIBLIOGRAPHY

Edwards, B., *The History, Civil and Commercial of the British West Indies Vol II* (1819) London, T. Miller.

Evelyn: *Silva, or a Discourse of Forest-trees and the Propagation of Timber in His Majesty's Dominions.*

Falconer, W., *A New and Universal Dictionary of the Marine etc* (1830) London, T. Cadell.

Farley, F.A., *Military Glory. A sermon etc.* (1848) New York, Henry Spear.

Fincham, J.A., *History of Naval Architecture etc* (1851) London, Whittaker and Co.

Galt, J., *The steam-boat* (1823) New York, J. and J. Harper.

Gilly, W.O.S., *Narratives of Shipwrecks of the Royal Navy between 1793 and 1857 etc* (1857) London, John W. Parker.

Gregory, A., *Robert Raikes, journalist and philanthropist: a history of the origin of Sunday Schools* (1877) London, Hodder and Stoughton.

Goethe, J.W. edited by Dora Schmitz, L., *Miscellaneous Travels of J. W. Goethe etc* (1884) London, George Bell and Sons.

Gomm, W.M. Sir, *Letters and journals of Field-Marshal Sir William Maynard Gomm* (1881) London, Spottiswoode and Co.

Gordon, J., *History of the Rebellion in Ireland in the year 1798 etc* (1803) London, J.D. Dewick.

Griffiths, R., *The Monthly Review; or Literary Journal: from May to August MDCCCIII* (1803) London.

Grimshaw, W., *History of the Wars of the French Revolution etc Vol 1* (1852) New York, Bangs, Brother, & Co.

Guy, W.A., *Public health: a popular introduction to sanitary science, being a history etc* (1870) London, Henry Renshaw.

Hall, B (Capt), *Fragments of Voyages and Travels* (1841) London, Edward Moxon.

Hall, S.C., *Retrospect of a long life Vol I* (1883) London, Richard Bentley & Son.

Hamilton, J.B., (edit), *Transactions of the International Medical Congress Ninth Session Vol IV* (1887) Washington DC

Hansard, T.C., *The Parliamentary Debates from 1803 to The Present Time etc Vol XIII* (1812) London, HM Stationery Office.

Hazlitt, W., *The Life of Napoleon Buonaparte Vol I* (1803) London, Office of the Illustrated London Library.

Head, F.B. sir, *The Defenceless State of Great Britain* (1850) London, John Murray.

Herbert, D., *Great Historical Mutinies* (1876) London, William P. Nimmo.

Howell, T.B., *A Complete Collection of State Trials etc Vol XXI* (1816) London, T.C. Hansard.

Howell, J., *Man-of-war's Man Vol II* (1833) Philadelphia, E.L. Carey & A. Hart.

Hughson, D., *Walks through London* (1817) London, Sherwood, Neely, and Jones.

Hutchinson, W., *A Treatise Founded Upon Rational Principles etc* (1791) Liverpool, Thomas Billinge.

Jackson, J., *Reflections on the Commerce of the Mediterranean etc* (1806) New York, I. Riley & Co.

James, B., *Journal of Rear-Admiral Bartholomew James 1752-1828* (1896) London, Navy Records Society.

James, C., *A New and Enlarged Military Dictionary etc Vol I* (1810) London, T. Egerton.

James, W., *The Naval History of Great Britain from the Declaration of the War by France in 1793, to the accession of George IV, Vol I* (1837), *Vol II* (1860), *Vol III* (1886), London, Richard Bentley.

Jenner, E., *An inquiry into the Causes and Effects of the Variolae Vaccinae, a disease discovered in some of the Western counties of England, particularly Gloucestershire, and known by the name of The Cow Pox* (1801) London, D.N. Shury.

Kelly, C., *History of the French Revolution and of the wars produced by that memorable event: from the commencement of hostilities in 1792, to the Second Restoration of Louis XVIII and the deportation of Napoleon Buonaparte to the island of St. Helena; including a complete account of the war between Great-Britain and America; and the memorable Battle of Waterloo etc Vol I* (1820) London, Thomas Kelly.

Knight, C., *A History of England etc Vol VII* (1861) London, Bradbury and Evans.

Knight, J.I., *Mechanics Magazine Vol I* (1821) London, Knight and Lacey.

Langford, J.A., *A century of Birmingham Life etc Vol II* (1868) Birmingham, E.C. Osborne.

Lara, B., *A Dictionary of Surgery; or, the Young Surgeon's Pocket Assistant* (1796) London, James Ridgway.

Lathom Browne, G., *Nelson, the Public and Private Life of Horatio, Viscount Nelson as told by Himself etc* (1891) London, T. Fisher Unwin.

Laughton, J.K., *Nelson* (1895) London, Macmillan and Co.

Lecky, W.E.H., *A History of England in the Eighteenth Century Vol VII* (1890) London, Longmans, Green, and Co.

Lockwood, J.A., *An essay on flogging in the navy etc* (1849) New York, Pudney and Russell.

Long, W.H., *Medals of the British navy and how they were won* (1895) London, Norie & Wilson.

Low, S., *Poetry of the Anti-Jacobin* (1890) London, Sampson Low, Marston, Searle, & Rivington.

BIBLIOGRAPHY

Lowe, J., *An Enquiry into the State of the British West Indies* (1808) London, C. and R. Baldwin.

Macaulay, J., *Doctor Johnson, his life, works and table talk* (1884) London, T. Fisher Unwin.

Macdonald, J.D., *Outlines of Naval Hygiene* (1881) London, Smith, Elder, Co.

Mackay, T., *The English Poor - a sketch of their social and economic history* (1889) London, John Murray.

Mahan, A.T., *The Influence of Sea Power Upon History, 1660-1783, Vol I* (1894) Boston, Little, Brown, and Co.

Mahan, A.T., *The influence of Sea Power Upon the French Revolution and Empire 1793-1812 Vol I* (1892) London, Sampson Low, Marston & Company, Limited.

Mann, J.H., *A History of Gibraltar and Its Sieges* (1870) London, Provost & Co.

Marshall, H., *Military miscellany; comprehending a history of the recruiting of the army etc* (1846) London, John Murray.

Marshall, J., *Royal Naval Biography Vol I* (1823) London, Longman, Hurst, Rees, Orme, and Brown.

Martin, M., *History of the British Possessions in the Mediterranean: Comprising Gibraltar, Malta, Gozo, and the Ionian Islands Vol VII* (1837) London, Whittaker & Co.

Massey, W., *A History of England During the Reign of George The Third, Vol IV* (1865) London, Longmans, Green, and Co.

Maw, W.H., and Dredge, J., *Engineering, an illustrated weekly journal Vol LIV* (1892) London, Offices for Advertisements and Publication.

Maxwell, W.H., *History of the Irish Rebellion in 1798 etc* (1803) London, Bell and Daldy.

McArthur, J., *Financial and Political Facts of the 18th Century etc* (1801) London, J. Wright.

Millar, A.H., *Roll of eminent burgesses of Dundee, 1513-1886* (1887) Dundee, John Leng.

Mivart, St.G., *Essays and Criticisms Vol I* (1892) London, James r. Osgood, McIlvaine & Co.

Moore, A.W., *The Manx Note Book* (1885) Douglas, G.H. Johnson.

Moore, J.J., *The British Mariner's Vocabulary etc* (1801) London, J. Cundee.

Morgan, W., and Creuze, A., *Papers on Naval Architecture and other subjects connected with naval science Vol II* (1829) London, G.B. Whittaker.

Mortimer, T., *A General Dictionary of Commerce, Trade, and Manufactures etc* (1810) Richard Phillips.

Murray, A., and Creuze, A.F.B., *Ship-building in Iron and Wood* (1863) Edinburgh, Adam and Charles Black.

Murray, M., *A treatise on ship-building and navigation etc* (1754) London, D. Henry and R. Cave.

Napier, Charles, Sir, *Lights and Shade of Military Life* (1850) London, Henry Colburn.

Neale, W.J., *History of the Mutiny at Spithead and The Nore with an enquiry into its origin and treatment etc* (1842) London, Thomas Tegg.

Neale, W.J., *Narrative of the Mutiny at the Nore* (1861) London, Thomas Tegg.

Newmarch, W., *On the Loans Raised by Mr. Pitt during the First French War 1793-1801 etc* (1855) London, Effingham Wilson.

Nichols, J., *The Gentleman's magazine and Historical Chronicle Vol LXXXIII* (1813) London, Nichols, Son, and Bentley.

Norie, J.W., *The Naval Gazetteer, Biographer, and Chronologist etc* (1842) London, Charles Wilson.

Norman, C.B., *The Corsairs of France* (1887) London, Gilbert and Rivington.

O'Brien, R.B., *The Autobiography of Theobald Wolfe Tone 1763-1798 Vol I* (1893) London, T. Fisher Unwin.

O'Shea, H., *Guide to Spain and Portugal* (1869) Edinburgh, Adam and Charles Black.

Pashley, R., *Pauperism and Poor Laws* (1852) London, Longman Brown Green and Longmans.

Pettigrew, T.J., *Memoirs of the life of vice-admiral Lord Viscount Nelson etc* (1849) London, T. & W. Boone.

Philp, R.K., *The history of progress in Great Britain* (1859) London, Houlston and Wright.

Privy Council *Regulations and Instructions relating to His Majesty's Service at Sea* (1808) London, W. Winchester and Son.

Rees, A., *The Cyclopaedia: Or Universal Dictionary of Arts, Sciences, and Literature etc Vol XXVIII* (1819) London, Longman, Hurst, Rees, Orme, & Brown.

Rendle, W., and Norman, P., *The inns of Old Southwark and their associations* (1888) London, Longmans, Green, and Co.

Robertson, R., *Synopsis Morborum: A summary view of observations on the principal diseases incident to seamen or soldiers etc Vol I* (1810) London, D.M. Shury.

Robinson, C.N., *The British Fleet: the growth, achievements and duties of the Navy of the Empire* (1894) London, George Bell & Sons.

Rush, B., *Medical Inquiries and Observations: containing an account of the bilious remitting and intermitting Yellow Fever...and a Defence of Bloodletting etc Vol IV* (1796) Philadelphia, Thomas Dobson.

BIBLIOGRAPHY

Sadler, H., *Thomas Dunckerley, his life, labours, and letters etc* (1891) London, Diprose & Bateman.

Schomberg, I., *Naval Chronology; or, and Historical Summary of Naval and Maritime Events etc* (1802) London, T. Egerton.

Schomburgk, R, Sir, *The History of Barbados etc* (1847) London, Longman, Green, and Longmans.

Scott, A., *British Naval Biography etc* (1853) London, Adam Scott.

Scott, W, Sir, *The Complete Works of Sir Walter Scott with a Biography and his last additions and illustrations, Volume IV* (1833) New York, Connor and Cooke.

Sears, R., *Scenes and Sketches in Continental Europe etc* (1848) New York, Robert Sears.

Shippen, E., *Naval Battles of the World etc* (1894) Toronto, C.R. Parish.

Slight, J., *A narrative of the loss of the Royal George etc* (1843) Portsea, S. Horsey.

Smedley, E., *Encyclopaedia Metropolitana; Or, Universal Dictionary of Knowledge, Vol VI* (1845) London, printer unstated.

Smollett, T. *The Adventures of Roderick Random* (1824) London, T. Davison.

Smollett, T.G., *The Critical Review; or Annals of Literature etc Vol XIII* (1800) London, S. Hamilton.

Smyth, W.H., *The Sailor's Word-Book etc* (1867) London, Blackie and Son.

Southey, R., *Life of Nelson* (1890) London, Macmillan and Co.

Southey, T., *Chronological History of the West Indies Vol III* (1827) London, Longman, Rees, Orme, Brown, and Green.

Standish Haly, R., *Impressment: an attempt to prove, why it should and how it could be abolished* (1822) Poole, Moore and Sydenham.

Steel, D. *The Ship-master's Assistant and Owner's Manual etc* (1801) London, H.D. Steel.

Stockdale, J., *The Parliamentary Register or History of the Proceedings and debates of the House of Commons etc Vol XI* (1802) London, Wilson and Co.

Taine, H., *The French Revolution Vol III* (1885) New York, Henry Holt and Company.

Taylor, C., *The Literary Panorama and National Register etc* (1816) London, C. Taylor.

Theal, G.M., *Compendium of the History and Geography of South Africa* (1878) London, Edward Stanford.

Thompson, G.A., *The Geographical and Historical Dictionary of America and the West Indies Vol V* (1815) London, Thompson.

Thompson, W., *The Royal-Navymen's Advocate etc* (1757) London, H. Slater.

Toynbee A., *Lectures on the Industrial Revolution in England: popular addresses, notes etc* (1887) London, Rivington's.

Trotter, T., *A Practical Plan for manning the Royal Navy etc* (1819) Newcastle, Longman, Hurst, Rees, Orme, and Brown.

Trotter, T., *Medicina Nautica, an essay on the diseases of seamen: comprehending the history of the health in the Channel for the years 1799, 1800, and 1801* (1803) London, T.N. Longman and O. Rees.

Trotter, T., *Observations on the Scurvy with a review of the Theories etc* (1786) Edinburgh, Charles Elliot.

Tytler, A.F., *Elements of General History etc* (1823) Concord, Isaac Hill.

Urquhart, T., *Letters on the evils of impressment with the outline of a plan doing them away etc* (1816) London, J. Richardson.

Voltaire, F-M. A., *Romances, Novels, and Tales by M. De Voltaire Vol II* (1806) London, Lackington, Allen, and Co.

Waterston, W., *A Cyclopaedia of Commerce, Mercantile Law, Finance, Commercial Geography and Navigation* (1847) London, H.G. Bohn.

Whitlock, G.C., *Prize money or, the right of Major-General Whitlock, K.C.B., and his troops, to the Banda and Kirwee Booty, tried by naval and military law, and the usage of the army* (1862) London, Harrison.

Willett, R., as found in *The Naval Chronicle Vol III* (1800) London, Bunney & Gold.

Wilson, J., *A Journal of Two Successive Tours Upon The Continent in the Years 1816, 1817 and 1818 Vol I* (1820) London, T. Cadell and W. Davies.

Winsor, J. (ed.), *Narrative and Critical History of America etc Vol VII* (1888) Boston, The Riverside Press.

Woodfall, W., *An Impartial Report of the Debates that occur in the Two Houses of Parliament, etc* (1794) London, T. Chapman.

Yonge, C.D., *The History of the British Navy etc Vol I* (1863) London, Richard Bentley

Journals, Articles, Reports Etc by Unknown Authors

A Collection of State Papers relative to the War with France etc (1799) London, J. Debrett.

A Narrative of The Proceedings of the British Fleet etc off Cape St. Vincent (1797) London, J. Johnson.

Abstracts of the British Navy; showing how it stood, in ships, tons and classification, at the commencement of every year, from 1793 inclusive.

American State Papers etc of The Congress of The United States Vol VI (1859) Washington, Gales & Seaton.

An Enquiry into the present state of the British Navy etc by an Englishman (1815) London, W. McDowell.

An Impartial Report of the debates that occur in the Two Houses of Parliament etc, Vol I (1794) and *Vol IV* (1796) London, T. Chapman.

Blackwood's Edinburgh Magazine No. CII (1825) London, T. Cadell.

British Minor Expeditions 1746 to 1814 - compiled in the Intelligence Branch of the Quartermaster-General's Department (1884) London, HM Stationery Office.

Chambers's Journal of Popular Literature (1877 and 1895) London, W. & R. Chambers Ltd.

Colburn's United Service Magazine and Naval and Military Journal Part I (1871) London, Hurst and Blackett.

Edinburgh Medical Journal etc Vol I July 1855 to June 1856 (1856) Edinburgh, Sutherland and Knox.

Encyclopaedia Britannica Dictionary etc Vol XV (1890) Chicago, R.S. Peale & Co.

Estimates and Accounts: army; navy; ordnance; civil list; public debt; the bank; the revenue; pensions; land tax; Session 21 April to 23 November 1820 Vol XI (1820) Oxford, Bodleian Library.

Fourth Report of the Commissioners for Revising and Digesting the Civil Affairs of His Majesty's Navy (1806) London, W. Winchester and Son.

Hansard's Parliamentary Debates etc Vol CIV (1849) London, Woodfall and Son; and *Vol CXXXIV* (1854) London, Cornelius Buck.

History of merchant shipping and ancient commerce, Volume III (1876) London; Sampson Low, Marston, Low, and Searle.

Illustrated Naval and Military Magazine etc Vol IV (1890) and *Vol IX* (1888) London, W.H. Allen & Co.

Impressment of seamen and a few remarks on corporal punishment etc (1834) London, Roake and Varty.

JOD/28012 - The Caird Library, National Maritime Museum Greenwich.

Journal of the Statistical Society Vol XVIII (1855) London, John William Parker and Son.

Life of William Pitt etc (1806) Philadelphia, John Watts.

Navy and Army Illustrated Vol VI (1894) London, Hudson & Kearns.

Niles' Weekly Register etc Vol XVIII (1820) Baltimore, Franklin Press.

Report of the Committee appointed to enquire into the subject of boy enlistment etc (1876) London, Harrison & Sons.

Reports from Committees of the House of Commons, Vol XIII 1798 (1803) London, publisher not stated.

Royal Commission of the financial relations between Great Britain and Ireland, first report etc (1895) London, HM Stationery Office.

Songs, Duets, Choruses etc called the Glorious First of June etc (1794) London, C. Lowndes.

Statistical Report on the Sickness, Mortality, and Invaliding among the troops of the West Indies (1838) London, W. Clowes and Sons.

The Annual Register or a View of the History, Politics, and Literature London, T. Burton and London, G.G. and J. Robinson

The Atlantic Monthly, Vol LXXI (1893) Boston and New York, Houghton, Mifflin and Company.

The British Critic, a new review etc Vol VIII (1796) London, C. Rivington.

The British Encyclopedia or Dictionary of arts and sciences etc (1818) Philadelphia, Mitchell, Ames, and White.

The Complete Works of Sir Walter Scott etc Vol VII (1833) New York, Connor & Cooke.

The Country Gentleman's Magazine January to December (1876) London, Virtue & Co.

The Debates and Proceedings in the Congress of the United States etc (1849) Washington, Gales and Seaton.

The European Magazine for 1797 (1797) London, J. Sewell.

JOURNALS, ARTICLES, REPORTS

The Field of Mars: Being an Alphabetical Digestion of the Principal Naval and Military Engagements etc Vol II (1801) London, G. and J. Robinson.

The Fifth Report of the Commissioners for Revising and Digesting the Civil Affairs of His Majesty's Navy (1809) London, House of Commons.

The Gentleman's Magazine Vol VIII (1872) London, Grant & Co.

The Graphic Vol 30 (1884) London, printer not stated.

The Hampshire Antiquary and Naturalist etc Vol II (1892) London, Elliot Stock.

The Journal of the House of Commons July 1796 to October 1797 Vol LII (1796) London, HM Stationery Office.

The Monthly Magazine, or British Register Vol XXV (1808) London, Richard Phillips.

The Monthly Review, or Literary Journal London, R. Griffiths.

The Nautical Gazetteer, or Dictionary of Maritime Geography (1847) London, Henry Hurst.

The Naval Chronicle London, J. Gold.

The Naval Chronicle Vol II July to December MDCCXCIX (1799) London, Bunney and Gold.

The New American Cyclopaedia of General Knowledge Vol 1 (1869) New York, D. Appleton and Company.

The New Annual Register, or, General Repository of History, Politics, and Literature for the Year 1797 (1798) London, G.G. and J. Robinson.

The Parliamentary Debates from the Year 1803 to the Present Time etc (1812) London, T.C. Hansard.

The Parliamentary History of England etc London, T.C. Hansard.

The Parliamentary Register etc Vol IX (1778) London, J. Almon.

The Parliamentary Register or History of the Proceedings and Debates of the House of Commons etc London, J. Debrett.

The Saturday Review Vol XIV (1862) London, Spottiswoode and Co.

The Scots Magazine, or General Depository etc for the year 1797 (1797) Edinburgh, James Watson and Co.

The Sporting Magazine or Monthly Calendar etc Vol 30 (1808) London, J. Wheble.

The State of the Nation etc Vol IV (1800) London, R. Shaw.

The Statutes at Large of England etc Vol XVII (1798) and *Vol XVII* (1811) London, George Eyre and Andrew Strahan.

The United Service Magazine and Naval and Military Magazine Part II (1840) London, Henry Colburn.

The Universal Magazine of Knowledge and Pleasure etc Vol XX (1757) London, John Hinton, and *Vol C* (1797) London, W. Bent.

Index

The words Britain, British, deck, England, fleet, France, French, Great Britain, guns, navy and squadron appear regularly so are not included in this Index.

INDEX

Anchorage(s), 1, 46, 76, 87, 88, 117-8, 126, 128
Andamans, 157
Anderson, James, 155
Anglo-Corsican Kingdom, ix, 127
Annual Register, 5, 140
Anson, HMS, 17, 103
Antigua, 50, 55, 146, 151, 156
Antilles, 156
Antwerp, 104, 106
Apprentice, 17, 23, 24, 28
Arden, Lord, 71
Armament 16, 105, 145
Armed neutrality, 88
ArmOe d'Angleterre, 105
ArmOe d'Italie, 122
Army, 7, 32, 55-6, 69, 83, 112, 147
Austria, 128
    commander, 127
    French, 5, 98-9, 119, 122, 140, 156
    of émigrés, 97
Articles of War, 34-5, 48, 67, 76
Artificers, 49
Artillery, 56, 79, 97, 121, 125-6, 150
    French, 123, 137
    Royal Corps, 29
Asia, HMS, 148
Assignats, 7, 115
Assurance, HMS, 148
Atlantic, 2, 83, 85-6, 89-91, 115, 146, 150, 156
Audacious, HMS, 91-3, 135, 137
Austria 4, 84, 88, 118, 122, 126, 128-9, 134, 159
Austrian Netherlands, 90, 104-5
Avenger, HMS, 148

Babet, HMS, 150-1
Badger, HMS, 79, 81
Bagonet, 124
Bahamas, 156
Baillie, Thomas (Captain), 52
Bakehouse, 51-2
    at Toulon, 116
Balaguier, 116, 121, 124, 126
Ball-scoops, 63
Baltic, 4, 28, 42, 104, 114
Banda, 157

Bank of England, 45, 68
Bank Restriction Act, 46
Bantry Bay, 101-2
Barbados, 146-7, 150-1
Barbary states, 114
Barfleur, HMS, 91, 131
Barlow, Robert, 1-4
Barometer, 1
Barracks, 43
Barrels, 52-3
    of powder, 101, 109, 125, 132
Barrow, John, 78, 84
Bar shot, 145
Bastia, 112, 127-9
Bastille
Bataille d'Aboukir, 139
Bataille du 13 Prairial An 2, 23, 95
Batavian Republic, x, 77, 90, 104, 106, 133-4
Bateaux à la Muskein, 80
Battery, 1-2, 20, 76, 113, 121, 124, 128, 137
Battle, viii, ix, x, 23, 35, 50, 63, 82, 84, 86, 91-5, 99, 105, 133, 136, 138, 143-4, 149, 158-9
    'line of', 19, 87, 93, 125, 137
Battle of the Nile, x, 118, 139-40
Baymen, 155
Bay of Biscay, 90
Bayonet, 28, 79
Bayonne, 90
Beaulieu, HMS, 148, 150
'Beau nasties', 30
'Beckett', 23, 25
Bedding, 57
Bedford, HMS, 123
Beer, 26, 51-3
Belgium, 6
Bell, John, 63
Belle-Île-en-Mer, 90
Belle Isle, 90, 96, 98
Bellerophon, HMS, 85, 91-2, 96, 135, 138
Belliqueux, HMS, 77, 154
Bell public house, 30
Bells, 11, 91, 94
Bentham, Jeremy, 49
Bentham, Sir Samuel, 49
Berbice, 149, 151

173

INDEX

INDEX

INDEX

INDEX

INDEX

INDEX